MAN AND ACTION

When Bill Hitches saw a derelict showman's caravan in Scotland, where he was convalescing after a major operation, he had no idea what adventures it would lead to. Aware of the loneliness and misery of disablement, he took the restored caravan on a journey across Europe as far as Romania, still in the thrall of the old regime, and visited homes and institutions for crippled, blind and mentally ill patients. He used the news media to highlight areas where improvements were needed and made great efforts to get action taken by the authorities. It is a story of bravery and tenderness brilliantly told by a man who understood what he saw.

MAX WILLIAM "BILL" HITCHES

Born in Solihull, Bill contracted osteomyelitis at the tender age of two, but was not diagnosed for nine years, during which time he suffered long periods of painful illness and many operations. As a consequence, he missed most of his schooling and endured great loneliness. He has two children, a daughter, Kerry, aged 28 and a son, Max, 31, who made the long journey across Europe with him. Max is very deaf, but he has a wonderful gift for languages, which was a tremendous help on the journey. Bill came to live in Tywyn, Gwynedd, North Wales in 1973. He is still working for the people of Romania and the children of Chernobyl, in the U.S.S.R.

A second volume of Man and Action,

MAN AND ACTION – Romania & Russia,

is in preparation and will be published in 1992.

To Richard and Sue

MAN and ACTION

by

Max William "Bill" Hitches

Best Wishes

Bill and Action.

Volume One

Scotland to Romania

Published in Great Britain by
Max William Hitches,
Top Flat,
Bryn Llewelyn,
High Street,
TYWYN,
Gwynedd.
LL36 9AD

ISBN 0 9517508 0 1

Edited and set by
ARIOMA Editorial Services,
Gloucester House, High Street,
BORTH, Dyfed. SY24 5HZ

Printed by
Bookcraft,
Unit 8,
Midsomer Enterprise Park,
Wheelers Hill,
Midsomer Norton,
nr Bath,
Avon,
BA3 2BX

Cover, map and drawings by J. Goodband.

This book in dedicated to Beth, who supported me from Wales, Max, my constant companion across Europe, and Action who walked all the way.

He is in love with the land that is always over /
The next hill, and the next, ...

He searches for last frontiers and lost doors.
He tries to climb the wall around the world.

"Portrait of a Romantic" A.S.J. Tessimond

The Collected Poems of A.S.J. Tessimond,
with translations from Jaques Prévert,
edited by Hubert Nicholson.
(Whiteknights Press 1985)

Border drawn by Lynda M. Codling

ACKNOWLEDGEMENTS

Action Research for the Crippled Child. All the staff and area organisers.
Alexander Hondon Ltd, London. Chris Mills.
Beefeater Inns. Various Managers and staff.
Cambrian News, Aberystwyth.
Cambrian Springs, Wrexham.
Collins Publications, Glasgow. J.D.Thompson.
Coopers Animal Health, Crewe.
Dalgety Spillers. John Stone.
Gaz Camping, Windsor.
Glasgow Herald. Andrew McAlam.
Kingsway, Rolland, London. Mr. John Cooper.
Laura Ashley, Carno.
Lloyds Bank, Cape Hill, West Midlands.
Mars Oil, Banbury.
Maxwell Tapes. John Durham.
Ministry of Agriculture, Fisheries & Food, Surbiton. Mrs. J.M.Payton & others.
Oban Times.
Olaf Line, Sheerness. Jenny Forrester.
Rotary Clubs at Tywyn and Rochester.
Sea Link, Dover.
Telford Tarpaulins, Telford.
Trail West, Oban. Andrew.
Veterinary Practice at Oban.
Wellcome Foundation. Keith Sharpe and office staff at Crewe.
Rt.Hon, Mrs Francis Shand Kydd. Oban.
John Keys. Dalmally.
All the poeple who helped me rebuild the caravan, and supplied goods and equipment in Oban and Tywyn.
Ted and Sue Batty. Tywyn.
Mr. Parry. Guilsfield, Powys.
Mrs. Beckett. Church Stretton.
Helen, Rachel and George. Oban.
Sandy Johnson. Oban.
Bob McTear. Oban.
David Clarke. Oban.
John Newton. Hadley Cannon.
Doug and Mary Lindsay. Kerrera.
Caroline Younger. Oban.
Mrs. Nora King. Edinburgh.
John and Mary Jackson. Accrington.
Henry Mulholland. Glasgow.

Tom Lee. Romany Guild, London.
Mark Lavender. Rochester.
Mr. Dunn. Steeton.
John Grieves. Tywyn.
Mr.Williams. Veterinary Surgeon – Tywyn.
Officers and men of Knightsbridge Barracks.
All the kind people who let us stop on their premises or who arranged same.
Blacksmiths and Harness menders.
Friends who provided Action with fodder along the way.
Newspaper, Radio and Television reporters throughout G.B.
The list is endless, so to all that I have missed: – Thank you for your help. Without you I would not have achieved it.
All our foreign organisations and friends.

To my friends, who are not mentioned by name because of political pressures or other for reasons, I offer my sincere thanks. I have not forgotten you; the memories I have will stay with me for ever.

CONTENTS

LIST OF ILLUSTRATIONS

Photographs

Other Illustrations

FOREWORD

Sometimes in life one gets an impulse to do something, an impulse so strong it cannot be resisted, the consequences of which lead beyond imagination. Such a momentous occurrence happened to me when I was in Scotland recovering from major surgery, my future prospects uncertain, and I happened to see a mouldering Gipsy caravan at the end of a driveway leading to a house.

From that moment my life was in the hands of fate, which took me to places in Europe of which I only knew the names. It revealed to me my own weaknesses and hidden strengths, it gave me an unexpected satisfaction and purpose for my life, and taught me to appreciate my good fortune. It gave me a rapport with horses, my own special horse, Action, in particular, and renewed the bond between my son, Max, and myself.

Short of money, in ill health, and unable to obtain the necessary documents to enter Russia, we could not stay and wait at the Romanian border, so we came back home and waited until such time as we could resume the journey and travel from Romania to Chernobyl, where we saw lingering devastation caused by the infamous nuclear accident that left so many young lives destroyed or devastated.

I came back from both parts of my journey with the firm resolve that I would do all I could to help the handicapped and disabled, the sick and the helpless in Romania and in Russia, especially Chernobyl, by collecting support in the form of clothing, books, medical supplies, money and sympathy from those who have anything to give. I cannot do it alone, but I can say where help is most needed and I know the people, who are there in Russia and Romania, waiting to receive it.

Profits from the sale of this and the second volume of my book will go to help these people; they have had to endure a long period of terrible hardship under the tyranny of dictatorial governments. I hope, if you enjoy this first volume, you will order a copy of volume two, due out in about 12 months from now. There is a postcard in the back of this book which can be used to notify me of your interest, in order that you can be advised when it becomes available.

SCOTLAND
Kerrera
Oban
Stirling
Glasgow
Lockerbi
Gretna Green
Carlisle
IRELAND
Kendal
Skipton
Halifax
Huddersfield
Sheffield
WALES
Derby
Coventry
Warwick
ENGLAND
Stratford
Banbury
Milton Keynes
Letchworth
London
Rochester
Sheerness
DENMARK
Rotterdam
NETHERLANDS
Vlissingen
Hasselt
Antwerp
Maastricht
Aachen
Bruxelles
Bonn
BELGIUM
Neuwied
GERMANY
Koblenz
Cochem
Bad Kreuznach
Karlsruhe
CZECHO SLOVAKIA
Stuttgart
Sigmaringen
Tübingen
Ravensburg
FRANCE
Kempten
Vils
SWITZERLAND
Innsbrück
AUSTRIA
Brenner
Bolzano
Trento
Rovereto
Vicenza
Verona
Venezia
Trieste
Zagreb
Chióggia
Ferrara
YUGOSLAVIA
SPAIN
Ravenna
Gulf of Venezia
Rimini
Pesaro
Ancona
ITALY
Pescara
Vasto
Termoli
San Severo
Foggia
Adriatic
Trani
Molfetta
Bari
Brindisi
Lecce
Otranto
Mediterranean

Chapter One

The Idea and Planning

It was another sunny morning as I drove towards Crow Haven, where I was to deliver a message to a man on a yacht moored in the Marina. It was the first week in June 1986. I had been living with Beth on the island of Kerrera since March. It was now eight months since the operation on my spine, and these last three months on Kerrera had helped me to convalesce. During the past year, Beth had been a tower of strength, not only through the operation, but helping me to overcome the effects of having sold a share of my business.

In many ways I was happy having the weight of business taken from me. I was tired of the building trade, in which I had been working self-employed for thirty years, since the age of fifteen. I felt free at last to do what I wanted, but I had not made up my mind what I did want. Our stay on Kerrera would finish in October. I had made no plans regarding work after my return to Tywyn, in Wales. I had settled well to island life, and working for Douglas and Mary Lindsay was a pleasure for me. Beth and I were living in the Lindsays' huge bungalow with their children, Calum aged thirteen and Iona eleven. Most weeks Douglas and Mary were away with *Corryvreckan*, their charter yacht. Beth's job was to look after the children and the home. She also took bookings for the charter yacht. My job consisted of keeping the garden tidy, generally maintaining the bungalow and helping to entertain the children.

Just before the turn-off to the village of Crow Haven, something caught my attention. At the end of a drive stood a large wooden caravan. It occupied my thoughts as I drove the rest of the way down to the Marina. When I was on my way back and still thinking about what I had seen, my car seemed to take over and I found myself in the drive. When I got close to the caravan I could see that it was a showman's caravan, large and probably towed by a lorry. I came to a cottage and I went there to make enquiries. The door was opened by a young woman holding a baby. I was in a dream. What did I want with her?

"I am looking for a gypsy caravan," I said. I had to say something.

We talked for a while and she gave me the name and address of a woman.

"The lady has one in her back-yard. I don't know whether she wants to sell it. You'll find it about five miles up the road."

I thanked her and headed towards the address I had just been given. As I drove I began to dream of buying a gypsy caravan, a horse and tack. Then I thought that it might be an idea to travel with them as far as possible – China even. I would need a reason for making such a trip, however, so why not do some good along the way? I woke from my day dreams when I found myself at the door of Caroline Younger's house.

"My name is Bill Hitches. I believe you have a gypsy caravan. Would you sell it?"

"No!" was her answer.

I slowed down and began to talk to her, telling her of my plans to travel to China and on the way do something for charity. She showed some interest in my story, saying she would consider it and write to me on Kerrera. Hopeful and excited, I went back to Kerrera and told Beth of my plans. She said nothing. I could see she was not pleased.

From that day, and for the whole of the following year, every day would be taken up with planning and making preparations.

The most immediate matter was to determine if it would be logistically possible to make such a trip as I had in mind. I began to make a list, as I applied my mind to it. At this stage I had no idea exactly how far away China was, what would be the best route to take or even whether a horse could pull a caravan such a vast distance. I had not the remotest clue how long it would take, what sort of terrain I would find in the countries I must cross and I had no idea what sort of weather conditions I might meet at different times of the year. One question brought more in its wake. How many miles could we cover in a day? Where should I stop each night? Where would I find fodder for the horses? If the horses required veterinary attention, would it be available? How did I get the horses shod?

Then it occurred to me that I would need permission to take my entourage abroad. What documentation would be wanted? Assuming I found answers to all these questions, would I be able to cope with such a journey, still weak as I was from my operation? Could I survive living, eating, cooking, washing, sleeping in my flimsy caravan? As I spoke about my plans, people began to show concern for my safety. What kind of reception would I get in each country I travelled through? I had not yet obtained suitable horses, harness and other tackle. I would also need some sort of back – up system of transport. My list began to proliferate as the days passed and the planning became more detailed. So far, however, I had been asking questions, not getting answers. But whom and where did I ask about such things?

My first need was to learn about horses and caravans. As I knew nothing about either, I should have to get tuition. As my list of equipment requirements grew, I began to worry about the cost of the venture. I decided to try for sponsorship from the business community.

By the end of June I had already selected my route to China. My method of selection had been based on looking at maps and finding the flattest possible way. Some mountains were unavoidable, but my priority was to be in certain countries at specific seasons of the year, aiming to avoid the bitter cold of winter, especially in the Eastern Bloc countries.

My journey would take me from Scotland, through England as far as Sheerness, where I would catch the ferry to Vlissingen in Holland. From Holland, I would go to Belgium, from there to Germany, then to Austria, Italy, Jugoslavia, Bulgaria, Romania, the U.S.S.R. and from there head towards Tashkent, which would bring me close to the borders of China.

I wrote to the London Embassy of each country asking what sort of papers would be required for myself and horse – drawn caravan, and asking for permission to walk across their country. Some embassies sent complicated replies, some did not answer at all. In the end I decided to set off without visas and entry permits, armed with nothing more than my passport.

Whilst all these preparations were going on, there were two items that were most important. Without them there would be no journey. The first was obtaining a caravan, the second was finding suitable horses.

As the days passed on Kerrera, when I was not doing chores for Douglas and Mary, I spent my time writing letters to possible sponsors and to embassies at home and abroad, and I visited Oban Library to gather information about the terrain and climate of those countries I wished to visit and to read books about horses.

By now I was driving Beth mad. For the rest of our time on Kerrera I spent every single minute thinking about and working on plans for the forthcoming trip. The distance between me and Beth grew as I pushed her aside, nothing else in my thoughts but the journey.

One morning a letter arrived. It was from Caroline Younger, the lady with the gypsy caravan. I tore open the envelope and pulled out her letter. I had been expecting the message contained in it.

"I have considered your request for the caravan and my answer is Yes – you can have it. You must pay £100 so that when you reach China you are not beholden to me in any way. I shall give the £100 to charity."

I was overjoyed. This was the start I needed. So far nearly all the replies to my letters asking for sponsorship or to embassies asking for entry and exit permits were negative. One exception was a letter from Mr. John Stone of Dalgety Spillers Foods Limited who generously agreed to help feed the horse until we reached Greece, as we would be travelling in countries where they had factories or franchises. On top of this, they also said they would supply waterproof clothing for me and blankets for the horse. The Wellcome Foundation also rallied to my assistance. They agreed to supply medical products for me and the horse, and the girls in their offices organised a sponsored run to raise money for me.

I had written to Mr. J.D. Thompson, Director of Graphic Publications at Collins, the publishing house, telling them of my plans and asking for help, which they gave in the form of detailed maps of my route as well as a donation of £350. These generous and practical responses, however, were not typical of the replies I received. Out of about 200 letters sent out to businesses asking for sponsorship, I received replies from about twenty per cent, and only five per cent agreed to help. I found that it was usually the small businesses that were the most willing to be of assistance.

By now the *Oban Times* newspaper had done an article about me, so

I decided to take advantage of the local publicity to ask the business people of Oban to help me with acquiring some of the smaller items I should need, things like pots and pans. Their overwhelming response was something I shall never forget. In fact, after about two months things were starting to come together, but I had not yet tackled the really important matter of obtaining horses, equine tack or basic tuition in horse and caravan care and management. This was the next item on my agenda.

I spent hours on the telephone talking to organisations connected with horses, asking what type of horse I needed and where I might purchase one. Most people were very helpful, but did nothing for my self confidence, sounding very unsure of my ability to accomplish such a journey with a horse and caravan. I seemed to be getting nowhere.

Thinking about things, I recalled that several people had mentioned a name that somehow stuck in my mind. They had all spoken of a John Jackson of Accrington, in Lancashire. They said he was a Gipsy. Every time I remembered this man, I would promptly put him out of my mind again. I would think about the caravan instead.

I arranged with the owner of Trail West, a trailer company in Oban, to take a transporter and collect the caravan from Caroline Younger. It would not have been possible to fetch it any other way as the wooden wheels were in a very bad condition, as was the rest of the vehicle. I was given permission to leave the van in the yard at Trail West's so that I could repair it. I should have to get a set of new wheels made, as there was no chance of salvaging the old ones.

Once the caravan arrived I was able to make a detailed examination and what I discovered was disappointing. The whole thing was in a much worse state than I expected. A large part of the top half was rotten, the canvas was torn and falling apart, the doors were broken, the window in the back was smashed and many of the struts that held the canvas were missing or broken. On the other hand, two major components: the floor and undercarriage were in reasonable condition.

By now it was early October and time for us to leave Kerrera and return to my home in Tywyn, in Gwynedd. I had managed to find a carpenter in Oban who agreed to attend to the woodwork and a painter who said he would paint the caravan. Reluctantly, I left them to get on with it, promising I should return in two months. I had not managed to find a wheelwright in Oban, so I took the wooden wheels to Wales.

Douglas, my employer in Scotland, said he was acquainted with the Right Honourable Mrs. Shand Kydd, mother of Princess Diana. He offered to approach her on my behalf and ask if she would be willing to lend her support to my journey. He also said he knew a man called John Keys, who lived in Dalmally, who had travelled extensively and was a travel writer. Douglas thought he might be able to help, and it was arranged for me to meet him at his home.

When I arrived, he took me into the kitchen and made coffee, and I began to tell him of my plans. He listened, at first with some scepticism. He interjected questions from time to time and offered occasional suggestions. His final question was, "What date are you leaving?"

"I don't know yet," I told him.

He walked towards the outside door, opened it and said, "You may as well leave. If you have no starting date, you must set one or else I shall not believe in you and neither will anyone else."

Having said that, he came back, got out his maps and began to work through the time scale for preparation and journey, taking into account the weather to be encountered at different seasons in the various countries and the terrain I should have to cross. We estimated that an average of 15 miles a day would bring me close to China in about two years. After much more discussion, we arrived at a date: June 1st, 1987, some nine months ahead. At that moment it seemed to give me plenty of time to make the final arrangements, but that was a view I would not hold for long, as a series of mishaps, almost catastrophes were waiting to take place.

As I left his house, John Keys said, "You have now set June the first as your setting off date and you must stick to it and leave on that date even though your preparations might not be completed."

I thanked him and went away with those words echoing in my brain. I was to realise just what sound advice he had given me when I began to formulate my plans. Knowing I had to leave on the first of June made me strive harder to be ready on time.

When I was collecting the caravan from Caroline Younger, she had asked me if I had chosen the charity I was to support. If not, she said, her mother was chairwoman of the Scottish branch of "Save the Children", her name was Norah King and I could have a word with her. Whilst I wanted to do something for the less fortunate, all the negative responses I had been getting from embassies made me start to think that it would help my cause if I were connected to a charity, preferably an international one. "Save the Children" could be the very one for my purpose, so, with Mrs. King, I approached them. They showed interest and asked me for more details. For the next four months I liaised with them, confident they would let me be connected to their organisation.

When I left Scotland, I arranged with Douglas Lindsay to have my mail forwarded to Tywyn. Letters kept arriving, most of them not very encouraging. One exception was a letter from Mrs. Shand Kydd, who asked me to supply details of my preparations. This I did, and within a week or so she wrote again saying she would be pleased to lend her name, particularly to support "Save the Children". I felt now that it was even more important to get linked to them. I had still had no luck with obtaining horse or harness.

One vital element of the caravan that was missing when I took possession was the pair of shafts. Once again resorting to the telephone, I tracked down a man in Stoke-on-Trent who agreed to make me a pair, taking the precise details from me as we spoke. I again mentioned my difficulty in obtaining horses and once again I was advised to contact John Jackson of Accrington or Tom Dooley of Kidsgrove. Tom has a gypsy caravan and horses. I decided to go and see him on the next day.

When I got to Kidsgrove, I found Tom Dooley easily enough. There was his mobile caravan and standing close by was his gypsy caravan, a beautiful sight. Two coloured horses stood patiently beside it. I had not chosen the best time for a visit, as Tom sorrowfully told me. On the day before, his best horse had died. He had left him tethered to a tree overnight and some youths with air guns had been taking pot shots at him. He was terrified and tried to run. His efforts had tightened the rope round his neck and he had strangled himself. By the time Tom finished his sad story, he was shaking with anger and distress. I imagined how close the man had been to his animal. As I made my journey, I was to learn exactly how he felt.

"John Jackson is your man," Tom suggested. "Nobody knows more about this type of horse than him."

I telephoned John Jackson the next day. I told him about my intention to travel as far as China with a horse and caravan.

"You'll never make it," he said. "The sheer volume of traffic and finding a stopping place every night is impossible to handle. It drove me off the road, and I was born in a barrel top *vardo*. (*Vardo* is the Gypsy word for their caravans)

I was having a job convincing him that I was serious about this and was determined to try.

"Right then. You had better get your arse up here. I'll then see what I can do to help you," he said suddenly. I set off for Accrington immediately.

John lived in a large house with stables surrounding the yard. He was a small man with black hair beginning to turn grey. I was struck at once by his confident and commanding voice. We sat together in his front room, drinking and discussing my plans. It was several hours later when he said he would help me. He told me he had just completed a charity run with horse and cart, travelling from John O'Groats to Land's End.

"Leave the horses, harness, shafts and wheels to me," he said. "I will be in touch. One thing, though. There is no way you can do it on your own. You need someone to help you, as you will need to have two horses for such a long way so you can change them over day by day. That takes two people."

Later on I would learn that I would need not just one person, but an army.

I discovered that it was tantamount to committing suicide to travel without public liability insurance, in case a horse bolted with the caravan, causing damage to other vehicles or members of the public, or in case a horse bit or trampled anyone. I failed to find an insurance company that would consider giving me cover, although I wrote to or telephoned about sixty companies.

Meanwhile, I was having to make occasional visits to Oban to see how my caravan was shaping. The carpenter was finished in January and the painter, John Jaks, said he would have to get it under cover before he could begin work. I found a man in Oban who let me put it in his shed.

News had spread that I was looking for a travelling companion and I had many offers from people, all strangers, some of whom even offered me money to be allowed to come with me. I had, however, been warned by experienced travellers to be very careful whom I chose to take with me as a great number of ventures had failed when the partners fell out. I was almost tempted to take one man who offered to put up £15,000, which would have been very useful, as I knew by this stage that the journey was going to cost easily £30,000. My son, Max, whom I had not seen for about two years, came to visit me in Tywyn and find out what I was up to. I told him I was planning to visit China with a gypsy caravan.

"You what!" he exclaimed in amazement, when I went on to explain how the idea had come to me and how I had spent the past three years of my life.

We went for a pint at my local and I asked him how long he was staying in Tywyn.

"I don't know," he said. "I'm out of a job at the moment."

"Why don't you stay with Beth and me?" I suggested. "You can help me with writing letters and such. I am having a job coping with all the paperwork."

Max knew what I meant. He knew that I had great difficulties with reading and writing. Most of the correspondence I had done so far was actually written by friends, relations and Beth. My problems owed their origins to childhood ill health. When I was a lad of three, I contracted osteomyelitis, an unpleasant bone disorder. It was during the second world war and I had to endure many operations to remove abscesses in many parts of my body. My leg, or rather, my hip gave me great pain during most of my childhood. The specialist treating me could not find the cause of my illness and I went in and out of hospital, and was often too ill to attend school. This disruption to my lessons played havoc with my learning, in particular my efforts at learning to read and write.

In 1950, when I was aged eleven, another specialist examined me and my illness was finally diagnosed as osteomyelitis. He operated immediately, removing part of my thigh bone. As I was still growing, they decided to allow the bone to grow together rather than pinning it. For me this entailed spending the next eighteen months in hospital and, later, in my bed at home, lying on my back and covered in plaster of Paris up to my neck. After this I was in a wheelchair for three months, then I went on crutches until I was able to walk again.

My schooling was resumed when I was 13½ years old, by which time it was too late to gain literacy skills. I left school not knowing much about it, and I have subsequently discovered that I also suffer from partial dyslexia, so I started off with a learning handicap apart from my physical ailments.

My experiences had a brighter side, however, as they left me with a feeling for all those who spend long hours alone because of illness, disability or for other reasons. Perhaps it all stemmed from a day in 1947. The summer was very hot. I had had an operation on my leg in the May and was allowed home, in plaster, but I had to stay in bed. My mother placed my bed near the window overlooking the back garden. The Stratford – on – Avon canal ran past at the end of the garden and a short distance beyond us was a lock gate beside a basin of deep water. For many years this water had been bathed in by village children and I saw many of my friends passing by on their way for a dip. I lay on my bed longing to be able to go with them. I wished with all my heart that one of them would stop for a moment and spend some time with me, as I was terribly lonely. Through the open window I could hear their excited shouts.

The village was situated on the other side of the house and I could hear the children playing games in the evening, the sound of bat hitting ball, the swish of skipping ropes, hopscotch. It was all so near yet so far. Many a night I cried myself to sleep, hoping tomorrow would bring someone to come and play with me. This sympathy for isolated people has always been with me and, maybe, has some bearing on my wish to help someone in the course of my travels.

I knew I needed a new canvas for the caravan, and I contacted Telford Tarpaulins who agreed to provide it free of charge. I was also given the sacking that lines the canvas. This was donated by a Mr. Parry of Guilsfield in Powys. The inner lining was donated by Laura Ashley's in Carno, Powys. From Mrs. Beckett of Cross Country Equestrian in Church Stretton came grooming equipment and hay nets. Mars Oil of Banbury supplied harness oil and hoof oil.

I had asked four leading ferry companies to sponsor me across the Channel and two gave me positive answers: Olau Lines from Sheerness and Sea Link from Dover. In the end I would choose Olau Line because their ferry docked at Vlissingen in Holland. Holland seemed to be the better choice, as it offered flat countryside and straight roads all the way through to the German border.

Several times I telephoned John Jackson in Accrington to ask how he was getting on with obtaining horses and equipment. He would usually tell me that he had been all over the place looking at animals. He said he had tested many, but they had not been bomb – proof and, secondly, they would none of them have been capable of pulling the caravan over such a distance.

"You need to get the best horses available. The problem is the owners never want to sell their best horses. Don't worry. I will find them," he assured me.

In December, he told me he had located two sets of horse harness and collars. These two, with various other accessories, would together cost about £2,000. He had also found a set of shafts costing £30. Rebuilding the wheels of the caravan came to about £450. He had made two tether chains each of which was 30 feet long. John was not a believer in using rope to tether horses as it could tighten round their necks and get entangled round their hooves. Chain was less likely to do this and, if someone wanted to steal the horse, rope could soon be cut, but chain required a hacksaw to sever it.

One insurance broker now told me not to worry about getting the public liability cover I needed. He said they would get an insurance company to undertake to provide this for me. I left it to him to prove his assertion. What a mistake that was!

Christmas arrived bringing a period of total frustration for me. Nothing at all happened for three weeks, as most people were off work. In January I tried to find out how to get a horse from Great Britain to Holland

and from Holland into other countries. A lady in the Ministry of Agriculture in Surrey was most helpful, always replying to letters and returning telephone calls. A letter from Mrs. Payton arrived on 25th March and told me all. It read as follows: –

Ministry of Agriculture, Fisheries and Food
Hook Rise South Tolworth Surbiton Surrey KT6 7NF

Telex 22203 Telephone 01-337 6611 ext 495

M W Hitches Esq
99A Plas Edwards
Tywyn
GWYNEDD

Your reference

Our reference
EK 5331
Date
25 March 1987

Dear Mr Hitches

A SPONSORED DRIVE FROM OBAN (SCOTLAND) TO THE ORIENT (CHINA)

Your letters of 24 and 27 February about the health and welfare requirements for horses on a sponsored drive to China, have been passed to me for reply.

As I explained to you when we spoke, this Ministry will only be able to provide certification to import your horses into the Netherlands and on to Belgium, providing you keep to your schedule of 2 days only in the Netherlands. I enclose a specimen copy of the health certificate that you will need to apply for. I understand that information on how to comply with welfare legislation has already been sent to you. From then on you will need to find out from each country on the route, the veterinary health conditions for import from the preceding country. I advise you to consider this before you leave Great Britain., as your horses may need to undergo tests for certain diseases.

I should also advise you that if you complete your journey to China, you will not be able to re-import your horses directly into Great Britain. You may therefore need to consider alternative arrangements for their care.

Finally, I wish you every success with your venture and do not hesitate to contact me again should you require further information.

Yours sincerely

Joan M Payton

J M PAYTON (Mrs)
Animal Health IB

Enc:

I gathered from this that the Ministry was only responsible for the export of the horse to Holland. After that it was up to me to enquire about the requirements of each country as I came to it. I began to feel that I was making no progress with any of the embassies or Ministry representatives, so I went to London to speak personally to people at each embassy. I spent three days working my way from one embassy to the next, but nothing new was learned with the exception of the embassy of the U.S.S.R. Here, I was told it was virtually impossible for lone travellers to be allowed to travel through the U.S.S.R. and they directed me to Intourist, Moscow, who had their office close by.

I duly presented myself and told my story, which left them at something of a loss. They said I should leave it with them and they would have to think about it. I trusted them, not knowing this was simply a way of getting rid of me. Now and again a note would arrive, soothingly advising me that the matter was now in the hands of Intourist, Moscow, or the British Embassy in Moscow.

I had, however, other matters to attend to. "Save the Children" had to be convinced that I was serious in my intention to reach China and they wanted convincing that it was practically possible and logistically possible. There was small chance of convincing anyone while I was being fobbed off by the Russians, still had no insurance cover and seemed to be beset by difficulties. I still pinned my hopes on establishing a link with the charity, in spite of all, but this was yet another mistake on my part.

In mid – January 1987, I received an invitation to attend the London Committee of "Save the Children" in order to spell out my plans and objectives for the benefit of representatives of the charity from all their U.K. regions. I felt confident that, after working closely with them for the past seven months, this meeting was a mere formality and I fully expected to get the final seal of approval and be told that we could work together.

To my horror, after spelling out all my plans, the chairwoman of the meeting said she was sorry, but the committee felt unable to commit volunteers to any more work this year and thus they were regretfully rejecting me for the present. I felt sick, shattered and depressed at hearing this. I went back to Tywyn in such low spirits that I came close to destroying all my plans. My deepest worry was that my sponsors had been so generous to me because of the assumed link to "Save the Children" and I felt my next step should be to contact everyone and return all their gifts. For a week I let myself wallow in misery, my future now in grave doubt.

Beth had become very withdrawn over the past few months, annoyed that I was planning on going away. Our relationship had become one of non – communication and I had been in the habit of putting her hurt look to the back of my mind, concentrating only on the journey ahead, but it was Beth who gave me the impetus to pick up the traces again after my bitter disappointment.

"Bill, you can't give up now, after all the work. Why not contact another organisation?"

She surprised me, as it must have been a hard thing for her to say. I took up her suggestion, however, and went to the library to find a book on registered charities. I selected several to which I wrote, amongst which was one called "Action Research for the Crippled Child". I telephoned their office and was advised to speak to Mr. Ted Raynor. He showed some interest and asked me to forward as many details and as much information as I could. By February 5th, Action Research had agreed for us to work together.

We agreed that I would display their posters on the sides of the caravan as I went along and they would provide me with Paddington Bear collection boxes for public donations. In each of their districts in Britain that I came to, their local organiser would be with us in the major towns. It all came as a huge relief to me, and I had learned the lesson about not putting all my eggs in one basket.

In the meantime, the caravan was still in Oban. It had been moved under cover and was being painted. When that was finished, the new canvas and interior lining had to be fitted and other repairs carried out. The leaf springs had become flattened out through much use over the years and I had to get them tempered by a firm in Wrexham, Cambrian Springs. Once again the work was done without charge. I was finding myself wanting to be in too many places at once by this time and Max volunteered to go to Oban, camp out and be on hand to work on the caravan, ensuring that it would be roadworthy in time for the big day. So, off he went.

In mid-April, John Jackson telephoned me to say he had found the two horses and they were in his yard.

"You had better come and see them," he said.

Off I went to Accrington. I shall never forget the first sight of my two horses, both black, about fifteen hands high, one with four white feet, the other with one white foot. Each had a tiny star on its forehead. John told me to come close and stroke them, but I was a bit apprehensive as they looked so huge. I went up and touched them both, stroking them gently and suddenly I felt good. At last I had my horses, something I had always wanted since I was a child.

There was a lot to learn and on the next occasions when I went to see Mr. Jackson, he would teach me many things about horses and driving, all the little tricks that he had learned during his years travelling the roads. The point he made most often and most strongly was the attention I must pay to the psychology of the animals. They were certainly valuable animals, one having cost me £1,000 and the other £900. By the end of April, John Jackson had kept all his promises about helping to equip me and get me organized.

During the first week of May, I travelled up to Oban taking the new wheels and the re-tempered springs to Max. John Jackson had agreed to arrange for transportation of the horses to Scotland from Accrington. They would come up in a horse box. When I arrived, Max told me he had made friends with two young ladies, Helen and Rachel, and a man called Sandy had provided digs for him in his house. Helen and Rachel knew the horses were arriving and they had spoken to a man they knew and arranged for him to take them, as he had a small stable on his smallholding.

It took some eleven hours for the horse box to come from

Accrington, and Max, Helen and Rachel were waiting with me when it arrived at 9.30 p.m. When we opened the back to unload the horses they were wringing wet all over. At this time, I knew next to nothing about horses, but they were obviously in distress and sweating. We fed and watered them and then let them sleep.

For the next few days we left them to get used to their new surroundings and on the fourth day we tried taking them for a walk. It proved impossible; we simply could not control them. They leaped, bucked and reared. There was no comparison between these animals and the horses I had seen with John Jackson. Unfortunately, the only place we could walk them was directly on to the busy main road and I was worried about the way they were playing up. Both Rachel and Helen were accomplished riders, but there was no way they could ride them.

We mentioned our trouble to Sandy, Max's landlord, and he told us he had a farmer friend who lived in a quiet spot in a lane leading off a village and who had a barn and fields. He offered to ask this friend if we could move the horses there to work with them. He was as good as his word and the next day we found a man with a horsebox and the horses were moved to the farm.

David Clark was a plant – hire man *cum* small farmer, dealing mainly in sheep. His barn and fields were a short distance out of Oban and offered an ideal spot for me and the horses to get better acquainted.

My next move was to get a vet to provide me with an influenza vaccination certificate for the horses and a document describing the exact details of each animal, its markings, breed, sex, age and name. As far as I had been able to determine, this was the only documentation I required to get me through the ports and onto the ferry. The influenza injections were in two stages, one was administered now and the second shot was to follow in three weeks time. It was now the last week in April, time was running out fast and we could not delay. I contacted the Veterinary Service in Oban and arranged for Mr. Ferguson to come out. He warned me not to put the horses to any exertion for a few days. I was growing impatient to press ahead. However, there were other important matters still to be dealt with.

The insurance had still not been sorted out; the caravan had not been brought to the farm where the horses were and John Jackson had told me I needed to be with the horses for two or three months prior to departure, in order for us to get used to each other. He had also told me that both horses were used to pulling flat carts on rubber tyred wheels, not something that towered nine feet above them and rumbled and crunched along on steel rimmed wheels while pots and pans clanked together and the undercarriage creaked. They would need time to get used to all this, John warned. There was not enough time left and everything was beginning to pile up on me.

Near the farm there lived a very kind man called George who helped us with feeding, watering and grooming. Rachel and Helen came over each day and were able to ride the horses, as they had calmed down by now.

We got the caravan to the farm. Now it had been fully restored, it looked smart and colourful. The undercarriage was yellow, the sides and ends maroon with splashes of decorative colour. The canvas top was bright blue. We put one horse in his harness, reversed him into the shafts of the caravan, hitched him up and I decided to try driving him straight away. The drive leading into the lane was rough and uneven. "Go on, boy," I said.

He leaned forward and began to pull and the caravan began to emit strange crunches and crackles as the wheels turned. The horse stamped his feet and then reared up to his full height, turning sideways as he landed.

"Steady, boy," I shouted. The horse tried to rear up again. "Get him out, Max. Quick!" By now the animal was trying to bolt and I could tell he was terrified. After a minute he was free of the shafts, still supporting his harness and swinging round in circles.

"We shall try the other horse, the one with one white foot," I said, trying not to panic.

He went between the shafts and was hitched up. I urged him to move forward, half afraid of what was about to happen. He began to pull, his feet stamping on the drive as he took the strain. Then, he was away, showing signs of fear but behaving well. I felt a surge of relief. That was not a bad effort for his first time, I thought. I could not foresee that it would be the last time he pulled the caravan before we set off on our long journey together.

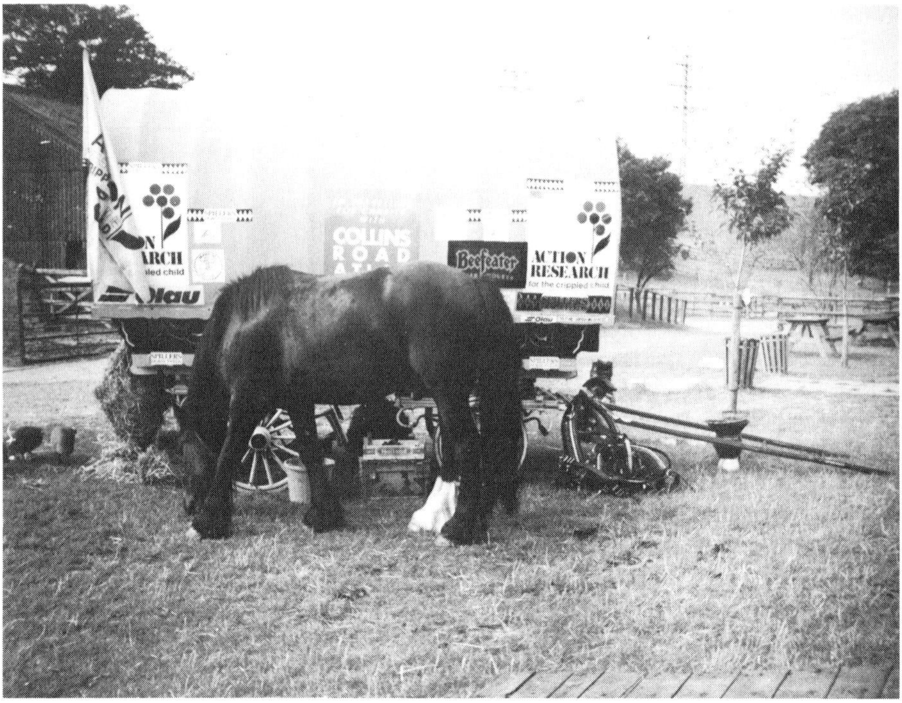

Action grazing in front of the caravan.

The caravan as it was when first seen.

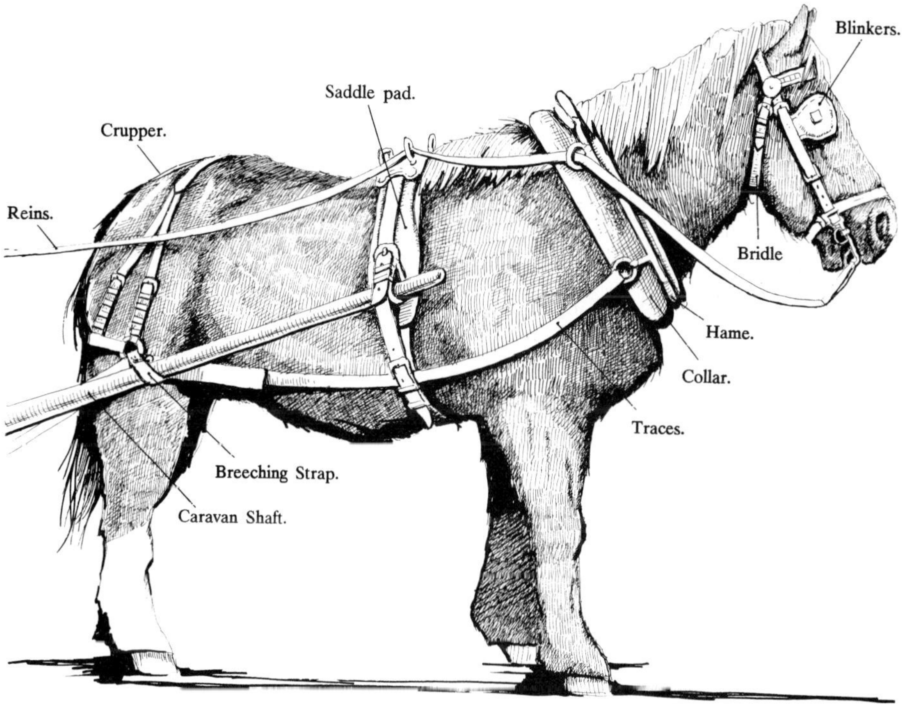

Detail of Harness

Chapter Two

Nothing Goes Right

My ignorance of horses would soon show. I found a few spots on the body of my horse with the one white foot. They were on his face, down his chest, between his legs and on his neck. Over the next few days the number of spots increased, grew larger and began to exude pus. David Clark told me they were from sheep ticks picked up in the fields used by the horses. He said things would be worse if we tried to pull the ticks out. On the fourth day I noticed the horse with one white foot was hanging his head and he was off his food. The weeping sores looked dreadful and I called the vet.

"He is very sick. I think it is tick fever," he said, having made a thorough examination. As we spoke the horse went down rather clumsily. "You must get him in the barn and keep him warm. I shall give him an antibiotic injection."

At first, when we tried to move him into the barn, the horse would not get up, but we managed it eventually. David Clark had prepared a thick bed of straw on the floor, and the horse went clumsily down again as soon as he was inside. He was staggering slightly and looked the way I was feeling at that moment. I spent the night in the barn, beside the horse. When he was lying down he could not support his head except by letting his chin rest on the floor. From time to time during the night I shone my torch on him. He never stirred, although sometimes his eyes were open. Even with my ignorance of horses, I could tell he was a very sick animal.

The vet arrived at 9.30 next morning and had another look at him. He shook his head sadly. "I don't know whether he will make it. His temperature is still far too high." My heart sank.

During the whole of that day one of us, Max, Rachel, Helen, George, David Clark's neighbour, or I stayed with him, but there was no improvement. He still showed no interest in food or water. That night I again stayed with him, this time lying by his side, my arm round his neck, talking to him and telling him to get better. I bathed his sores, those I could reach, with warm water. I did not know what else I could do to help him. At last I fell asleep by his side. There was no fear of him getting up. He was too ill to move.

Max arrived and I woke up. I looked at the horse and saw him lying with his head flat on the floor. I thought he was dead.

"White Foot, White Foot," I said eagerly, fear in my voice. He opened his eye and looked at me, moving his head slowly. This time he did not have to rest it on the ground. I pushed his water under his nose and he stuck his head in and had a little drink.

"Max," I shouted, "He's getting better, I think. He's just had a small drink. Get some apples and carrots." Max cut them into small pieces, put them in a bowl and put them in front of the horse, but he didn't want them yet, so we left them there. I left Max on watch while I went to David's house for some warm water. I set off to fetch the water and returned half an hour later, by which time, to my amazement, the apple and carrot had gone from the bowl.

"Max," I shouted, "Have you moved his food?"

"No, Dad."

"Well, it's gone. He must have eaten it. Get some more. Let's see if we can get him up."

We tried unsuccessfully to get him to his feet, then left him to it, amply provided with hay, apples, carrots and water.

During my time spent with White Foot, as I now called him, I had been thinking how to get the other horse used to pulling the caravan. I was almost certain it was only the noise that frightened him. I decided to put horse and caravan in the field, as the iron shod wheels would not make a noise as they rolled along in the grass.

We settled the horse into the shafts and I went aboard to do the driving, George holding the bridle. Slowly stomping with his hooves, stopping now and again with fright, then moving on again, trembling at first. Gradually he calmed down a little, which pleased George. I said, "Take him out." I was satisfied. It had been a great improvement over the last time.

I went back to the barn to look at White Foot. My heart thrilled when I opened the door and saw him standing, nibbling gently on the carrots. I was over the moon. I ran to him, hugged him, kissed him on the nose and told him, "You've made it!"

The vet called again later and took his temperature. He said it had come down a bit, but it was still high. Then he gave him a jab of antibiotic in his neck.

By the following morning, many of the sores were scabbing over and looking much better, so I led him outside the barn and onto a nice piece of green grass. He tucked in with enthusiasm, something he had not done for many days, and I knew he was on the mend.

Meanwhile, things were piling up in Tywyn so I decided to return that morning and arrived home, very tired, at 8.00 p.m. Almost before I was indoors, the telephone rang. It was Max calling from Oban.

"There's been an accident, Dad," he said. "The caravan is smashed up."

"What do you mean – smashed up?" I asked.

"George decided to put the horse with four white feet into the shafts on his own. The horse bolted, turning the caravan over and smashing it up," Max explained.

"How bad is it? Can it be repaired?" I enquired, clutching at a last grain of hope.

"No, I don't think so," Max said flatly.

"I'm coming straight back," I told Max. Beth had been listening to the conversation and I could see she felt for me.

"Bill, don't go straight back. Stay and get some sleep tonight. You need rest and you will think more positively in the morning."

She was right. In the morning, however, came another bad blow to my hopes. A letter arrived from the insurance brokers I had been depending on to get me the necessary cover. It was eight months since I last had contact and they were now advising me that they had been unable to find any insurance company willing to take me on. I thought to myself, not for the first time, that I had made a grave error in trusting in one source alone. I vowed that I would never again make the same mistake, but in future would have several options open to me. It had happened several times during my preparations that I had been let down. It was a serious matter, as several embassies had advised me that any permission to pass through their territory was dependent upon me having public liability cover.

Before leaving for Oban, I tried in vain to speak to other insurance companies, but with no joy. In the end I gave up, feeling that everything was against me.

From Tywyn to Oban by car takes about eight and a half hours, if one drives non-stop. I drove up non-stop and it was a miserable drive. I kept going over in my mind all the things that had gone wrong and the things I had not done at all or had started but not finished. My head was full of problems and I found it impossible to sort them out. My brain was in a fuzz. I reached Max's digs at 8.30 p.m. He was waiting for me, torch in hand, and we made directly for David Clark's farm. It was getting dark when we arrived.

"It's in the barn, Dad," said Max. He opened the door and stood back. I shone my torch on the caravan. The whole top half was shattered and broken, hanging to one side.

"What do you think, Dad?" Max asked.

"It's a write-off," I replied. "I think that's the end of the journey for us."

I walked away from the barn, almost in tears and unable to think what to say or do next. "Take me to Oban, Max. I need a drink."

When we got to Oban, I took my pint and sat down alone feeling utterly dejected. I knew many of the people in the bar, as I had drunk there often in the past and my carpenter, my painter, Rachel, Helen and Max's landlord, Sandy, were regulars there. They were all present, coming up and saying "Sorry, Bill, Sorry, Bill." I was overwhelmed by people trying to sympathise.

By 11.30 p.m. I had drunk many beers. Meanwhile, Sandy and his friends had been consulting together, and he now came over with Max and asked me what I intended doing next.

"I don't know, Sandy. Give up, I suppose." Saying these words, I burst into tears. I covered my face with my hands and sobbed loudly. My grand plans for the journey now lay in ruins. After a time I pulled myself together and slowly people came over, one by one, to ask what they could do to help. By now Sandy had taken control.

"Don't worry, Bill. One way or another these boys will get you on the road again," he said gently. "I have a friend in Connel Village. Bob McTear is his name and he is a retired shipwright. He might help to rebuild the caravan, if it is possible. I'll go over early in the morning and ask him. I'll go myself, as he hates the English. He's a strong Scottish Nationalist, so he may help or he may not."

I slept that night at Sandy's home. True to his word, Sandy went off early to speak to Bob and came back at 9.30 a.m. Next morning he said that Bob wanted to see me right away. Sandy said he was coming with me.

We arrived at Bob's bungalow and Sandy knocked at the door. A man came to answer it. He had grey, wavy hair, wore glasses, had a round face and was rather plump and elderly. Sandy introduced us and Bob led us into his lounge. He asked us to take a seat and he offered us tea. I accepted gratefully, as I still felt rough after the previous night.

"Well, Bill, Sandy has told me about you and what you plan to do. It is a marvellous thing." His next statement shocked me. "I don't know what you are doing sat in my house. I hate the English, but because you are a friend of Sandy and you have big problems, I will try and help you. I don't know how much, as I have a bad heart. Come on. Let's get to it."

"What, now!" I said.

"Yes," said Bob. "Time is not on your side."

That day we dismantled the caravan, salvaging whatever we could. It was a warm day and Bob was sweating profusely and breathing hard. By 5.00 p.m. everything was done. The next stage was rebuilding. That same afternoon, Sandy had gone along to a local timber merchant and he returned with a load of timber.

"How much do I owe you, Sandy?" I asked.

"Nothing," he said. "The timber merchant has given it to you. The boss had already heard about what happened to the caravan."

During that day my thoughts had turned often to George. He had not turned up and I guessed how bad he must have been feeling. I could understand that he did not want to face me. I felt no ill towards George, however. He had only been trying to help me and he knew how important it was to get the horse used to the caravan. There were only two weeks left before the big day. I went round later to see him at home and I told him I put no blame on him. He was obviously very upset. I knew how he loved the horses. They were visible from his kitchen window.

"I will not come to them again, Bill," George said sadly, turning away from me and walking into the kitchen. Sometimes in life we might be permitted to tell a little, white lie, and this was one of those times.

"Oh! That's a shame, George. I was relying on you to work them for me tomorrow morning. Max and I might be late and the horses will need water and White Foot has to have his special food." This was something we had been giving him since his illness to build him up. "If you can't do it, I shall have to ask Rachel."

"I'll do it, Bill," said George. My ploy had worked.

I was not going to be late at all. In fact, it was quite the opposite. We arrived early.

All day and for many days thereafter, Bob, Sandy, Max, Rachel and I, with occasional help from David Clark, worked on the caravan. I cannot give enough thanks to these people.

When most of the woodwork had been completed, I had to return to Tywyn where there was much unfinished business to complete. I decided not to waste any more time trying to get entry permits for the various countries I should be visiting, but to try getting as far as I could with nothing. I still had not decided on a travelling companion, I had no insurance cover and I had not actually driven my horses. I now had to make some decisions. There remained only a few days until June 1st.

The first step was to make up my mind not to take the horse with four white feet, but to try and get another horse during my journey. Secondly, I would ask Max to come with me. He had been helping me now for several months and he seemed to me to be the obvious choice. The snag was that Max had no money and I should have to support him. When I put it to him, he agreed to go as far as Sheerness and see me aboard the ferry. In the meantime, he was hoping I might find someone else.

There was nothing to be done about getting practice at driving the horse and caravan. Even if I had had more time, the horse with the white foot was still convalescent, but the other horse was too dangerous.

That left me with the financial side of things to worry about. When I had done my initial budget I had not made any allowance for the extra costs of telephoning, travelling and incidentals that had cropped up. In the past year those extras had made a large hole in my money, the fund I would be relying on to provide for my needs as I travelled during the next two years. I decided, when I got home, that I would ask the bank to help me.

At the back of my mind was the matter of insurance, as yet still unresolved. If I failed to sort this out in the remaining ten days, I should have to call everything off.

When I got back to Tywyn I found a pile of mail awaiting me. One letter was from Mr. Sharp at the Wellcome Foundation asking me to go to Crewe Hall, their U.K. Headquarters, to collect a cheque from the office staff and some medical supplies for myself and my horse. Another letter was from my bank, asking me to get in touch as I was overdrawn. I did not realise that things were that bad already. I had to act at once to remedy the situation. The only way out was to cash in my insurance policy.

I rang my insurance agent and explained the predicament, so he promised to set things in motion right away. I made an appointment to see the bank manager on the 24th, hoping to have the insurance money in my hand by then.

On Friday, May 21st, I went to Crewe Hall to collect the cheque and supplies. Mr. Sharp and his staff had laid on a lunch for me. I was introduced to Mr. Cooper of Kingsway Rolland, London Publicity agents. It was he who presented me with the cheque. Later on, Mr. Cooper asked me if I needed any help. I could have given him a list of things, not least of which was finance, meaning sponsorship. However, I told him about my difficulty in obtaining Public Liability Insurance. He leaned back in his chair, clasped his hands behind his neck and stared at the ceiling for a few minutes. He was a small, dapper man, his hair greying. With his glasses and his pin-striped suit, he looked every inch the typical London City gent. When he walked, he had a distinct limp, as he had lost one leg during the war and now had to rely on an artificial leg.

He suddenly leaned forward and said, "On Tuesday I am going to the Houses of Parliament for a meeting. I will see what I can do for you." He handed me his card. "Ring me at home on Wednesday night."

When I got home, I found that the cheque from the insurance company had arrived. It amounted to £4,300 and with it and the £600 I had just received from the Wellcome Foundation, I went to see my bank manager. I felt confident that with this £4,900, enough to cover my overdraft, I could borrow another £6,000.

When I opened the door to his office and entered, I saw a second person present.

"I am sure you don't mind Mr. Phillips being present. He will be the new manager here next month."

"No. I don't mind," I said.

I sat down and began to talk to them about my journey, gradually building up to the sensitive matter of borrowing £6,000.

"Mr. Hitches, your overdraft is now £4,700. You say you have with you two cheques totalling £4,900, enough to clear the overdraft?" the manager said.

"That's right. I need another £6,000 to see me on my way. It can be set against the deeds of my house, if that's all right," I told him.

His reply shook me to the core. "How do you intend paying it back? You say you will be away for at least two years. You will have no income. I am sorry, but I can lend you nothing."

I have never felt so sick. I felt myself trembling with temper, or some other intense emotion – I am not sure what. I began to plead with him, raising my voice at times, but the answer remained the same. I walked dejectedly back to my car. After all the other mishaps and disasters, this was the final crunch.

Beth was sitting in the car waiting for me. I got in beside her and collapsed in tears, telling her of the manager's refusal.

"Bill," Beth said, catching sight of a crumpled envelope clenched in my hand, "Have you remembered to pay in those cheques?"

"Oh dear! I forgot, with all the upset I had in there. I'll go back and pay them in," I said.

Beth's eyes met mine. We were both on the same wavelength. I started the car engine and drove off. My feeling of guilt grew as we drove along. I felt it was a dirty trick not to have deposited the cheques – or was it fate!

Finally, I deposited them in another bank in Tywyn, then I wrote to Lloyds Bank's Head Office in London explaining what I had done and why, adding that I had been backed into a corner by the manager and that one year's planning had gone into my journey already and I was not going to throw all that away.

Although I had deposited £4,900 in Tywyn, I knew this would not last for longer than a few months. There would be day – to – day expenses to be met for myself and for Max. The horse would have to have new shoes, a vet must be paid at every border crossing, there were visa payments to be made, there would also be a green card for the horse box, and I had no idea how much any of these would cost.

I made one more decision, one that would enable me to complete my journey, and in so doing I put a wall between Beth and myself that would be hard to break. I put my house up for sale. That meant that if it sold while I was away Beth would be homeless. I was blind to her dilemma; only my journey mattered to me. At this late stage I had no other way of raising the cash. I would not be able to raise it any other way while I was travelling.

On the night of Wednesday, May 26th, I telephoned Mr. Cooper about insurance. He gave me a number to ring and said I should ask for John Newton. I rang and was given the name of a man called Chris Mills of Alexander Howdon Insurance Brokers. This man was expecting my call, I was told. When I rang his number, however, someone said he was not there and would be away all day. It dawned on me that I only had one working day left before June 1st, which was on the coming Monday. Once again I felt like abandoning my plans.

I went to see Beth at her workplace, as I had decided I must get back to Oban and see how things stood up there. My parting with Beth was frosty, to say the least. Her last words were "Goodbye. I hope you enjoy it all and that it is what you wanted." She sounded sarcastic and stern.

I left, feeling miserable and sad. On Friday, I met the vet and the horse with one white foot had his final influenza injection. We had decided to wait until the last moment, to give the poor animal a good chance to get over his illness.

At 11.30 I went to see Bob McTear, the retired shipwright, at his home. I asked if I could use his telephone to try and get hold of the elusive Chris Mills and talk about insurance. Bob and his wife had always been most kind to me, often allowing me to use their telephone for long distance calls and never accepting payment.

I got through to his office, but his secretary told me he was out at the Market at present. She said he knew all about me. She asked me to call back between 4.30 and 5 p.m. I waited until 5 o'clock and tried again, only to be told that Chris Mills was still not back. She took my number and said they would ring me back.

I sat waiting in Bob's house, thinking that there would not be anybody in that office now until Monday, it being Friday evening and getting later by the minute. If I had no insurance cover, I certainly could not risk going out with an untried horse and a caravan, especially in view of my lack of experience in handling either.

It was six o'clock when the telephone went. Chris Mills was apologetic, explaining that he had been all day trying to get some ships insured for passage through the Straits of Hormuz. He said he had all the information he required and all I had to do was send him £100 and I was covered. I was speechless; first of all just to hear him say all was well, and secondly, to know how little it was costing me. During my search for a company to accept the risk various large sums had been bandied about, the reason being the extremely unusual nature of my requirements. So many reasons for turning me down had been given that I was expecting a premium of at least £1,000 would be the price I should have to pay. I thanked Chris Mills very much and promised I should have his cheque for £100 in the post that very night.

"If you do that," he said, "You can leave on Monday as planned."

Now, with only two days to go, I had a feeling of numbness as I went about putting the finishing touches to the caravan and equipment. The mishaps in the last few months had left me feeling very tired. I wished that I had another few days just to get away from it all and rest my brain, but I had set June 1st as my leaving date and I would stand by it.

The vet had recommended that for the first few days I put the horse to little strain because of his recent illness and the influenza injections. On Sunday, I decided to give my horses proper names; not a difficult decision to make. The horse that was coming with me I would call Action. He was the one with one white foot. The horse with four white feet would be called Research. The names derived from the charity Action Research for the Crippled Child, the charity to which I would be connected while I was in Great Britain.

Refurbishing work on the caravan.

Chapter Three

The First Stage – Through Britain

I arrived at the farm at 8 a.m. and found Max with a hangover from the previous evening. The Great Day had arrived.

I groomed Action, fed and watered him. A little later, Max arrived with Rachel, and I put Action into the caravan shafts, then it was time to say goodbye to David Clark and thank him for letting us use his fields and barn. I had already agreed with him that he would keep Research, my second horse, at the farm. I walked over to say my farewells to Research, who had been leaning over the fence watching us get ready. I felt sorry that he was not coming along.

"Go on, Action," I said, taking up the reins. Action pulled forward, the caravan creaked and squeaked as it began to move. The steel rimmed wheels hit the Tarmac with a mighty rumble and Action stamped his hooves for a few seconds then continued walking. We were on our way at last.

It had been arranged that we should arrive in the town of Oban at 10.30 a.m., where many friends would be gathered to see us off. Among them were representatives from "Action Research for the Crippled Child", whose posters adorned the canvas sides of the caravan, and people from Spillers, as well as the Right Honourable Mrs. Frances Shand Kydd. From the farm to the town centre was a walk of about twenty minutes for Action. The vet had warned us not to subject the horse to too much strain and I considered this short walk could do him no harm. After many hand–shakes and photographs, we at last set off on our mammoth journey, heading towards China.

Once outside the town, we took Action out of the shafts and hitched the caravan to a small van. Max drove ahead and George and I followed, with me leading Action. It was a warm, sunny day, but that walk was a nightmare. Action was terrified by the traffic which passed in both directions and we were on a twisting, busy road. Whenever a lorry overtook, Action was frightened and he swung out into the road. George, Rachel and I spent most of that first day soothing him.

Max returned to us in the afternoon, having found a parking place for the night in Tynuilt. At the end of a thirteen mile walk I was a weary man. It was here that we said goodbye to Rachel and George. I was most grateful to both of them for all the help they had given me over the past few months.

I tethered Action to a tree and then went to the village pub for a pint with Max before turning in. I had longed for this day to come so that we could start on our long journey, but now the day was over and I had never felt so shattered.

The second day was even worse than the first. As I walked with Action while Max took the caravan ahead, every minute was torture. Action was even more nervous than yesterday, but I was now on my own with him and he was still swinging out wildly whenever a lorry overtook us. We got as far as Dalmally where, having obtained permission from the management, we were able to spend the night on a hotel car park.

I had already discovered that one problem with Action was his phobia about steel grids or manhole covers in the road. As we walked along, he would do anything to avoid having to step on them; this included swinging out or rearing up. By the hotel were five steel grids about 18 inches apart, so I spent an hour trying to walk him between them. It probably did nothing to overcome his phobia, but I had at last done something to get us more used to each other.

During this time, a lady stopped her car and spoke to me.

"I keep a hotel four miles along the road to Tyndrum," she said. "When you come past, stop and have a coffee and something to eat. I'd like to help you if I can."

"Thanks very much. We'll be ready for something to eat when we get to the hotel. We'll see you at about eleven o'clock."

I set off ahead, leading Action, and Max drove the truck behind. After a couple of hours we arrived at the hotel and were glad of an excuse to stop as Action had been behaving in his usual nervous manner. We tethered him by the roadside and went into the garden of the hotel to have coffee and cake.

The road was busy at that time of day and the hotel is situated on a very twisting section. It was lovely to relax and to have a bite to eat. The day was overcast, but fine and warm. I thought life was getting better. Lorries roared past on the road. Suddenly I heard the sound of galloping hoofbeats. Action had broken free and was galloping off along the road.

Max jumped into the truck to drive after him. I ran along the road, terrified that I would round a bend to find an accident caused by the runaway horse. I ran for two miles before catching up with Max. The horse had stopped and was cornered, but Max couldn't catch him. I was out of breath after my two mile run, but I calmed myself and talked to Action, until he let me take the reins.

Because it was so difficult to walk the horse, I had put on his harness that morning so that he had a bit in his mouth, which I hoped would give me better control. It had not helped much, but I felt that at least we were trying everything that we possibly could to manage him more efficiently. He must have been an awe inspiring sight as he galloped down the centre of the road with his reins streaming out behind.

I was so relieved at seeing him that I showed him no anger. I could tell he was excited, so I talked to him, telling him he was a good boy, patting his neck to calm him down. He was breathing heavily and so was I.

We led Action back to the hotel where the worried hotel owner was waiting for us. She was marvellous. No sooner had we tethered Action than more coffee was produced.

"Mr. Hitches," said the lady, "When you get back from your journey I'd like to buy your horse. I don't care how much you want for him; give me first refusal." This was the first of very many offers that were made to me as the journey proceeded. Where ever we went someone wanted to buy Action.

In spite of my determination and relief at having started out, I was having enormous doubts about carrying on. I was the first to admit that I didn't know enough about handling the horse, especially a horse that was not schooled. Man and horse were learning together. Every time there was a crisis, especially with the horse, I felt the full weight of responsibility. In between major crises, there was the constant worry about Action's behaviour on the busy roads. At the end of each day, when we stopped for the night, I was exhausted.

After the first week of walking, I considered that Action was now fit enough to pull the caravan, so this he did. We continued to travel east across Scotland, by Tyndrum and Crianlarich, then turned southward towards Callender and Stirling. We were on our own now, Max and I. We had to be self-sufficient and look after Action. We progressed slowly, making good about fifteen miles each day.

The days began to take on a familiar routine. Waking at about seven or seven-thirty, our first job was to feed the horse with the high protein feed which had been given to us by Dalgetty Spillers. Because the horse would be pulling a caravan for long distances through countryside which would not always have good grass along the roadside, this supplement was essential. Next, we all three needed grooming, Max, the horse and I. Conscious that we were working for "Action Research for the Crippled Child" and that we were constantly in the public eye, I insisted that Action be groomed after his feed. Max usually did this while I did the washing and tidied the van.

We had a small Gaz stove on which we heated water for our morning brew and for washing ourselves. This meant we did not have to light the stove. If we were near a river, we would wash ourselves and our clothes in its cold water.

A few days after leaving Oban it began to rain and continued to do so for almost all that miserable British summer of 1987. It rained so much that we were always wet through and often unable to dry our clothes. We hung them up in the back of the van to let the breeze blow through them, but still finished up wearing damp shirts and trousers.

I eat no breakfast, but Max would try to make himself a piece of toast on the stove, then we would make sure that the site of our overnight stop was left as clean and tidy as it was when we found it. By about nine-thirty we would be ready to leave.

In the early days, when I considered Action was still too weak to pull the van, Max would go ahead with the truck and the van. When he had found a suitable spot he would park the vehicles and make his way back to help me. After going for about five or six miles, we would stop for something to eat, if we could find a café. We carried no stocks of food because we were passing through towns or villages every day and we bought all we needed as we went along. After resting the horse for an hour or two, we would carry on through the afternoon until we found a place to brew tea or a café. Here we would rest again, not just for the sake of the horse, but because the time on the busy road played havoc with my nerves and I needed time to compose myself.

One afternoon, as we travelled slowly, a lorry travelling in the same direction came very fast round a corner behind us and, unable to stop in time, left the road and ploughed into the woods at the side. The effect on Action made him try and bolt, caravan and all, as the noise of the lorry crashing into the woodland was horrific. Actions' instinct was to get clear of it, so he went up the verge pulling the caravan and me in his wake. He was uncontrollable, and I began to realise his immense strength. As he climbed up the verge, the caravan tilted to an angle of thirty degrees, but luckily Action could go no further as his way was was blocked by the trees. He halted, trembling violently.

"Steady, Boy. Steady." I was shaking with fright, but I knew I had to show him who was in control. "Back, Action. Back, back." I fully expected the caravan would turn over on its side as we reversed down the slope and back onto the road. Max stayed to make sure the lorry driver was uninjured and I led the panic stricken horse out of the way.

On another day, a lorry had been following us with its air–brakes hissing loudly, the driver growing ever more aggravated at being delayed by us. He pulled out to overtake the horse and van, went into the path of an oncoming car and the two vehicles collided head on. Once again Action tried to bolt and veer off the road. I really could not blame him as I was again frightened and I thought that if it was going to be like this all the time we should never make it. Fortunately, both vehicles were travelling slowly at the moment of impact and nobody was hurt.

After a tea break, I felt strong enough to carry on, but from then on I was worrying about finding a place to stop for the night. At first we had tried to carry on until dark so as to travel the maximum distance in the day. Some days it took us two hours to find a place to stop for the night and this meant that we finished up driving the horse in the dark. After just one night of this, I insisted that at five o'clock we began looking for a place.

During our day there were two other important tasks. We always had to have a supply of water for the horse, who drank six to eight gallons every day. We kept a lookout for water and filled our buckets where ever we found it. As we drove along, we also kept an eye out for pieces of wood and twigs for our evening fire. As we collected them we put them in a sack hanging on the back of the caravan.

To me, my nerves shattered by the horse continually playing up and the constantly wet weather, the days were drudgery, one task after another, and always at the back of my mind the problem of finding somewhere to stop for the night.

Max and I are "townies". Although I was born in the country, I spent most of my life in the building trade in towns. Like so many people, I thought of the countryside as consisting of leafy lanes along which the horse would trot, with myself sitting on the step of the van as we bowled along. Every evening we would find a grassy verge at the roadside, tether the horse and turn in for a good night's rest. The reality was vastly different. I found that the rural parts of Britain are inhospitable places with no room for travellers who spend each day on the move and each night in a different location. Country people are deeply suspicious of travellers. Generations of country children have been brought up with the threat that if they stray from the straight and narrow the Gipsies will kidnap them.

I found that instead of spending the nights in idyllic rural seclusion, we made for a village or, if at all possible, a town to stop in. In towns and villages there was always a car park, either a public one or one at the pub. Landlords were always willing to let us stay for one night. Sometimes council officials tried to stop us staying the night in the public car parks, but generally they turned a blind eye when I assured them that we would move on the next day.

Max and I always cleared up any mess the horse had made, though I wryly admit that horse's urine is more offensive than manure. The smell of horse urine drying in the sun on a Tarmacadam carpark was enough to make sure that we moved on as quickly as possible.

Life was not all doom and gloom. There were a few high spots, even during the first weeks of the journey. I had promised to attend the fair at Cumbernauld to collect for "Action Research", so when we got to Crianlarich I took the road east towards Stirling. One afternoon we were passing a large hospital where the wards were like separate billets with space between, each ward having an entrance at the end. It was one of the rare days that summer that was not spoilt by rain, and I could see a few patients sitting outside. Completely on impulse, I swung the horse and van round into the hospital entrance and went up to the reception.

"Do you think the patients would like to see my horse?" I asked the bewildered young woman at the desk.

"I'll ask the administrator," she said.

"Take your horse and caravan to the back of the children's wards and the wards for the old people," said the administrator. "We'll ring the wards and tell them you're coming and the nurses will bring all the patients that are fit enough out to see you."

I took the horse round to each of the wards that were pointed out to me, and first the children then the older patients came out to see Action. The horse was well behaved away from the noise of lorries and other frightening sounds of the roads.

At the last ward the nurses wheeled out an old man in a wheelchair. I could see that he had suffered a stroke. One side of his face was paralysed and one arm. When they brought him near the horse he struggled up from the chair with help from the nurse. He looked carefully at Action and then tried in vain to stroke him. I saw that his problem was, that whilst he clung to the nurse with his good arm, he could not raise his weak arm to the horse. The old man sobbed with frustration, so I took hold of him and held him upright so that he could stroke Action and feel his silky hair. After a while he sank back into the wheelchair and the nurse returned him to the ward. She came back to say goodbye to me.

"He used to have horses," she said. "You know, he hasn't made an effort like that in the two months that he's been here. That's the first time that he's actually shown interest in something."

I went on my way in a thoughtful mood. I felt as though I had been of some use in giving the children little rides and letting the older patients get a break from the monotony of hospital life. Action had brought pleasure to them, but most of all I remembered the old man stroking the horse, with tears rolling down his cheeks.

We carried on along the busy roads to the fair at Cumbernauld. Action was still frightened by everything that he saw or heard on the road. Sometimes it was not only what he saw or heard that terrified him. One day he reared and whinnied as we were passing a grassy bank. It took me a few minutes to lead him on a little way and calm him. I looked over the bank and there was a billy goat quietly munching away. The horse could not have seen the goat as it was not making any noise. Action had been terrified by the smell of the animal.

At Cumbernauld arrangements had been made for us all to spend the night in a safari park. I led Action, who was pulling the van, and Max drove the truck in. We tethered the horse, unhitched the stove from underneath the van and lit the fire. Suddenly the peace was shattered by the most appalling howl that I have ever heard. On and on it went, more howls being added to the first one. Looking over the fence, I saw that Action had been put into the paddock right next to the wolves' enclosure. I rushed round the van to go and comfort the horse, only to find him unconcernedly cropping grass. The wolves howled for an hour until they were fed, but Action never raised his head from the grass. Max and I were convulsed with laughter to see the horse that reared and bolted when it heard the sound of a pig snorting or a hen clucking by the side of the road calmly eating while a pack of wolves howled for food ten yards away.

A few days afterwards, I made for Airdrie and arrived at the town later than I liked. Worse still, we had not been able to find a suitable place to stop in the town so we had to go on a bit further until we came to a small wooded area with enough open ground to tether Action for the night. The wood was only a few hundred yards outside the town, but by the time we had fed and tethered the horse it was dark.

Tethering Action was easy. John Jackson had made up a length of chain with a collar to go round the horse's neck. The chain continued through the collar and could be shackled back on itself so that it was difficult to undo. I always tightened the shackle with a spanner so that unless someone came along with tools they could not free the horse. The other end of the chain was shackled round a tree or post in the same way, again tightened with a spanner. After I was satisfied that Action was secure, Max and I went off to a pub nearby to get something to eat and drink. We were gone for about an hour, returning to the van at eleven o'clock. By now it was pitch black, but I could see that Action was not there. By the light of a torch I saw that the chain had gone from round the tree. Max also saw footprints in the muddy soil near the tree, and we knew that someone had intentionally set the horse free.

We started to search the wood, looking for signs that a forty feet length of heavy chain was sure to have left. The marks of the chain went through the wood and then disappeared on the Tarmac leading to the town. One might not think that a horse would go far with a weight like that behind him, but it has to be remembered that Action can pull a caravan with a man on board.

I was desperate. Just then a car drove up to a nearby house and the driver came over to us to see what the matter was. He offered to help by telephoning the police, which he did, then he offered to drive us round the town to search. The only problem was that this quixotic driver was as drunk as a lord. Fortunately, we had gone only a few hundred yards when we saw two policemen in the road. They stopped and I quickly got out of the car and went over to them.

"Have you seen a horse?" I asked.

"Is it yours?" came the reply. "It's down there. You catch it. I'm not going near that bloody great thing."

I went down the road to where Action was cornered and after a few minutes was able to calm him and lead him back to Max, who was trying to explain to the police how we came to be out in a large Mercedes with an obviously drunken driver. I told the police that it was an emergency and that the man had come out of his house to help us. True, he had only gone into the house to telephone for us, but to our relief the policemen got back into their car and drove off. In two minutes I had led Action back to the tree and Max had got the car and driver safely home. Our irrepressible helper then invited both of us to come in and join him in a nightcap.

We carried on with our journey south through Scotland towards the border with England. It was July by now, but the weather was terrible. It seemed to rain every day, so that Max and I were constantly wet. Action was fit and well, the walk through Scotland, at first without the weight of the van, had strengthened him and he was looking well and was obviously strong again. On the other hand, his behaviour had not improved. He was just as nervous as ever. Of course, now that he was stronger it was more difficult for me to hold him if he started to bolt or swerve.

By this time Action's shoes had worn thin and were coming loose, so when we got to Carluke, just south of Airdrie, we found a farrier. He was an old man, tall and wearing a leather smock. His hands were gnarled from years spent fitting horse shoes. We had parked in the Municipal Park, beside a large hedge and it was here that he came and fitted new shoes.

Near the Border, we decided to go to Gretna Green and see the famous blacksmith's shop. Juggernauts, cars and lorries roared past and Action trotted calmly along. Max had gone on ahead to check the road and we were only a few miles away from our destination when, without warning, Action stopped in his tracks, raised his head and snorted, sniffing the air.

"What's up now?" I thought. "Go on, Boy. Go on."

He moved forward trotting, still excitedly snorting. He was growing more excited, trying to take me off the road and onto the grass verge. I pulled him up and jumped down from the caravan. As I reached his head he tried to bolt, this time heading across the road and into the oncoming traffic. I could see Max approaching.

"Max," I shouted, "Something's the matter with Action. I can't control him. We had better get him out of the shafts and try to find out what's the matter."

Slowly we unhitched him and as soon as he was free from the shafts he lifted his hooves and tried to bolt, swinging his rear end out into the main road. Luckily the lorry coming towards us must have spotted the danger and had slowed down. A few yards away was a small cul–de–sac and I headed Action towards it, passing a barn full of sheep. Once in the cul–de–sac, I removed Action's harness to see if there was anything sticking in him or rubbing him. He was still snorting, head raised and body stiff.

Max checked his hooves and legs, but we could find nothing wrong with him or his harness. As we attended to the horse, a tractor and trailer arrived at the barn and the driver began loading the sheep. I knew something was badly wrong with Action. Normally, as soon as he was free of his harness he would dive his nose into the nearest grass, but not this time. I began to walk him slowly up and down the cul–de–sac, trying to relax him and talking gently to him. He began to calm down a little.

"Let's try him again, Max," I suggested. We put him back in the shafts and went back to the main road, where he started his antics all over again. I had a job to control him for the next 300 yards or so, then he suddenly relaxed and trotted on as though nothing had happened. I puzzled about what had been happening and supposed I might never find out.

That evening, after parking, Max and I went for a pint in a pub and we got talking about horses to a young woman who herself owned horses. During our conversation, I mentioned to her about Action playing up that afternoon.

"Where you say this happened did you see on your right a farm standing back across the fields?" she asked.

"Yes," said Max.

"Well, that is a slaughter house. It was the smell of blood that frightened him. I cannot ride along that road with my horses. The smell drives them crazy," the woman explained.

This was another thing I had learned about Action – that the smell of blood terrified him. Later in my journey I would come across similar events.

When we arrived at Gretna Green, we parked the van close to the forge. It was midday and we were amazed to see the number of couples that went inside, presumably to have a link forged between them. One couple asked if they could have their photograph taken with Action and the van. I was delighted to oblige them. They spoke with a foreign accent and I learned that they were from West Germany. They had flown from Düsseldorf very early that morning, arriving at Manchester where a hire car was waiting to take them on the three hour drive to Gretna. They were married in ten minutes, and had their photograph taken with Action. The car was standing by to whisk them back to the airport so that they would be back in Düsseldorf for the wedding reception that evening. I was pleased that Action had added yet more colour to their crazy wedding day.

We had a minor celebration for crossing the first national boundary on our journey. I drank a couple of pints, the toast being "To many more border crossings!"

After crossing into England, I did not find the going any easier. The weather was still terrible with almost continual rain as we took the road across the bleak moorland south of Carlisle. Action was no better behaved, still shying and rearing when lorries passed. Altogether, I was at a very low ebb.

When we came to Penrith, I remembered that a relative of John Jackson's wife lived in the town. George Bowman is a wonderful horseman and the world champion four-in-hand carriage driver. We went to see George and he offered us space to spend the night in his yard. I poured out my troubles with regard to Action to him. I told George I was having difficulty in controlling the horse and hadn't yet succeeded in driving with any sort of comfort or style. George offered me a demonstration. He put a small cart behind four of his horses and invited me to get up next to him. Then he drove the four round his practice course at world championship speed. It was a remarkable demonstration, almost frightening the life out of me as the horses galloped round the tortuous course.

When it was over, George went back to his stables to see that his horses were groomed and to carry on with arrangements for his next competition.

We set out again. I felt worse after the experience than I did before. I was ashamed that I couldn't handle one horse at the trot, having seen George control four horses at the gallop with such ease.

Soon after we left Penrith, I was trying to drive Action up a fairly steep road when a lorry came down the hill towards us. It was still two hundred yards away when there was a loud bang as one of the tyres blew out. The lorry driver braked hard to control the vehicle and this unsettled his load of stones. A huge boulder dropped from the lorry and began to roll down the hill towards Action and the van. It thundered down on us, picking up speed. I didn't have time to move, but stood clinging to the horse to stop it bolting. The boulder leaped into the air, left the road and crashed into trees at the side. Action was shying and rearing and I was as frightened as he. It was all over in a minute, but the effect on me lasted for days. It was the last straw.

The next evening I said to Max, "I can't go on like this. I'm going to give the journey up."

"Give John Jackson a ring," suggested Max.

I did. I told John all about Action and about the latest accident. John knew from the tone of my voice that I was desperate.

"You'd better come down and see me," he said.

I went to Accrington the next day, leaving Max to look after Action and the van. I poured out my troubles to John and for an hour he just sat and listened. He had told me at the very start that I wouldn't get to the ferry to cross the Channel, never mind China, so I expected him to say I told you so.

After he had listened to me for a bit, he said instead,

"You've done well to get as far as you have. I told you that traffic is terrible on the roads. However, you've stuck it for over six weeks and you've travelled three hundred miles. You've learned a lot and you've learned the hard way. If you want to carry on you can do, but first you must believe me when I tell you there's nothing wrong with the horse. He's most likely been used to one master and he's not used to you yet. Whoever had him probably treated him different to what you do. He's the right horse for the job, and I'll tell how to go from now on if you want to carry on.

"Don't even think of driving him. Walk by his head and talk to him all the time. You might have to walk five hundred miles if that's what it takes, but you must be there at his head telling him what you want him to do. If you do this, you and he will get to know each other and he will come to trust you and do what ever you want him to."

I spent the whole day talking to John, then drove back north to where Max was waiting. I felt as though a great weight had been lifted from my mind.

Chapter Four

The Second Stage – Through Britain

By now I had started to learn certain things about driving and about Action. I was soon to find out about going down hills. John Jackson had said that this was the most dangerous thing to do. The sheer weight of a caravan full of pots, pans, clothes and many other items necessary for the journey made a total load of some fifteen hundredweights. During the re-building of the caravan, the brakes were the last things to be made and, as time ran out, the construction was not good, so for much of the two years they were either broken or poor.

As we came to the crest of a hill, Action would twist his body into a straight S-shape, his bottom pushing against one side of the shafts as his front feet moved slightly diagonally to the shafts. In this way he knew that the caravan was pushing slightly sideways and in doing so made it more difficult to dislodge his feet. There would be times, however, when he would have difficulty in holding back the caravan, as the road surfaces in some countries were like glass.

There was one other quirk about Action that I noticed. If, while we were walking along a road, he came to a white painted fence or gate, he would automatically try to turn into it. I quickly deduced that his previous owner must have had a white fence or gate to which the horse would return each night after work. It is known that horses are creatures of habit, but they also remember best those who feed them and where. As we seldom stayed longer than one night in any place, it took him some time to lose this habit.

Although by now we had encountered many hills, the sight of Shap Fell was in front of us. We stopped at the bottom to check the caravan wheels and the horse's harness and shafts. As we prepared to set off at a trot, it became very overcast, then it started to drizzle. Very soon the upper part of the long hill facing us had vanished under a heavy mist. For the first part, Action had taken the slope in his stride, the cars and lorries passing us with headlights blazing, then, suddenly, we were in a soup-like fog.

The traffic came towards us in streams. The vehicles behind us were piling up into a long queue, and I felt frightened as cars and lorries tried to squeeze past. On our left hand side, for a great distance, was a concrete retaining wall, and I knew that if anything was to go wrong now we would have no chance of escape.

By this time the wind was blowing the rain into our faces and we were soaking wet and cold. Then we came to a clearing in the clouds and I prayed that the top would soon arrive. I pulled the caravan as close to the side as I could to let the traffic pass and Max chocked the wheels to take the weight off Action. He was breathing heavily, his nostrils blowing out air.

"We must let him rest awhile" I said. But it was not to be. Within a moment the mist came down on us like a blanket. I yelled to Max that we must move on or risk being run down. "Go on Action" I shouted. He pulled, but his feet could not grip on the greasy road and I thought he would fall. I felt panic, and realised that Mr. Jackson's advice, to wind from side to side up steep hills to lessen the gradient, would be impossible to follow in this volume of traffic, with visibility down to twenty yards. We were stuck!

"We have to do something quick" I said, "Let's put some of his hay under his feet".

"OK" replied Max, hurrying to follow the suggestion.

With the hay promising a better grip, I shouted, "Go on, Action. Pull," and turned him diagonally into the road as the caravan moved gradually forward, gathering speed as his hooves dug into the road surface.

Slowly, with great effort, we reached the summit. Here we stopped to rest awhile then slowly descended the other side. Soon the rain and mist started to disperse and at last we could see the traffic more clearly. To climb over Shap Fell had taken us four hours. We descended the other side slowly, heading for Kendal.

We had been on the A6 since leaving Carlisle. I was now walking with Action, talking to him continuously while leading him by the bridle; praising him when he did well and cursing him when he was bad. Following John Jackson's instructions, things seemed to be improving between us and we were now averaging the fifteen miles a day target I had set. In Kendal, we turned off onto the A65 and headed for Skipton, in Yorkshire. The caravan had stood up well so far, with few problems. About every 200 miles we would remove the wheels, grease inside the hubs and generally tighten any bolts holding the caravan together.

I was having difficulty with the harness; with the amount of rain we had encountered all the leather was permanently wet, making it sticky and slimy. Each night we would wipe it with a cloth to dry it, but in some places it was showing its age. As the stitching was breaking up, I knew I should have to find a harness maker to get it re–stitched.

Arriving in the lovely town of Skipton, we found a large municipal car park, but no grass for Action, so I fed him hay which I carried in a hay net hanging on the back of the caravan. With his high protein pellets, this was sufficient for his needs. I got water for him from a local shop. In the evening, we took a tour of the town with horse and caravan, and many people gathered round us when we stopped, asking us questions. One woman said she knew someone in television and she would telephone him to see if he would be interested in doing a story about us.

She returned an hour later to tell us that a team from the "Look North" programme would be arriving from Leeds in the morning. A few minutes later, a newspaper reporter arrived to do a story and take a photograph of the horse and caravan. The caravan always looked good in photographs, in its yellow, maroon, green and red, with the light blue canvas cover. We had two big posters, stuck one on each side of the canvas cover, advertising "Action Research for the Crippled Child", and hanging from a flagpole on the back was a silk flag also advertising the charity. I always felt it was important, when we were on television or in newspaper photographs, that these posters and the flag were clearly visible.

We had started collecting, using our Paddington Bear collecting boxes, which were sealed afterwards. Every major town had an organiser and helpers who would assist us in making the collection and who would take away the money at night. This sort of collection took place all the way through the U.K. I found the district organisers most helpful to us on many occasions. They arranged overnight stopping places for us, and often fed us and arranged hay and water for Action also.

As we came along the main road on the outskirts of Halifax, I saw a sign that said "No Horse-Drawn Vehicles on this Road", so I turned off to the right, hoping I would soon end up in the town. As soon as we turned we found ourselves on a short, very steep hill. Max wound on the brake to full lock. We started down slowly, then there was a sharp crack – bang. Action lunged forward, the weight of the caravan on him.

"Dad, the brakes have broken," shouted Max.

I was trying to get Action under control. He was trying to stop, but the sheer weight of the caravan was too much for him to hold back. His steel shoes had no grip against such a force. He went down on one leg. He knew he had to get up again quickly or the whole caravan would be on top of him. With his enormous strength, he managed to get up and bring the caravan under control. Quick thinking Max put the chock under the wheels to take the weight of Action. I grabbed the knife that I always kept close at hand for emergencies, and cut his bracing straps instead of undoing them, which would have taken too long. The danger was that if Action was frightened enough he might decide to try and bolt. If this idea entered his head there was no way of stopping him, so I quickly released the other straps that held him in the shafts and led him out with relief.

Close by was a large area of grass and a few small trees. The grass was lush, so I tethered him to a tree on his chain, doing up the bolts hand-tight. While all this had been going on, two men had been watching from over a wall.

" What's up, mate?" one shouted as he walked towards us.

"The brakes are knackered," Max said.

"Bring it down to the factory and we'll see what we can do for you."

With the help of more men, we got the caravan off the steep hill and into the factory building. For the next two hours many men worked on the brakes, making new parts and fitting them. About every fifteen minutes, while this was going on, Max or I would look over the wall to check on Action, who was busy eating the lush grass, still moist from the previous night's rain.

Although the brakes were better than before, they were still not perfect. The problem was, that as the wooden wheels were not properly bound, when we wound on the brake wheel, which in turn pulled the brake block onto the steel rim, the block did not always make a good connection.

"Go and fetch Action," I told Max, "While I go and thank the men."

A few minutes went past before Max came running back panting.

"He's gone. Chain and all's gone," he said.

"Who's gone?" asked the men.

"Action," Max replied.

Immediately, I thought of the danger, knowing that the busy main road lay 100 yards away. If he had got onto that who knew what might happen; the danger to both horse and public could be immense. I ran from the factory, with Max in hot pursuit, racing towards the main road. On reaching the road, I took a good look round, but there was no sign of Action. Max suggested that he must have headed for the city centre. I started running towards the town, looking down every turning. Max, meanwhile, had jumped into the van and was touring the streets.

I ended up in the city centre about twenty minutes after we had first discovered the horse was missing. I had begun to panic, remembering the way he had bolted, harness flapping, in Scotland. If he did the same here, in the city, with so much traffic, the damage he could cause would be enormous. Max found me standing in a street.

"Have you found him Dad?"

"No."

"I've been all round," Max said.

There was a telephone box near me. "I'll ring the police and ask for help," I said.

I dialled 999 and explained the situation to the police. It took a moment or two before they understood what I was trying to tell them.

"Where are you calling from?" the officer asked.

I described to him the whereabouts of the call box and he told me to wait there, promising to have a car with me in two minutes. The car, driven by a policeman, arrived and the driver told me to jump in. He asked me to tell him where the horse had last been seen, so I described the hill, the factory and the land. Max said he would go back and take another look round.

With me as passenger, the police car blasted around the streets, searching in vain for my horse. The driver kept in contact with his headquarters by radio, asking everyone if a loose horse had been sighted, and always the answer came back – no. After fifteen minutes of this I was in a real panic.

"What I can't understand," said the police driver, "Is that if someone has been injured in the road, we might not hear about it for a long time, but if an animal gets loose it is normally reported immediately. It's a funny thing. I think we might have to get more cars out on the streets to look for him."

Just then Max came speeding back, brakes screeching. I feared the worst.

"I've found him, Dad. He's in a dangerous place and I can't get at him. Come quick."

Max jumped in the police car and directed us back to the grassy island where Action had been tied.

"Someone took him," Max said. "I went back to the tree to see if I could find evidence of his hoof prints to see if I could discover which way he had gone. I found them and followed them from the tree, across the road, up a steep bank and into some trees and bushes up a gully. There he was, with a fence in front of him, and to one side a sheer drop of some 50 feet. He is wedged between the fence and the drop, in a three feet wide gap. I'm frightened in case he panics and goes over the edge."

We arrived at the island and Max pointed across the road. I ran over and up the bank, through the trees and along the gully. I saw Action standing motionless. I called encouragement to him as I approached. He turned his head to look at me and gave a soft neigh to which I paid little attention at the time. Max was right about him being in a dangerous spot. With a sharp drop to his right, he was wedged in a three feet wide gap, unable to move forwards or sideways. The only way out was to reverse him.

I walked calmly to his head, talking to him. It was not going to be easy backing him out. His long reins were wrapped round his right legs, the side with the sheer drop. It would be necessary to crawl under his belly and lift each leg clear in turn. His harness was caught on the fence post, acting like a strap to prevent him falling over the drop. I had to decide how to release him without causing him to panic.

To free his legs by lifting each in turn, not normally a difficult situation for a horse to be in, was not quite so simple in this case, balanced as he was at present. The other option was to cut his reins and harness away from him. I decided this was better than trying to disentangle him

"Have you got a knife, Max?"

"No, Dad," Max replied.

I knew there was a knife in the caravan, but there was no time to go and fetch it. I must act quickly. Hesitantly and slowly I crawled under Action's belly, between his legs, talking to him, reassuring him. He seemed to understand what I wanted when I tried to lift his hoof. His leg was heavy to lift from a normal standing position, let alone when I was on my knees underneath him. Gently, I lifted his front leg, praying he would stand steady. If he did not, I could have been trampled by more than half a ton of horse and we could both have gone over the precipice together. I pulled his hoof gently, telling him what I wanted. he understood and lifted the leg while I unwound the rein. I went to his back leg and again he lifted his hoof and let me free him. He put his hoof gently back on the ground.

Before I could relax, however, he tried to move backwards while I was still underneath him. While the reins were round his legs he had been unable to move. I was frightened for a moment, until I realised that he was held to the fence by his harness. I told him to stand while I quickly crawled out from under him. He obeyed as the fence held him.

Once out, I undid a buckle and slowly released him. He was now free standing, but his front and back right legs were only eight inches away from the edge of the drop. He would have to come out dead straight. Holding his bridle, I told him to come straight back. To my relief, he came straight back and out. The agony was over. We were safe.

"Dad," Max said, "He was stolen. When I followed his tracks here the first time there were footprints of a man as well as Action's."

While leading him back, Max showed the policeman and me the prints. They were plain to see through the trampled grass.

"I think that whoever took him must have panicked when he got him on that ledge and he scarpered across the fields. I don't think we have much chance of finding him," the policeman said. I agreed and thanked him for his help, then we went back to the factory, hitched up the caravan and set off towards Huddersfield.

This was to be the first of some thirty–seven different occasions when we would be robbed or have things stolen from us, often violently, on our two year journey. There would not be one country where we would not have things taken from us.

Chapter Five

It Was Harder Than I Wanted

On arriving in the small town of Steeton, I pulled up in front of a grocery shop for a packet of crisps. It had been a sunny day and Action was in good form. I had noticed how shiny his coat was now, with his hair short after his winter coat had gone. As his body moved, his muscles rippled and showed in the sunlight. His eagerness to pull the caravan was evident to me.

As I walked from the shop, a young man approached. He asked many questions about our journey, and in the end he invited us back to his home for a meal. Both Max and I were hungry, so we agreed. His name was Brian Dunn and he was a teacher in the local Primary School. I said to him that we must first try to find a parking place for the night.

"I will see if you can park in the school playground," he said. "Wait here." He returned shortly and said, "Come on. Follow me. It's O.K. to stay in the playground."

Next to the playground was a small area of grass on which children played. We tethered Action up and went to Brian's home for a meal which his wife had been cooking for us. It was delicious, and afterwards we went for a pint in the local. Brian asked me if, in the morning, I would give the children a talk about our trip. I agreed.

In the morning the main hall was full, not only with children, but also parents and teachers. The children had been taking part in some activities, and the head asked me to present the prizes, which I did. After this I gave the children a talk about the journey so far and gave them an idea of what lay ahead. Then it was time to let them ask questions and I was surprised at their interest and understanding. As a result of this, I decided that talking to children was important, particularly in helping them to avoid prejudice towards handicapped people. This was the first of many visits to talk about handicapped people we would make to schools and colleges, mainly abroad. The children all had an opportunity to watch a local blacksmith fitting a shoe to Action. At about 11 o'clock we left the school to the cheers of children and teachers. I felt that although things so far had been hard to handle, this had been worthwhile.

With Action Research organisers meeting us each day, it was easy for Max to go ahead every morning, leave the van and get a lift back in a car. However, it was not always thus, so I acted on advice from John Jackson and bought a second hand bicycle from a shop in Keighley. Max could take it ahead with him and ride it back to meet me. Then we would tie it on the back of the caravan and continue together. Unfortunately we did not have the bike for long, only a matter of a few days.

We visited Huddersfield Town and were allowed to park in the main shopping area, make a collection and get publicity for Action Research. While here we met an unbelievable woman. She introduced herself as Brenda. She had a strong character, a pronounced Yorkshire accent and an evident fear of no – one. She was in a wheelchair, and I would guess her age was about forty. She was overjoyed by our presence in the shopping area and she quickly took a Paddington Bear collecting tin, positioned herself by the entrance and began to rattle it in front of everyone who walked past. Later she told me about her life, saying that from the age of twelve until just recently she had been in a home. Since she had been allowed to leave, she had had two heart attacks which had confined her to the wheelchair.

That evening we moved just outside the town and parked on a piece of wasteland close to a pub. We tethered Action to the caravan, which had the bicycle strapped to the back of it, and went for a pint. After about twenty minutes, Max went to check on the horse, and when he came back he was not happy.

"Dad, someone's pinched the bike. It's gone."

"No, Max! I can't believe it – not in daylight, in a built – up area." But, he was right. It had gone, never to return. Whoever took it was not afraid of horses, as Action had been tethered right alongside it.

On a couple of occasions when Max had gone on ahead he had difficulty in finding me, as I had turned a different way. This was the case when we headed for Denby Dale and I took the wrong road. It was 4 o'clock in the afternoon when Max caught up with me. He was fuming and frustrated and I was concerned also, in case anything had gone wrong with the van. When he found me I was just entering Denby Dale.

At the southern end of this village was a pub and a small lane leading to farm. We parked here, expecting to be moved on. Soon an old farmer arrived and asked if we would like some water for the horse. He told us to follow him. He took us into a yard, pointed out the tap and told us to help ourselves when we wanted. We unhitched Action and tied him to the back of the caravan, but there was little grass so I gave him hay and bulk feed, which is high in protein and vitamins. About three quarters of a bucketful per day seemed to be enough to maintain his stamina.

Max and I went to the nearby pub, both of us preoccupied with the matter of losing each other. We got stuck into a pint, ending up having had a fair few. Ah, well, it was a Saturday night!

"Dad," Max said, "I've got an idea. Chalk marks on the road. If I put a mark on each turning to show you which way I have gone, you can follow my route. If you have to change routes, you can use chalk of a different colour to show me where you went."

It was an idea we used during the next two years; the only disadvantage being that the marks vanished when it rained. When we got to Bulgaria, Romania and the U.S.S.R. we had to suspend our marking. One reason was that children would rub them out. The other was continuous begging by adults and children for our pieces of chalk. Sometimes crowds would pursue us down the road, often on the carriageway, which was intolerable to us as well as dangerous for them.

Max had another way of picking up my traces in dry weather. In some countries the steel rims of the wheels left a white scratch on the road surface which he could soon detect. In Greece, Bulgaria, Romania and the U.S.S.R. there were so many vehicles using steel rimmed wheels on the roads that this method was useless. Max and I conjured up signals to warn me of obstacles ahead, like long bridges, construction sites, manhole covers and cattle grids.

Later, in the pub, Max and I fell into conversation with a young man and we asked him what he did for a living.

"I'm a chicken sexer," he replied, at which Max and I burst into laughter, thinking he was pulling our legs. "I'm serious," he insisted. "There are only about fifty of us in the country and we have just formed a union." We were still laughing, but he was not. "We needed a union. The Japanese are moving into the business in a big way, and unless we stop them it will end up like our electronics industry."

I was having difficulty in keeping a straight face, and Max had gone to the toilet as he did not wish to laugh in the man's face. I am still not sure whether he was having us on or not.

The Sheffield area organiser for Action Research was a lady, Sue Mace. She was delightful, full of fun and every inch a woman. With her rather Oxford English voice, she was very impressive. We had arranged to meet on the outskirts of the town where she had obtained council permission for us to take the horse and caravan into the shopping precinct. There we would meet the Major and various reporters. It was a lovely day and everything went as she promised.

We made good progress during the next few days, as we headed for Derby. Once there we entered the city centre and collected money in our Paddington Bear tins for Action Research. There was a generous response as we toured round. I had now come to realise what a great attraction we were. In big cities thousands of people wanted to talk to us. When we moved across open country, people would stop and question us, often offering food and drink for Action and ourselves. Much of this enthusiasm was due to us having been on TV and radio or in newspapers. Lorry drivers would hoot as they passed us and would use their CB radios to tell each other to look out for our horse and caravan. They were all most courteous to us.

The drivers we found most impatient were ordinary bus drivers. We had often been shouted at or had a two finger salute. Max, who has a shorter temper than I, would retaliate in kind.

At Ashby-de-la-Zouche we attended the annual fair. Mr. Stone of Spillers had arranged to get some more horse nuts delivered to us here. We spent most of the day hiding from torrential rain which cleared in the afternoon and allowed us to take Action round the show. I was driving between the exhibitors' stalls and we came to a hot dog cum beefburger stall.

Action started his old trick of snorting and shuffling his feet, showing reluctance to go past the stall. When we were passing this stall once more he began playing up again. At first it puzzled me, then I understood. It was the smell of raw meat. I was cooking our evening meal a few days after this and the same phobia showed itself. I lit the fire and prepared to fry some liver which I had first washed. I put it in the pan using my fingers. Without washing them, I went to speak to Action. As I began to rub his nose he shied away, snorting and would have bolted had he not been tethered on his chain. The smell of blood had scared him.

On another occasion, when I was travelling round an island, a lorry containing animal skins overtook us. How I kept control of the horse in so much traffic I do not know. It was more by luck than judgement.

Darkness was closing in as I drove towards Hinckley with no lights on the caravan. I was worried about breaking the law as well as the danger. Max walked ahead. Recently he had acquired the habit of walking in the centre of the road, to get the best view back and front. Often a vehicle would overtake just as another was approaching and the overtaking vehicle would pass very close to Max and Action, almost touching Max. Suddenly Max shouted that there was a pub ahead. I told him to see if there was room for us to park at the rear of it. He told me there was, but it was a squeeze to get in.

By now we had a good collection of newspaper cuttings about our journey as well as an official letter from Action Research for the Crippled Child. I went into the Kiw Pub lounge and a lady came up and asked if she could help us. I told her I had a horse and gypsy caravan outside and I thrust our book of cuttings towards her. The front page was open and showed an article about our visit to Derby. She read it briefly then said I could put the caravan round the back and the horse on a patch of waste land, then I could come in and get something to eat.

This, in brief, is the way we presented ourselves to publicans, farmers and others when we stopped for the night. As we crossed Europe, the scrapbook became our passport to foreign countries and parking places. On literally hundreds of occasions it would save our bacon when we had dealings with the police, and without it we should never have travelled so far.

With Action settled, we went inside for a meal and a drink. The lady introduced herself as Viv. Her husband was Pete. She produced a plate of sandwiches, at which Max's eyes lit up. He was starving.

Sitting next to me at the bar was a very smartly dressed man sporting a black dicky bow tie. He looked rather over dressed for this pleasant lounge.

"My name is Norman Dagley. Pleased to meet you."

Viv, Pete, Norman, Max and I made conversation together for a couple of hours, and it emerged that Norman was World Billiard Champion, hence his smart appearance. Pete asked us where we were spending the following night and I said we hoped to reach Nuneaton.

"I have a friend with a pub in Nuneaton. I could ring him and ask if you can stay there with the horse and caravan," he said, making for the telephone. He returned to tell us that we were expected at the Grif House, and he gave us directions on how to find it.

Next morning we thanked Viv and Pete and set off towards Grif House. It stood close to an island in Gypsy Lane. How appropriate, I thought. Plastered across the front was a sign "Beefeater Inn – Whitbreads." The manager welcomed us, found a spot for Action to be tethered and the caravan parked, then invited us to come inside for a meal on the house. Our acceptance was not long in coming.

The manager asked us if it was alright for him to contact the TV and newspapers while we were there. I agreed and it was arranged that they would come at 8.30 next morning. The meal was delicious, starter, steak and sweet with a couple of pints for good measure. During the evening the manager asked where we were going next. I told him Coventry.

"Would you like to stop at another Beefeater Inn? I can phone the City Arms just outside the city and ask if they can take you there." He went to telephone and then came to confirm that we could go there on the following evening.

On our journey to Sheerness we were to be the guests of another ten Beefeater Inns, there was always room for Action and the caravan and food for Max and myself. In fact, by the time we reached Sheerness we had almost become sick of steak! My thanks go out to all those kind managers and manageresses.

In Hinckley we met with a lady representing Action Research and decided to make a collection. While we were rattling the collecting tin a policeman came up and asked what we were doing. There was enough publicity material on the caravan to make the answer to his question quite obvious. The charity's representative intervened and began to explain who we were, but he ignored her and asked us to produce our documentary evidence of association with the charity, and our driving licences. He studied and returned our papers before turning on the lady and asking her to prove her association with the charity. She did so and he left without comment.

Our entry to the main shopping centre in Coventry was difficult. I had learnt that we could collect most money and publicity by taking horse and caravan right into a precinct. I drove round for ages looking in vain for the way in before I spotted a van driving up a ramp leading into some buildings. When I followed, I found myself right in the shopping centre. We parked in a busy spot and for the next three hours hundreds of people came up to ask questions. A kind man brought a kebab each for Max and me. Then a lady came with cream cakes for us and carrots for Action. Another lady came with apples for the horse. Feeding Action was like an epidemic. One starts and then everyone else wants to do it. It was the same in every country, people bringing sweets, peppermints, apples, carrots, plums, peaches, grapes, oranges, lemons, potatoes, cream cakes, bread of all kinds, melons, cucumber, candy floss, ice cream, ice lollies, sugar, even onions.

While Action was being fed, a Gipsy woman stood close to us selling posies of flowers. She moved closer, hoping for more customers. She gave the caravan a more authentic look and I hope she did better business.

In every country people would ask me if we played music or read palms. As we were about to leave the precinct, the Gipsy woman did something I had never seen before. She touched the caravan and then went to stroke Action. "Now I have luck," she said. "I have stroked both horse and caravan. You must always stroke the caravan first, then the horse. To touch just the one is no good." After this she took a posy and tucked it behind Action's headband.

The next few days in the Midlands, having been in the Coventry newspapers and on Midlands TV, we were overwhelmed with food for us and Action, and good luck wishes for our journey.

We arrived at the Beefeater Inn at Earlsdon by early evening. Parking was difficult as the carpark was small, so the manager let us put the caravan in a small yard belonging to the Inn. Action was tethered close by. There was no grass, and I fed him hay and nuts for his tea, although his belly was still full of goodies from Coventry. Just as we were going in for our meal I head someone call my name, and I turned to see coming towards me my father and my brother Richard, who had come over from nearby Warwick, where they were living. It was nice to see familiar faces after all these months.

We went inside together and the kindly manager fed all of us and gave us each a pint. The telephone rang and it was a reporter asking for me. I gave him my story and had just sat down to finish my meal when a man carrying a black tape recorder arrived from the B.B.C. He asked me to do an interview for radio.

As we were leaving next morning, I angled Action too far round while trying to negotiate a turn in the small carpark. Suddenly, with a crack and a crunch, Action was left standing in shafts and harness, but without the caravan. The cross member attaching the shafts to the van had been broken off. Now we were in big trouble. Max and I were stumped. This job would need a carpenter with the right tools.

We were on our way towards my home territory, Stratford – on – Avon and Warwick; I had family in the area. Max and I tied and bound the broken bits together, hoping the temporary repair would hold as far as Warwick. We travelled along gently and got as far as Warwick, where my Uncle Bill directed us to a craft centre in Hatton. In this village was a woodworker and he made a new cross member which he bolted to the caravan's undercarriage. The job took most of the day, so we parked at the back of the craft centre for the night and tethered Action to a thick, rough hedge straddling a steep slope leading to fields below.

When we came back to the craft centre late at night there was no sign of Action. Max and I began to panic. It was pitch black and we hurried along the hedge to where he had been tethered. We heard a neighing and the sound of something heavy crashing through the thick hedge. The noise, coming suddenly out of the darkness, scared us stiff. It was the very first time Action had given us a neigh of welcome when we came back to him, and from that day forward he would always acknowledge our return in this way. It was a sign that mutual trust was developing between us.

Action was less excitable now when something on the road upset him, and I felt this was due to me talking continuously to him and getting to know him better. In Warwick we took Action to the main park. It was sunny day at last and a good number of people, mostly children, stroked Action. It was here that I started something that was to give enormous pleasure to people during the next two years: giving rides to children. There was a family of Asians who had come over to speak to the horse, and after several minutes the father told the children it was time to go. Everyone except one small girl walked away, but she said she wanted to stay with Action. She was stroking his nose and I felt quite touched by her awe of him. Her father marched back and began to drag her away and she began to cry. I called after them and beckoned them to return.

"Would she like to sit on the horse?" I asked. Max intervened to say it was too dangerous. "You hold the horse, Max, and I will lift her onto his back."

The father was all for this, so up she went. I held Action by the bridle and he never flinched. The little girl was ecstatic, her tears already forgotten. She was the first of many thousands of people who would sit on his back, hundreds of them handicapped. I shall never forget the joy it gave them, as many had never stroked a horse, let alone sat on one.

Next we went to what I call my home town, Stratford-on-Avon. The Beefeater Inn, named Encore, had no direct parking place, so I pulled into a field just outside the town, by the River Avon. There was plenty of grass here for Action, but I was bothered about whom the land belonged to. We toured Stratford many times, the traffic was the busiest we had yet encountered. In the early afternoon the "Midlands Today" TV film crew came to film us in front of the Shakespeare Theatre, after which we spoke to some reporters on the streets and many of my friends and relations came to see us. It was lovely to see all these people.

A young lady came up and introduced herself.

"I would like to do a painting of your horse and caravan, and when it is finished I shall give it to Action Research for the Crippled Child to auction, sell or do what they will with it." She then took a number of photographs from which to work.

While we were in Stratford the cameras never stopped clicking at us. In the evening we ate steak again at the Encore Beefeater Inn. I had been a busy day and we went early to bed. So far I had been sleeping in the caravan. At the rear end was a bunk bed with a sprung mattress and a quilt. It was still summer and I had not yet found it cold at night. Winter would be the testing time. When we crossed the Alps and on the Romanian-Russian border we would encounter temperatures 20° below zero.

Between Stratford and Banbury is Edge Hill, famous for a battle between Roundheads and Royalists in the Civil War. We reached the bottom of this hill when it was almost dark and I knew it well. Over the years there have been many accidents, particularly with lorries, on its bends. We debated the matter and decided to chance going up it that night, as there would be less traffic than in the morning. To my amazement, Max, who is always more cautious than me, agreed. We carried small torches in the caravan. I fixed one on the back of the van and one on the front, then, with Max following behind in the horse – box, we started climbing.

At first it was not too bad, then Action started slipping on the shiny Tarmac. He could not hold the van and I had no helper to chock the wheels. I was in trouble again. At last the horse came to a stop, even his great strength not enough to take us further. He could not retain his grip and the caravan began to roll slowly back down the hill. I dashed to the back, but it was too late. With an almighty bang it stopped. I could hear the crunching of wood and smashing of glass. I thought we had hit another vehicle. I was right. It had rolled back into the horse box driven by Max.

"It's O.K., Dad," said Max with a grin. "It's a good job I saw it rolling back. I thought I could stop it with the van."

Luckily, not much damage had been done apart from a broken lens, a broken broom handle and some chipped paint. From this incident we learned the wisdom of Max driving behind the caravan when we were ascending steep hills. There were some steep roads ahead of us, in the Alps, in Greece and in southern Bulgaria.

We were just outside Banbury when Max said, "This place sells harness oil. Let's go and see if they will give us some."

We turned into a drive leading to a farm. In the farmyard was a lady to whom we introduced ourselves and asked if we could obtain a supply of harness oil. She told us to speak to someone else. Then a tall man approached us and we explained our needs. He said he would supply the oil if we would carry publicity for his company on our caravan. We followed him to his office in the farm building. He gave us five litres of oil and some stickers advertising Mars Oil, and we then set off for Banbury, where we found two newspapers' reporters waiting to interview us.

That evening we decided to head for Buckingham. We were just outside Banbury when a car came alongside and the driver told me that one of our wheels was coming off. I checked Action and jumped down to investigate. The man was right; the rear nearside wheel would have come off in the next few yards. Max looked at it and said, "We've lost the nuts that hold it on. They must be on the road somewhere."

Two nuts, one with a right hand thread and the other a left hand, held the wheel, and if we failed to find them we were in trouble. Just at that moment a head poked out of a house window and a voice shouted,

"Hey, mate! You're on TV. I've just been watching you. What a coincidence, you pulling up here."

By now several people had joined in our vain hunt for the lost wheel nuts. One man said,

"I work at Alcan. Maybe they can make you new nuts. I'll telephone my boss."

He came back and escorted us down the road towards Banbury, stopping now and again to push the loose wheel back on the shaft. The Alcan factory was huge and there were guards on the main gates. We were expected, as they let us in immediately and the caravan was wheeled inside the building. Within a few minutes a man arrived to tell us that they would mend the wheel in the morning by making two new nuts. Two men were allocated to us and new nuts, bushes and washers were made for all four wheels. The job took two days to complete. After thanking all concerned, we set off towards Buckingham.

It was not easy to find a stopping place for the night, so we headed for a village where we found a small piece of land in the centre. I suppose you could call it the village green. It was getting dark by now, and although I knew it was wrong to park there, as the grass was well kept and the trees were nice, it was too dark to continue. Although we were not told to move off, we had many frosty looks from the locals next morning, when they saw the mess Action had made on the grass and the trees he had nibbled. We tidied up and left quickly.

Max had been claiming unemployment benefit while we travelled. He had been told to report to the nearest benefit office once every two weeks and he could go on drawing his money. When we got to Milton Keynes they said he could not be regarded as available for work while he was travelling, and they refused to pay him any more. From now on I would have to support him. This was another cost I had to take into account. I knew that without him I should have to go home.

Although it had been arranged for us to go to another Beefeater Inn when we got to Milton Keynes, something went wrong with the arrangements and we were told we could not stay. We learned that there was another Beefeater Inn at Bletchley, a few miles away. The managers, Brian and Pam, turned out to be a delightful couple.

The Bletchley Park Beefeater Inn stood at the end of a *cul-de-sac*. Next to it was a scrap of waste land adjacent to the railway track. Here we parked and tethered Action. Trains thundered past every few minutes, and Action showed no sign of fear as he munched away at the grass. During the evening a man from local radio arrived for an interview and he was closely followed by a newspaper reporter.

We ate another steak and turned in for the night. I was just about to fall asleep when there was a tap on the caravan door. When I opened it there were two policemen standing there.

"What's going on here?"

Again I thrust the book of press cuttings at them. They began to read it carefully, but just then the peace of the night was shattered by the sound of hoof beats and breaking branches as Action ran through the scrub. They were not just startled; I thought they were going to have heart attacks. Action came to a halt close to the caravan, and by now one policeman was some twenty odd feet away, ready to run. Action, now a silhouette against the bushes, had frightened him out of his wits. I called the horse by name and he gave a little neigh.

"Bloody Hell! It's a horse!" said one policeman.

They left after warning me that I had parked on a double yellow line.

"I'd make sure you move it, if I were you. The traffic warden will have you if you're still here in the morning!"

Early next morning Max went to move the van, but the clutch had gone, and true to the policeman's word, the traffic warden arrived.

We told Brian of our problems and he arranged for a friend to bring us a new piece for the clutch. Luckily, Max is mechanically minded and knew what had to be done. In the evening we were ready to move on, but not by caravan. I was getting concerned about reaching the Alps before winter and we were already more than two weeks behind schedule. To make up for lost time I decided to hitch the caravan to the van and tow it, with Action inside the van.

We had gone some 500 yards out of Bletchley when there was an almighty bang. Max yelled that the caravan had come off. I looked back and saw it impaled against a wall. When I got down from the van, I saw a policeman leaning on the top of a car.

"Christ!" said Max, "Now were for it. He must have seen it happen."

I looked at the policeman and he looked at me. I waited for him to say something, but he just lowered his head and wagged his finger as much as to say, "Naughty boys."

"Let's get out of here, Max."

We hastily re-hitched the caravan and made it more secure before leaving. The policeman just stood looking.

Chapter Six

London and the Home Counties

During the next few days we went through Kempston, Biggleswade, Royston, Saffron Walden and to the Beefeater Inn at Harlow. Once again we had steak and a few beers at the Harlow Mill. I went to say good night to Action, something I always did. I found him lying down and he made no attempt to rise when I bent down and began to stroke him. Horses have no defence when they are lying down, but he did not move. He was wide awake and loving every minute as I stroked and scratched his neck. Without warning, I sat on his belly and he remained motionless as I scratched him. I felt this was the ultimate proof that trust between us was now almost complete.

I went to bed feeling good, and as I lay there thinking, I made the decision to enter London and take him to Oxford Circus, Piccadilly Circus, or wherever the road would lead us. My main point of contact in London was at the offices of Collins, the publishers in Grafton Street. I had kept in contact with Collins's representative, David Swarbrick, and I telephoned to tell him of my decision to enter London. I asked if he knew where I could park the caravan and horse. He said I was to leave it with him and telephone again that night. He came up trumps. He gave me the number of Knightsbridge Barracks and told me to ask for Lieutenant Colonel Clark. We could stay at the Barracks.

It was Sunday morning when I drove Action to London and headed for the Thames. We came to a road lined with coaches from all parts of Europe and found ourselves overwhelmed by foreigners asking us questions. We made our way to Hyde Park and the Barracks. As Lt. Col. Clark was expecting our arrival, guards at the gate let us pass. Lt. Col. Clark met us and showed us where to park the caravan, putting us in the care of a soldier. He led Action to his quarters which were approached by way of a concrete ramp and along a large passage way. Doors led off this passage at intervals of a few yards, each leading to a large building in which were stabled the black horses of the Queen's Household Cavalry. At the far end we came to our building. In the corner was a single stable knee deep in straw. I thought how smart it looked, as I let Action go inside and start on the hay already provided for him in a rack.

As I turned to walk away Max told me about Action's stable.

"You know what it is, Dad. It's the stable used by the Queen's Drum

Horse. The soldier told me they had put him out to grass so Action could use it." I never discovered the truth of that story.

Security inside the Barracks was very strict, but in the evening we went for a walk down Kensington High Street. We had to prove our identity before being allowed back inside. We were woken next morning by the sound of hooves passing close to the caravan, and we looked out and saw soldiers walking the horses round the yard for exercise. The horses themselves looked to be in fine condition, but I was surprised by the state of some of their hooves, which were cracked and worn by continuous fitting of shoes. I knew there was no way Action could walk as far as China if his feet got into that condition.

That morning we watched a parade in the yard as the cavalrymen prepared for the changing of the guard. It was a colourful display of horses and riders, so we asked for, and were given, permission to take photographs. For security reasons, it was not normally permitted to photograph inside the barracks.

I received a message from the Lieutenant Colonel that two camera crews, one from B.B.C. and the other from I.T.V., were waiting at the gate for us with two reporters, one from the Evening Standard and the other from the Communist Morning Star newspaper. He explained that all these people could not be allowed inside because of security, and only the two reporters were permitted to enter. One was a young woman and one a man. We gave them our story before hitching up Action and the caravan and coming out through the gates. The TV crews were still waiting and they followed us, filming as we made our way towards Buckingham Palace.

There were removable barriers across the gates of the Palace, so we cheekily moved them aside and took Action right up to the main gates. He stuck his nose between the bars and sniffed. A big crowd gathered round us, mostly foreigners, then a uniformed man emerged from the throng and asked us politely to move away. We spent the rest of that day roaming the town, visiting Piccadilly, Oxford Street, the Strand and Downing Street.

Max had a friend at home who was anti Mrs. Thatcher. He told Max that if we could get Action to do a mess outside Number 10 he would give £20 to Action Research for the Crippled Child. We tried, but without success.

Action was great in all the traffic; taxis, vans, lorries and cars sometimes coming abreast of him and he remaining quite unconcerned in the middle of it.

The next day the Lieutenant Colonel arranged for Action to have new shoes fitted and his harness to have much needed repairs made. Meanwhile, Max and I had many things to sort out, one being to talk to Jenny Forrester of Olau Line at Sheerness, the people who were sponsoring us on the ferry. We were able to give her a rough idea of when we should arrive at Sheerness. I also spoke to Mrs. Payton at the Ministry of Agriculture, Fisheries and Food in Surbiton because I needed to find out what needed to be done to get Action onto the ferry. I was told that he had to be taken to an approved Ministry stable near the port for a veterinarian to inspect him and furnish me with a certificate of his fitness to travel. I was told that I could get nothing more here and must comply with Dutch regulations for him to land at the other side. I should have to comply also with regulations in every country I visited with him.

I told Jenny Forrester and she said she would arrange about the stables and the vet. I also mentioned to her my qualms about driving him on the right hand side of the road.

We made our way to Rochester, staying at Beefeater roadside lay-bys and at a farm where the public visit to see the animals. While here, I discovered that Action could still get upset. At one point he was amongst goats or sheep that kept pinching his food. Max had been cleaning out the van, shovelling the muck into a wheelbarrow. Suddenly Action lined up his back legs and let fly, catching the barrow dead centre and sending it soaring about ten feet in the air. It was the first time I had seen him get angry and I made sure it was the last time, as I determined to keep him clear of goats or sheep who might steal his food in future.

The lovely old town of Rochester was not an easy place to park as nearly all the centre has been pedestrianized. We took him in and many people strolled around. Lots of these were visitors from abroad visiting the town because it was Dickens's birth place, and to see the cathedral and castle. We pulled up outside a restaurant, Mr. Topes, at the end of the precinct and close to the castle. A young man introduced himself to us. He gave his name as Mark Lavender and invited us to join him for dinner that evening.

By the time we had eaten it was getting dark and we had not found anywhere to park. Just around the corner, by the castle wall, was a small street and although it clearly said NO PARKING, I decided to park here over night. The only problem was a lack of grass for Action, apart from a small piece against a wall, which had a large tree growing on it. There was always the castle moat, with its beautifully kept grass, but I decided against this, fearing that Action might do too much damage to the turf. I tied him to the tree.

Next morning a tapping on the caravan door woke me and I found a policeman outside.

"Max Hitches?" he asked. "I have a warrant for you, for non-payment of a fine. You damaged a lamppost in Worcestershire and you have not paid."

I was dumbfounded. "I did no such thing," I said. "You have the wrong man."

"You are Max Hitches, are you not?" the constable asked. Then it registered with me what he was saying.

"I think it's my son you want. I'll go and wake him up."

I roused Max and the constable explained what he had come for. The fine amounted to £300, which Max did not possess. The policeman said that if he could not pay it, he would be taken in. This left me with the one option of paying it myself, which I did.

As one policeman left another arrived. "Is this your horse?" he asked. We admitted ownership of the horse. "We have had a complaint from the

Deacon. That grass is part of his garden and your animal is chewing it up. You must leave immediately."

In the middle of this, Max was trying to start the van. "Dad," he said, "It won't go. I think it's something in the distributor. I'll have to take it to pieces."

The policeman kept saying we must move the horse, but where could I put him? I eyed the moat. "Can I put him on there? I asked, pointing towards it.

"As long as you move him from here, I don't care where you put him," he replied.

I led Action across the road to the moat. The only thing to tie him to was a stone post. I secured him and left him to eat the lush, short grass.

"This morning," said the policeman, "The postman came to that door where your horse was." He pointed to a door in the wall beside the tree. "That's the Deacon's house, and the postman couldn't get past your horse. The Deacon is not happy."

Max was still trying to get the van going. He told me we needed some parts. We asked a passer-by how to get to the nearest Bedford dealers and he told us it was in Chatham, the next town. We decided to walk there and get the parts. When we came back with them, Action was nowhere to be seen. There was a big hole in the moat and a trail of deep gouges running along it. The once lovely turf was in one hell of a mess.

Action had torn the post out of the ground. Max pointed ahead, saying the horse must have gone in that direction. We followed the gouges out onto the road where they showed up as scratch marks. Further up the road a man shouted to us that the horse was there and bleeding badly. When I reached him, Action was trembling on the end of his tether. At the other end of the chain was the stone post weighing about two hundredweights. I could see that he had torn the post free, and as he raced along it had banged against his legs. The more he tried to race away from it, the more often it struck him. I found cuts on his legs and his tummy, none of them really serious, but I remembered how his blood had become infected in Scotland and I set off to find a vet.

A young lady came and examined his cuts. He would let no-one touch them, and she said they were not serious as far as she could see, but there was no way of telling how badly he was bruised. She gave him a sedative and an antibiotic injection and told us to let him rest for a few days.

At this point a lady arrived and said she was the deacon's wife. She said how sorry she was about the horse and offered to let us put him in her garden to recuperate. We put him in the deacon's garden and I thought how ironical it was that he should only have been there because the deacon had wanted us to move him away. When I left him there, I found a newspaper reporter waiting to get a story from me about the moat.

Then a van pulled up and a man jumped out shouting, "Look at my moat! It's ruined. Ruined!"

It was then that I cracked. I had just had to face discovering about Max and the fine, which I had had to pay; the broken down van and the injuries to Action. I had had enough. "F*** your moat," I yelled. "Piss off!"

He jumped back in the van and drove off, shouting, "You ain't heard the last of this."

By now Max was up to his elbows in grease, cursing and swearing. It had been a bad few hours for both of us. Then Mark Lavender, the restaurant manager arrived.

"Let's have a look, Max," he offered. After tampering with the distributor for a few minutes he asked Max to switch on the engine and away she went.

For the next two days we parked by the castle on a small car park. I went to pay the veterinarian, but she would take nothing; and I never heard any more from the council. I have wondered since if the deacon had a word with them.

When we set off again, we went to Chatham to collect for Action Research. Two lovely things happened here. An old lady, clearly a local, came up and asked, "Does your horse like sugar?" When Max said he did, she said, "If you stay here, I'll go and get some." A few minutes later she returned with two boxes of cube sugar. "I have saved this since 1939, when war broke out. I have been waiting to do something with it," she said, feeding Action with lump after lump. She left the remainder with us to give him later.

Not long afterwards, two elderly ladies stopped and one began to talk to and stroke the horse. The other stood well back although her friend tried to coax her to touch Action.

"I am frightened of horses," she said repeatedly. They walked away together, but returned after a while. The first lady was trying to persuade her friend to touch Action. She guided her frail hand towards his head, but as her fingers touched she drew away quickly. Then, gathering confidence, she tried again, this time enjoying the feel of him. Soon she was stroking him freely. She turned and said, "I am 84 years old, and this is the first time in my life that I have ever stroked a horse. Maybe it is also the last time."

It had been arranged that when we got to Sittingbourne we should meet Liz Knopp, the representative for Action Research, the owner of Mars Oils, and Jenny Forrester, who would give us final details of our sailing arrangements. She had arranged with a Mrs. Friday, owner of stables in Sheerness, for Action to be examined there. We had been booked to sail on the Britannia at 10.00 a.m. She told us that her opposite number in Vlissingen, in Holland, had arranged a police escort for us on our first day and a camp site for the night.

We went straight to Mrs. Friday's stables and she telephoned for the vet. I was very worried about what he would say about all the cuts and scratches on Action, and I showed him a letter from the vet in Rochester, which seemed to satisfy him. He signed a certificate of fitness, which he handed to me. It was only valid for a few hours, so we had to be on the boat that same night.

At lunch time, we took Action into Sheerness. It was to be our last visit in the U.K., and it poured with rain, as it had done on almost every day this summer.

We entered the dock at 7 o'clock, accompanied by Liz Knopp and her husband. Here we met Jenny Forrester, who quickly arranged our tickets. We said goodbye to the Knopps and trundled aboard the ferry. They had decided to put us on board last, so we were near the rear doors. Once inside, I gave Action some food and water, but while I was doing this there was a loud noise that startled him and he began to jump about in his horsebox. I realised it was the ramp that forms the door being closed. Action settled down to eat and the ferry pulled away from the dock. We were on our way to Holland.

As I lay in my bunk that night, I thought about what John Jackson had said when I first met him. "You will not make it to the ferry boat, let alone China." But we had made it. It had been hard though, and I prayed it would get better.

Touring the London landmarks.

Tackling City of London traffic.

Passing Buckingham Palace.

Chapter Seven

Arrival in Holland

On disembarking from the ferry, we found Paul Cramer, Freight Manager of the Olau Line, waiting for us. Holland was our first foreign country and I was concerned about Action, who had been standing in his horse box for over ten hours. After introductions were complete, I said to Paul, who spoke perfect English, that I had to get Action out of his box and let him stretch his legs. Paul showed me where we could pull up, as we were still within the area between the ferry and the customs post. Action looked stiff and awkward as we led him down the ramp. When he reached the Tarmac, he looked around, as if he knew he was on foreign soil. Max began to clean out the horse box while I walked Action round.

A motorcycle police sergeant was with Paul, who introduced us and told me this was our escort as far as the first camp site, a distance of some six kilometres from the port. Action was walking steadily by now, so we hitched the caravan and moved forward to the customs barrier.

A customs official emerged from a nearby building and began to talk with Paul. After a minute or two, Paul came across to me and said,

"Bill, you cannot enter Holland." My heart sank. Then Paul explained, "There are no laws here that allow horses from other countries to walk across Holland. You must put him back in the horse box, the officer will seal the door and put him on the ferry back to England."

Paul and the officer spoke together again, this time in a different tone of voice, more excitedly. The policeman just looked on. I could see Max was becoming agitated at what was taking place. Paul came over and asked what documentation we had for the horse. That was a good question and one I dreaded. I produced the only things I had, which were the vet's certificate of health, but this only confirmed that he was fit to travel on the ferry, and the vaccination certificate from the vet in Oban, which said he had been injected against influenza. I knew neither of these was of sufficient importance to gain us entry to any country. In fact, the only documents we had for ourselves were our passports and the vehicle documents. Paul passed the certificates to the customs officer, who looked through them, shaking his head.

Paul continued the discussion, only more sternly this time. He was gesticulating and showing that he felt it was ridiculous not to let us into Holland. The policeman, who had been a silent observer, now started his motorcycle and drove away towards Vlissingen.

"Dad," said Max, "I think we've lost our escort. He's got pissed off with waiting."

Paul came over and asked us to put the horse back in his box and wait. The customs man went back into his office and Paul walked towards another building.

"What do we do now, Dad?" Max asked.

"I don't know," I told him. "Just wait, I suppose."

We had just put Action back in his box when I turned round to see our policeman return, followed by a Mini which stopped on the other side of the barrier. A young woman got out and had words with the guard on the barrier before approaching us.

"I am from the local newspaper," she said. "I understand you are having difficulty entering Holland. Would you give me a story about what you have been doing and your purpose in trying to reach China?"

I spoke first about what I understood to be our present situation, about the horse about to be sealed in his box and shipped back to England. Then I told her about our journey through Great Britain and our connection with the charity Action Research for the Crippled Child.

"What do you want to do in Holland?" she asked.

I was not ready for the question. I had not thought this out in detail. I wanted to help the handicapped, remembering the enjoyment we had brought to the old and the children in the hospital we had visited in Scotland. I told her we would like to visit a hospital of some sort. She had written down everything I had told her.

Paul now returned. "I have spoken by telephone to our Ministry of Health in Rotterdam. They are now in contact with the Chief Customs Officer to see if a special document can be made to permit you to enter Holland. You will have to wait," he explained. The reporter was still busily writing it all down.

Someone came from one of the buildings and beckoned to Paul. Before he left he told us we must wait for a Ministry vet to come and inspect the horse. "If the vet says he is O.K. he will give you a document to travel across Holland." The vet arrived twenty minutes later.

Once again, I was apprehensive on account of the cuts and bruises the horse had acquired in Rochester. The vet walked over to Action, lifted one of his eyelids, walked round him and lifted one leg, then got out pen and paper and began writing. He handed me the paper and Paul said, "That's it, Bill. You are in."

"How much do I owe the vet?" I asked.

Paul spoke to the vet. "Nothing. It is his present to you," he said. With that, the vet left. I showed Paul the note and asked him to translate it for me, as it was in Dutch.

"It says that he has examined the horse on this day and in his opinion he is fit to travel across Holland. He has given today's date. That's all it says. The Ministry in Rotterdam have spoken to the customs people here and it is all in order for you to go now."

The policeman was already on the other side of the barrier and he signalled to us to move forward. The barrier slowly went up and out we went with never a backward glance. Max and I shouted our thanks to Paul.

When we came to the road, I moved over to the right hand side. Action showed no sign of amazement at this change to the wrong side, but what amazed me was, that after we had gone a few yards, there was a two feet wide strip of steel running right across the full width of the road. In my eagerness to get away from the customs post, I had failed to notice it. With a sudden jolt, Action stopped and I almost fell off the caravan step. I tried to get him to pass over it, but he was stubborn. He was determined not to cross over, in spite of me shouting at him. Suddenly he took a flying leap, the caravan still firmly behind him, and he was over it. I nearly fell out of the van.

We went a bit further and came to a point where a set of railway tracks crossed the carriageway. Again Action stopped, then tried to go sideways as he reversed away from the rails. I jumped down, grabbed his bridle to lead him gently across them. Our escorting policeman had been keeping behind us and holding back the traffic, and he stopped most courteously while I extricated us from this situation.

I started moving Action forwards, then there was a bang, clonk, clonk, and we found ourselves on a steel bridge spanning a river. The sound of steel on steel, and the hollowness and bounce terrified Action, who began to bolt. I managed to stop him when we were about half way across. He stood still, trembling, and other drivers had stopped for us.

I tried to urge him forward, but he refused to move forward or back. I began to panic. What would our escorting policeman think? If he reported us, we could be be stopped from crossing Holland; we could be seen as dangerous to the public. I had to try something. There was the choice of coaxing him across or taking him out of the shafts, which was not a good idea. He would be more dangerous if he were loose and if he were to bolt with harness dangling.

I went in front of him and stamped hard on the steel plates of the bridge, telling him that it was alright. Then, still stamping hard, I began to walk forward and Action began to follow me when I got ten feet ahead of him. I continued to stamp my way across and he came slowly after me until we found ourselves safe on Tarmac again. I stopped, put my arms round his neck and told him, "We did it, boy. I know we can make it together."

As I held him, I remembered when he lay in the barn in Oban, unable to rise to his feet, and how as I lay with him I felt as if he was saying, "Thank you for your help." I knew now that his trust in me had grown and that we had a bond between us which would strengthen as we continued our travels together. While I was still holding the horse, our policeman guided the traffic past us. He walked over and put his hand on Action's neck, saying something to him in Dutch, which I knew meant "Well done".

We arrived at the camp site and had just parked up when the reporter in her Mini arrived with a photographer to take pictures of us. I asked here where the nearest food shop could be found and she told me it was in the village about two kilometres away. She offered to drive me there. We found a small supermarket and the reporter asked me what I wanted. I had made a list of about a dozen food items while we were on the ferry, and this I handed to her. She went round, filling a basket, then went to the check – out where I attempted to pay with a handful of guilders I had obtained while we were making the crossing.

"I want to pay," she said.

"No, you can't do that," I protested, but by now she had handed over the guilders from her purse. When we got outside, I insisted on reimbursing her. She refused, saying it was her present to me to help me through Holland.

This was the first of many hundreds of times that foreigners gave us food as we travelled along.

When we got back to the camp site, the policeman had come back on his bicycle. Speaking through the reporter, who had good English, he said, "If you have any problems in Holland, you can get in touch with me at the Police Station. Here is the address and telephone number." He took a sheet of paper from his notebook and handed it to me, then he wished us good luck and took his leave.

That evening we went to a small bar to sample our first Dutch beer. We got talking to the owner's wife, whom we told about our desire to make contact with a handicapped organisation. She said she would contact one on the following morning. The beer was good, but expensive, and by the time we left, at 10 o'clock, the £20 I had changed into guilders was nearly gone. Max had already come to terms with the Sterling/Guilder exchange rate.

I was sleeping soundly in the caravan when I was woken by the sound of tapping on the door. A woman's voice was calling us by name, and when I opened the door, I found it was the woman from the the bar. She spoke some English and explained that a man named Mr. de Vos would meet us on the road to Middelburg at about 11.00 a.m. She drew us a plan showing how to reach the road then departed. I made a cup of tea while Max harnessed Action, who had been on good, green grass all night.

The road to Middelburg, like most roads in Holland, was flat. Major roads have cycle tracks, usually on one side only, sometimes on both, and the countryside is well tended. Dividing the parcels of land are many dykes. Houses and gardens are kept very tidy, and I was struck by the profusion of flowers in house windows, on patios and in window boxes.

This day was the warmest day we had had on the journey so far. The first kilometre took us down a narrow lane that joined the main road to Middelburg. As planned, a man on a bicycle stopped us and introduced himself as Mr. de Vos, President of Stichting Sports Steunt. He was about sixty years old, tall, smartly dressed in grey flannels and a hound's tooth check sports coat. He wore a collar and tie.

He beckoned to us to follow him into the town centre. As we made our way round the town, people stopped to talk to us, asking questions about our journey. These questions were mostly the same as those we had been asked in Britain: – "Where had we come from; where were we going; what is the horse's name and his age?" – Many of the Dutch people spoke English. – "How can you get him shod; can I give him a sweet or whatever? How many kilometres can you cover in a day; what about the heat and the cold?" – These were the standard questions we would be asked everywhere.

We parked Action and the caravan in the main square in Middelburg and a crowd gathered round us. It was a busy town and it was Saturday morning. Mr. de Vos had brought a collecting box with him to get money for his own organisation. People frequently dropped money into it. Max and I wore official identity cards of this organisation, the Stichting Sports Steunt Group.

A smart looking waiter carrying a silver tray loaded with coffee cups and cream cakes crossed the square and came over to the caravan, where he deposited the tray of goodies in the doorway. He told us they were for us, then he left. I said to Max that if we were going to be treated like this all the way, it would be great.

Mr. de Vos told there was to be a big fair in the small town of Kappela, but he would be unable to come with us as, unfortunately, he had a previous engagement. I suggested that we went, and as the collection for Stichting Sports had been so good in Middelburg we would collect in Kappela. However, if we had no representative of theirs with us, how should we dispose of the collection? Mr. de Vos said he would give us the number of their bank account and we could deposit the money at our leisure.

We arrived at the fair by lunch – time and within a minute an entourage of people approached us. One man sported a large gold chain. He introduced himself and also another man, wearing an even larger gold chain.

"I am the Mayor of Melton Mowbray and this is the Mayor of Kappela. The Mayor would like to welcome you here. Melton Mowbray and Kappela are twin towns. He wants to ask if you would would address the crowd over the public address, and tell them about your journey and the purpose behind it."

I agreed to do this, but first we wandered round the fair collecting. I had an interpreter to help me make my speech to the crowd, although many people in Holland could understand English. I felt a bit nervous, but managed to get through it.

We made good progress towards Belgium and were nearly up to the customs post when we decided to camp for the night. Just outside a small town Max noticed a gathering of static caravans. He said he thought it must be a camp, so we pulled in to ask if we could park there. No – one seemed to speak English, but they understood what we wanted. They fetched a man loaded down with gold rings and chains and he signalled us to come in. It was a Gipsy site and quite up – market. Action was tied on a grassy area amongst trees, and the children and youngsters loved him, pampering him and catering to his every need.

I woke next morning to hear Action neighing close to the caravan. I opened the door and found him waiting for me, surrounded by many children. Either they had brought him or he had brought them to me. It was something he had started to do as soon as I moved inside the caravan. His instinct was to get as near to me as possible. He neighed again when I said his name, and shoved his head through the open door of the van, fearlessly, but as if he needed me. Although he had been pampered by the Gipsy children, I was the only one he wanted.

From this day on, I could never remember Action putting a foot wrong in all the thousands of miles we travelled through eleven countries. My love for him was very strong.

The wheels needed regular greasing and this was as good a time and place as any in which to do it. We found one young man who was able to understand what we intended to do, and he went off and found four men, who went to the back of the caravan and lifted it bodily while the young man put blocks under the axles. Max removed the wheels and greased them. The same method was employed to deal with the front wheels.

Over a cup of coffee, we explained to the young man about having our bicycle stolen. I was not sure he understood. A few minutes later he vanished. It was now time to leave, so we hitched up Action and all the camp site people came to wave us off. I looked at the children and suggested to Max that we might give them a ride first. So, for the next hour I trundled up and down the main road, the caravan full of children and mothers.

I was just about to leave, when the young man came back. He tugged at my arm and told me to come. Curious about what he wanted, I let him pull me across the road and into a field of maize standing about five feet tall. Some twenty yards inside the field, he stopped and, bending down, he lifted a bicycle from the ground.

"For you, if you want," he said.

My reactions were quick. Why was the bicycle hidden among the maize and where had the young man been for the past hour? I declined his offer, but he would have none of that. He carried the cycle to the caravan, while I tried to stop him. Insisting that it was for us, he shoved it inside then turned with a smile and shook my hand. Everyone else was standing around watching in silence, then the chief stepped forward and gave me a name and address on a piece of paper. "Friend. Friend," he said.

"Dad, it's the address of some more Gipsies in Antwerp for us to visit," Max said.

After thanking them all, we left, but a few hundred yards up the road I stopped, opened the caravan door and removed the cycle. I told Max to get rid of it and there was no need to explain why. I had no idea where it came from and I was taking no risks, in case we were stopped by the police. Stolen or not, I felt the young man had given it to me with kindness in his heart.

Again it was a nice day, the sun was warm, Action had been on good grass all night – so he was content, the road was flat and smooth, and on both sides of it were cycle lanes. It was Sunday morning and cyclists kept passing us, sometimes singly and sometimes in two's. Others cycled in groups, occasionally whole families with children.

By now, Action had become accustomed to things coming up on the inside of him, but for the first few days in Holland it had sometimes startled him. He now had to listen on both sides, on his left for cars and lorries, and on his right for cyclists and those scooters that chose to use the cycle lane.

It was about 15 kilometres to Putte and we arrived in mid afternoon. It was a small town, the main road its high street, and Max and I decided to go straight to the Customs Post which we could see at the far end of it. The buildings covered both sides of the road and had that certain look common to all Customs Posts, large or small. The post was quite plain in appearance, with many signs directing one where to go and what to do; some in the three native languages plus a selection in foreign languages.

I pulled Action up; there was no barrier, and the small Customs office was right on the side of the road. By the front door stood two men, one in civilian clothes, tall with a small moustache and leaning against his bicycle, the other in uniform, but without his jacket, a short well–tanned man of about 45.

As we stopped neither man moved; they just stared. The civilian spoke first, in Dutch.

"We are from England", explained Max.

"Oh! What's this?" came the reply in good English.

I said, "We are trying to reach China with it."

A short silence ensued, then the conversation continued for a few more minutes. Meanwhile, the uniformed man had not spoken, but was wandering round the back of the caravan, touching things, pulling at the wooden wheels and looking at the horse. I felt slightly uncomfortable, but kept talking to the civilian, who by this time knew all about us. He spoke briefly to the still silent officer who then vanished into the Customs office, where I could see him in conversation with a colleague. These two re–appeared together, chatting away, and spoke to the civilian in Dutch. He translated into English for us.

"They say that you cannot travel through Belgium on those wheels." My first thought was that perhaps iron bound wooden wheels were not allowed on Belgian roads, but he continued more reasonably, "You will have to wait till tomorrow morning, as the matter has to be referred to another official for possible approval. You must park on that car park," he added, pointing to a large area of rough gravelled space. "The officer will be here at 7.00 am." And with that he got on his bike and trundled off, while the two officers returned to the Customs Post with no further comment.

We pulled onto the parking lot. Running down the back of it was a large, rough, unkempt hedge, and beneath that a patch of grass and weeds.

"Let's park next to the hedge," I said to Max, "We can tie Action to it."

Already thinking that this would be tonight's sleeping place, I released Action from the shafts, took off his harness, and looked in the hedge for for somewhere to tether him. In one corner was a big gap, about eight feet wide, leading to another rough looking car park, and here I tied the horse where the grass looked best.

For the past few days Max and I had not eaten too well, our diet being particularly lacking in meat, so I said, "We'll make a stew that will last a couple of days."

"Good idea, Dad" replied Max. "Let's go and get what we need. There are still shops open. I saw them as we were passing down the High Street."

There was one other thing that we had to do before leaving Holland. It was to deposit at a bank the money we had collected for Mr. de Vos.

We found a supermarket where we bought carrots, onions, beef stock cubes, leeks and swedes. At the rear of the shop was a large display of meat, butter and cheese. We looked along the meat display and, of course, it was priced in guilders, which we could follow. What we could not follow was the type of animal the meat came from. In the end I decided on a light pink coloured meat that looked like pork to me. Max was not so sure and carried on working out the writing on the tickets.

"No!" he said, "This is pork. This means pig in Dutch. I think the one you are buying is horse meat."

My stomach turned over to think that I was about to eat horse. The man behind the counter was already picking it up to weigh it on the scales.

"No, No. I said, "Sorry. We don't want that one."

The man looked a bit confused, but got the message and put it back. I apologised and walked further along to something more recognisable.

"There are some chickens. Let's play safe and buy one of these." So chicken stew it was to be.

Back at the caravan I set to preparing the stew. We had no large cooking pot so I decided to cook it in Action's new galvanised bucket.

Said Max, "I'll scrub it out first."

"Well he only drinks from it," I replied.

"If you won't scrub it out, then I will," replied fussy Max, and for about half an hour he scrubbed with great vigour, while I chopped and gutted. He returned it to me, gleaming.

I had collected some sticks from under the hedge and lit a fire, and for an hour the stew boiled merrily, with many tastings. And then I said,

"It's good, Max, and I think it is ready. Let's try some."

We dipped our red mugs into the bucket, trying to catch some chicken as well as gravy. Then we sat down with mug and spoon, and some of yesterday's bread.

For a few mouthfuls it did taste good, but soon I felt that didn't want any more. It crossed my mind that perhaps I had become over-hungry in the last few days, but Max, by now, was on his second mugful, proclaiming the stew to be very good. There was plenty left for tomorrow, so I washed up and stored the remainder in airtight polythene containers before going to look for Action.

I could not see him at first when I went through the gap in the hedge as he was on the other side, eating away. I told Max where he was, in case he wondered, and he replied,

"Dad, you'd better get him back. I think he's wandered into Belgium."

I told Max to take no notice, it would be OK, and I left it at that.

In the evening I decided to try to walk through the Customs Post into Belgium and I showed my passport to the Customs Officer. He let me through and I went into a bar about 100 yards from the caravan, and sat down alone while Max stayed with the horse for security reasons.

In this bar I had the best drink of beer of the whole journey, served by the best barmaid I have ever seen. She seemed to be serving ten people at once. I returned to the caravan and turned in.

Bang! Bang! "Hallo! Hallo, Mister." It was just daylight and, still half asleep, I opened the caravan doors. Standing there were two Customs Officers.

"Papers. Papers," one of them said. He was dressed smartly in his uniform, and not a man to argue with, I thought.

"Where is your horse?" he asked.

"Behind the hedge," I said.

"Where? In Belgium?" he snorted. He was flipping through my passport as he spoke. I was slightly nervous, not knowing what harm we had done in letting Action on to Belgium's soil without permission. Next came "Horse documents please." I produced the only thing that I had, which was the vaccination certificate the vet in Oban had made out for us. The Customs man flipped it over several times before thrusting both documents back into my hand. Then he sternly said,

"You must go. You must go," and pointing at the watch he held in his hand stated, "Six o'clock. Six o'clock," before he turned and walked away.

The second Customs Officer, our friend of the previous day, had been walking round the caravan once again, muttering a few words to his chief, who was obviously the man we had been waiting for. He now also pointed to his watch and said firmly, "Six o'clock. You be gone." Then with his hand he made a circular movement, and with a "Brmmm – Brmmm," he walked off.

Max had been sleeping while all this was going on and I roused him with, "Max, Max, we can go." He woke up in his usual slow and ponderous way.

"Oh good," he said, pulling on his trousers.

"You must hurry. The Customs chief kept saying "six o'clock," and I think we have to be out of here by then. Come on Max, hurry!"

It was ten minutes to six, and I knew that to get everything ready to leave in ten minutes was impossible, particularly with Max as he is for the first half hour of the day.

We were ready by about 6.30 a.m., but by this time we were surrounded by juggernauts. Now I understood what the Customs man had meant when he said "Brmmm – Brmmm." There was no way out of the vehicle park. We were locked in.

"There is only one way out Max," I said, "Through the hedge and into the other car park, then onto the main road". Max was not impressed with this idea, but I went on, "I don't fancy going back to see that Customs Officer again; he was quite adamant about us going through by six o'clock."

"Right! We'll chance it," Max agreed. So through the hedge with horse and caravan we went, across the car park and onto the main road. We were in Belgium. As I nosed out luck was on our side. Parked empty on my left was a juggernaut, and I realised that we could not be seen from the Customs Post if I pulled in front of it. It worked perfectly and without looking back, we set off towards Antwerp.

As we had not crossed the Holland/Belgium border officially, for the rest of the day, as we travelled we expected at any minute to be stopped by police and told to go back. We saw many customs and police cars, but none of them stopped us.

The road to Antwerp was flat. We stopped several times on the way to water and feed Action, and at about four o'clock we decided to cook the rest of the stew. While Max washed out the galvanised bucket with his usual care, I got a fire going.

We had stopped in a lay-by, where sticks were not easy to find, but I found enough to get a good boil on the go. After a while I noticed a greenish froth on top of the stew, and as the boiling continued, froth and bubbles completely filled the bucket. I thought, "That's a bit odd," but no more than that. In went the two red mugs and I took the first spoonful. It had a very funny taste indeed.

"What do you think, Max. Does your's taste queer?"

"Yes it does. I can't eat mine," he replied.

"Nor me," said I.

To describe the taste and by now, the smell, I would say it was like eating metal, and it smelled like a rusty old tin. Max then said, "You know what you've done. The stew has taken the galvanising coat from the bucket!" Then I told him about the green froth, and we both realised that, even on the previous night, when I could not eat the stew, the metal was already in it and it had fermented during the day. We poured the rest into the bushes. So much for Belgian Border Stew! I wonder we survived.

As we got closer to Antwerp the road surface started to get more bumpy. Then as we entered the outskirts of the city, many streets turned to cobblestones, very uneven and sometimes with large holes. We headed for the dock area, as we thought that we might find somewhere to camp for the night, perhaps on some waste ground. As we crossed the city it seemed there was a tram-line or pothole every few yards. By now the wooden wheels were taking considerable punishment and I was worried that the caravan might fall apart with the vibration. I was so concerned that I considered the damage we were doing could force us to turn back. I conferred.

"What do you think, Max? At this rate we will ruin the wheels."

Max pointed out that it was now 5.30 p.m. and at the slow pace we were travelling and allowing time to find a parking place, it could be two or three hours before we were settled, and darkness would be upon us. It would be very difficult to camp in the city, so we decided to proceed to the docks.

It was a decision I soon regretted, as the cobblestones became worse, the tram-lines more numerous, and the surface even more uneven. To top it all we became lost in the side streets. Eventually we did find the dock area. Along the front ran a long, uneven road with more potholes and more cobblestones.

"Max, we must get out of here," I said, and Max agreed. "Let's head out of Antwerp as quick as we can. Which way, Max?" I asked.

This was a question I was to ask him often, as I had come to realise that my son had an uncanny sense of direction and a memory for buildings, monument, streets, shops etcetera, that was very special.

"Let's go that way," he said.

So, turning away from the docks, we headed out from Antwerp's cobbled streets for about an hour until we reached a decent road. I noticed a signpost for Aarschot, showing that Max's sense of direction was right. I was relieved to be on a smoother road. The damage to the wheels would not become apparent until later on.

Max was away parking the van. We were in the centre of Lier, a small Belgian town, and I knew Action was thirsty, for he had walked about seven miles. I waited for Max to return, but as time went by it crossed my mind that perhaps he was having a job finding a space. A man asked me if I would like a drink and I said, "Yes."

"Come with me to that café," he said.

"I can't leave the horse alone," I replied.

"Come on."

I had never left Action unattended before, but I said, "Alright, I'll come." Action also needs water and I can get it from the café, I thought, and so I left him. I could see him from the café window, standing there with many people around him. He never moved an inch, and in the future I was able to leave him on his own for many hours, with little fear that he would not stay. He understood when I said, "Stand and wait." The only danger came when something startled him; like polythene bags blowing towards him, or a noise such as children with balloons that went off `Bang!' or people waving flags in front of his face.

Action was miserable. It had been drizzling all morning and he walked with his head hanging almost to the ground, the posture he took to let the rain drip off him. We decided to keep moving.

It was late afternoon when Max came back to me after parking the van. He told me he had found a spot for us in a pub car park. We drove for another hour before he pointed it out to me in the distance, at the end of a small road on our right. No sooner had I turned the corner when there was an almighty bang as a high sided lorry overtook us. Action jumped. It looked like a firework display going on round the lorry. The vehicle had cut some electrical cables and they had come down right in front of us. Where they touched the ground they twisted and turned, the power shorting and sending out flashes and crackles. The display continued for several seconds.

Action wanted to leave the road and go into the ditch. I managed to control him as the flashes and crackles subsided and became merely an occasional burst. The lorry had not stopped. This had been a very dangerous time for Action and myself.

Max ran to the pub to notify the police, who arrived inside two minutes. It was not easy for us to give them a statement, but we managed it by providing a series of drawings. It seemed that people building a new filling station were taking electricity from a pole on the far side of the road. They had slung the temporary cable too low, and the lorry had hit it. From what I could understand from the police, the culprit was in for big trouble.

Safely parked beside the pub, I found a tree by an allotment and secured Action to it. It was now late, Max and I had not eaten, and with all the fuss with the cables, we had not had a chance to buy food, so we were both starving. Besides this, I had run out of Belgian money and there was no way of changing any more Sterling. The only thing we could do now was raid the allotment.

As it had been raining most of the day, the ground was wet, and as it was dark, I sent Max while I kept watch. He vanished over a dyke, over a fence and into the night. I could hear a few curses and sounds of anguish! I was tempted to call out to ask if he was alright, but that could have alerted someone. Then I heard the sound of him running through the mud, then I heard a splash followed by some unrepeatable language. After this it went silent for a time.

At last I heard him climbing back over the fence. He lined himself up to jump the dyke, and just about made it to my side before he began to slide slowly backwards into the ice cold water. When he emerged he was in a terrible state, covered in black mud, wringing wet and without vegetables, as he had lost them when he fell.

The next morning that allotment looked as though a bomb had hit it. Worse than the damage done by Max was that done by Action, who had slipped his chain in the night and had been gorging himself with everything in sight.

"Let's get out of here, Max, before we find ourselves in big trouble. You should see that allotment," I said.

I had never seen Max wake up so quickly. Inside ten minutes we had left the place at full trot. We would not stop for the next ten miles, remembering what that policeman had said about the big trouble in store for the man who slung the cables.

I had started to grow bored with driving Action. Contrary to popular opinion, there was no ambling gently through the countryside, admiring the view and listening to the birds, the smell of nature in your nostrils. Certainly there were times when it was like this, but the normal situation was one of juggernauts, tractors, trailers, buses, coaches and cars scorching past; road works with compressors, J.C.B.s, and cranes to negotiate. It seemed as if life depended on all these things, and it was only because of all the publicity we had received that we were treated courteously. I tried to imagine myself in the position of a Traveller or a Gipsy with a horse in front and caravan behind. I concluded that it would be hard in today's society. They were looked on as scroungers or thieves and I should have been seen in the same light, but for the charity's banners and posters that we carried. Without them I would not get very far.

In the afternoon we met a group of English soldiers, and Max asked them if there was a mechanic among them, as the van was playing up again. They invited us back to the camp, where there was a mechanic. I asked if they knew of any homes for the handicapped, as we had not yet made any contacts in Belgium. How he knew it, I do not know, but one of the men supplied us with an address in Deist.

We arrived at the army camp, but there was no sign of our friends from the morning, and we could not gain admittance. I tried to explain what we wanted, but the answer was always no. So we left. I felt hurt; since being in Holland and Belgium, everyone had helped us, and this refusal of entry to land held by our fellow countrymen left me disappointed and angry, as may be seen from what I did. There was a nice, green bank by the entrance gates to the camp, and I let Action feed on its grass. His big, deep hoof-prints made some mess, I can tell you!

Making Belgian stew in Action's bucket.

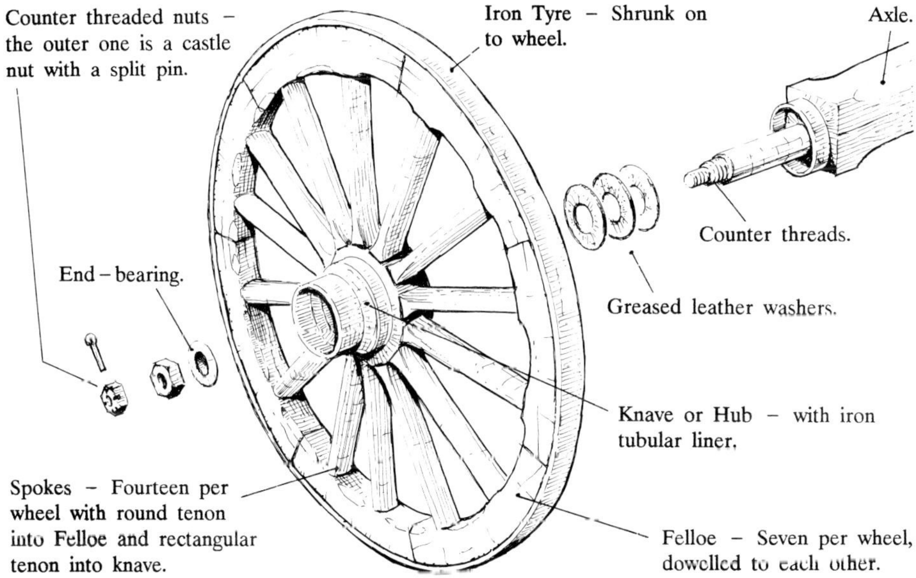

Detail of wheel construction

Chapter Eight

Getting into Germany and Visiting the Handicapped

Shortly after leaving the army camp, we were approached by a group of students who were interested in our journey. We showed them the newspaper cutting from Holland, and they told us of a home for the handicapped in Diest. We decided to visit this place, and arrived at lunch–time. There was a small yard with a little school on one side and a large, new building on the other. From the latter emerged two ladies, keen to know what we were doing there. We showed them our book of newspaper cuttings by way of explanation and they quickly understood.

They escorted us inside, sat us down and fed us, after which a number of handicapped people, most of them adults, came to stroke Action. Their faces showed delight. Presently, a crowd of small children came out of the school and began to touch the horse. We were about to take our leave when a representative of the home came over. He told us that this home had been built with funds from the Lion Club. We talked for a while before he vanished back inside. He came back with a letter of thanks to us for visiting his home and offering best wishes for the rest of our journey. This was the first of many such letters from homes for the handicapped. They would be our passports to every country we were to visit. There would be times when we went to as many as three such places in a single day, and always Action and the caravan proved tremendous attractions; something I had not envisaged at the start.

Darkness was closing in as we reached the outskirts of Hasselt. Max had gone ahead to find a stopping place and he came back to show me the way there. It was a small patch of grass under a motorway bridge, but it lay between a steep, wooded bank on one side and a field of maize on the other. I tethered Action to a tree on the bank, leaving him insufficient chain to reach the maize plants. Against the trees the horse was barely visible, and it was a secure spot, so we decided to leave him there and go into Hasselt, a town famous for its gin distilleries, for the evening. Action still needed water, so we put a five gallon container in the horse box and set off.

We entered a small bar and I went to the counter where I found myself flanked by two men. I asked the one on my left if he knew where we could see some night life.

"Yes, Ducky," said he in a very sweet voice. "Where do you want to go?"

The man on my right leaned round me and began to talk in the same sweet way, so I slunk back to Max, who was grinning.

"Sit down, Ducky," he said, "And drink your beer."

We had quite a bar crawl that night and were well away by midnight, when we made our way back to the horsebox for the water container. We had found it by half past midnight. Then Max discovered that we had a puncture in one of the tyres, and we could not possibly drive back to the camp site, but even in my drunken stupor, I knew Action needed his water.

"Which way, Max?" I asked.

"Haven't got a clue," he said. For the first time, his uncanny sense of direction had left him, possibly because of the gin. "I know it's about four miles away."

There was no chance we could have walked it in the state we were in, assuming we could ever have found the right road. I proposed finding a police station and asking for help. After scouring the town, we found it and, still clutching the water container, we went inside. No – one spoke English.

We tried, through bleary eyes and gin fumes, to explain our dilemma; that we needed to water our horse and had a puncture on our vehicle. *Aqua* – Water, they understood, but to explain where we had left horse and caravan, under a bridge near the motorway, took considerable time, much hand waving and many drawings. Once they got our drift, two officers ushered us into a Black Maria. We still had no water for our horse, and Max was convinced they were taking us to the cells.

After a short drive, the car stopped and one officer opened the door. To my amazement, we were beside the caravan. I shook his hand and thanked him, shaking the container and again saying "*Aqua* – Water".

"Morning, morning," was his only reply.

"I need it for Action," I said. On hearing his name the horse appeared, charging through the bushes, in which he had until now been hidden from sight. I never saw policemen move so fast as those two when Action hit the end of his chain, only feet from where they were standing. One man put his hand to his heart, tapping it gently as if to reassure himself that he was still alive.

"He won't hurt you," I said, going towards the horse. "Come and stroke him."

At that moment I felt my feet going from under me, not because I was drunk, however. I was falling into a big ditch full of mud and water. Max was glowering at me, and I knew he was thinking that the policemen were wondering what the hell we were up to. With a great effort I crawled out of the ditch. I was wringing wet and plastered with mud.

One officer approached and I thought my troubles could only get worse, but he reached out and took the water container, climbed back in the van and the pair of them drove off. Max and I went wearily to bed, but were not quite asleep when we heard the sound of a vehicle approaching. It was our policemen again, with water for Action. One of the men carried the water towards Action, stumbled slightly, then began to empty the container into his bucket.

After they had left, Max said,

"Dad, I was scared stiff when he stumbled. I had nicked a bag of sweet-corn from the field. Action must have got at it and opened the bag. I am sure that policeman knew what it was, but he said nothing."

It might appear that Max and I spent an inordinate amount of time frequenting bars, but the prospect of sitting, hungry and tired, in a cramped caravan until bed-time was not one we could contemplate night after night. Had we been of more temperate habits, we should have missed striking up some very useful friendships and meeting people who were able to help us along the way. Most evenings, we were content with one glass of the local brew and a light meal, but sometimes, after a very trying day, we were tempted to over indulge ourselves.

My head felt awful as I drove Action back to the horse box on the following morning. I did not feel like mending that puncture. When we arrived, we found a lovely surprise awaiting us. The tyre was fully inflated and a police car stood by the horsebox.

"Good morning," said a policeman. "Everything O.K. now. We fix tyre. Good luck on your journey."

Our next stopping place was on the Gipsy site recommended by our Gipsy friends from Holland, and we found on the site many beautiful, mobile caravans, and dotted amongst them were several older vans with wooden extensions that looked like permanent homes. We pulled up and someone came to ask our business. Max handed him the note from our friends. He called out to an elderly man, who came up, walked round us and then pointed out a vacant patch of land beside one of the caravans. I needed no explanation and we went over and parked.

For the rest of that day we were inundated with children of all ages and most with grubby, dark little faces. They flocked round the horse and some entered our caravan and wanted to sit on the bed. A youth came over, after talking to the horse, and warned us to keep the children out of the caravan, as they would steal anything they could. I ignored his warning at my peril.

Food had not been too plentiful of late. There was more than enough in the shops: meat, pasta, sausage of many types, fruit and vegetables, but we had not had time to buy it or cook it. For this occasion we had the sweet-corn and butter. After our experiences with the bucket, we had acquired a boiling pot. We put the heads of corn in water and left the pot to boil merrily for about fifteen minutes. When I thought they were ready, I took them out, but when I bit into one my teeth made no impression on it. They were still hard and green! Another culinary failure.

Although there were plenty of women and young girls about the place, none came near us. I did not find this surprising, as I know that women generally keep clear of strange men, especially if they are not of their own kind.

As we ate, a car drew up, a man jumped out and threw two sacks on the ground. An old woman came and emptied them onto the ground. Out cascaded fresh sea fish of all sorts. Women converged on her and she distributed it among them. One hour later, the old woman served us fish stew.

It was a Sunday. At 6 p.m. the children vanished, returning at 7 o'clock, clean and dressed in their best clothes. It was the time for an evening chatter for the womenfolk, who stood about in small groups or strolled casually up and down. One young woman came up with a four year old girl wearing a pretty dress and a pair of red Wellingtons, which seemed odd, as it was a dry summer evening.

At seven next morning, dogs barking, cocks crowing and children's laughter signalled that the men were preparing to go to work, climbing into Tarmac or scrap lorries. We were ready to leave by 8.30 a.m. It was my aim always to tidy the caravan and make my bed every morning before setting off. A large, soft Paddington Bear, given me by Action Research for the Crippled Child, hung in one corner. He had a pair of scarlet Wellington boots and a suitcase. The suitcase was still there, but the famous Wellingtons had vanished. I deduced that a child had stolen them, but I did not feel inclined to try and recover them.

Mid morning, when we were close to the Dutch customs post, we decided to visit a café. We should have to cross a small part of Holland to reach Germany, and I was thinking about the first time we entered Holland, at Vlissingen.

A crowd gathered as soon as we stopped, and most people spoke English. I left Action unattended while Max went to post letters home to his mother and sister. A young man invited me to have coffee and something to eat, and I never refuse an invitation. Besides, I needed water for Action, so I left the horse surrounded by admirers while I followed the man into a restaurant. I watched him through the window as I tucked into ham, bread and cakes. He stayed put, and it was small wonder; people were going into a shop and coming out with carrots and apples for him.

I was thinking with dread of the customs post which lay ahead of us, and I mentioned my concern to my companion. He consoled me by saying the post would not be manned on this particular day. Then Max returned and was treated to his food and drink.

When we reached the barrier to Holland, there was no – one on duty, the barrier was up and we were able to drive through towards our next destination, Maastricht, where there is a square surrounded by hotels, shops and cafés. There are many items of interest to tourists, churches with wall paintings, medieval tunnels under the town and, most prominent of all, the war graves of the Allied troops that surrounded the town during the last war.

In the evening we took a stroll around. The town was full of young people enjoying a drink or a meal outdoors. The shopping precinct was full of shops displaying beautiful goods.

I was very impressed to hear many buskers singing in English. In a bar that evening we met two Englishmen, Danny and Klaus Fairbrother, who had been working in the building trade in Maastricht for a number of years. We drank together and had many a laugh. At one point, Danny set fire to the brandy in his glass, but he was so drunk he spilled it down his arm. The flames followed the trail of spirit. He had no idea what to do next and ended up by dropping the glass on the bar. He was not badly burnt, but I am sure he never repeated the trick.

We had been invited to visit a sports complex next day. It was part of Stichting Sports Steunt group and many handicapped people arrived to what turned out to be a carnival. Fire service and police vehicles were there to give demonstrations, and we had been asked to give children rides in the caravan. The police asked if Action would be upset by their sirens, as their route came close by us. Action took no notice of them when they did some trial runs, and many children enjoyed rides in our caravan.

We were now close to the German customs post. In all my preparatory correspondence, it was Germany that had provided the most forms to be completed and had most regulations to be observed, none of which I had attended to, so I was expecting problems. I was feeling uneasy until a tall, blond man came up to us in Maastricht and gave his name as Johann Mettringer.

"I see you carry Olau Ferry Company publicity on your caravan. I work for them as purser aboard a ferry. Is there any help I can give you?" he asked in perfect English.

I mentioned my doubts about crossing into Germany. He asked me to hand over all my documents and promised to drive me to the border and see me safely across. I gave him everything, our passports and the folder of press cuttings included, and arranged to meet him again on the same spot at 3 o'clock.

He arrived punctually and told me that I was to be at the customs post next day, at 7 o'clock in the evening. He said our safe crossing had been arranged and that he would be there himself to make sure we encountered no snags. At Vaals, a few kilometres from Aachen, we went through the Dutch customs post and it was 7 o'clock when I arrived at the German border crossing, but there was no sign of Johann. As darkness was soon to fall, I decided not to wait for him, but to go across, knowing permission had already been given and assuming it would be no more than a formality.

Two customs officers caught sight of Action and came rushing up waving their arms and speaking in German, which I could not understand. I got the impression that they knew nothing about us. They directed us to park just over the border, in German territory. We sat and waited while frantic comings and goings went on at the customs post. Then we heard someone calling our names. It was Johann. He called out to ask if we were having problems.

"I don't know", I called back.

Johann went inside the customs office and came back after five minutes looking less than pleased.

"It seems these men have been told not to let you across. I told them their chief had given permission for you to cross tonight, and I have played hell with them. They're on the telephone to him now, while we wait."

Presently a customs officer came over to tell Johann we could enter

Germany. I unhitched Action from the caravan, and Johann asked if we could leave him on a patch of grass beside their building for the night, as it was getting dark and we could not travel. They agreed and we shook Johann warmly by the hand.

"I should like to do one more thing for you. I will take you for your last meal in Holland."

We left the caravan and horsebox in Germany and walked back into Holland, to a nearby restaurant. Johann bought beers for us before we all sat down to a big steak apiece. Max and I were both hungry and we finished our meals before Johann, who had been talking, had hardly started on his. During the meal, one of the customs men came up and spoke to Johann, who threw his knife and fork down angrily.

"I don't believe this! They say you can't enter Germany. Their chief has changed his mind. You must bring everything back into Holland, including your horse."

I stood up and prepared to go and fetch my belongings, but Johann told me to sit down while he finished his meal. He swore about the Germans and ordered another bottle of wine, which he said would help him think. The waiter brought yet more wine when Johann set off for the customs post, telling us to stay where we were until he returned.

"I have spoken by telephone to the chief, and he is on is way, the little shit," he said.

The chief arrived and Johann went for him, talking in German for which I needed no interpreter. I could sense that the man was getting embarrassed. We all went into the office, where other customs men wearing holstered guns sat around.

"He had a change of mind after talking to one of their Ministry vets," Johann explained. "He can't take responsibility for letting us in without a valid Coggins test certificate and the right documents for Action, so he's chickened out."

Johann spoke to the chief again, and I could make out the occasional word of abuse. The chief paced up and down, sometimes holding his head. Suddenly, Johann banged his fists on the counter, which made an officer with a gun begin to slide his hand towards his thigh. Johann ranted on for a bit longer then told me we should have to wait for a vet to arrive, but this would not be before 8 o'clock the following morning. Meanwhile, we had to move everything back into Holland.

Johann gave us the gist of what he said to the chief, adding that the chief had asked him what part of Germany he came from, as his German was so fluent.

"I am Dutch, I told him," Johann said, "And if you do not let them through tomorrow morning, I shall get television and newspaper reporters here." He left us to find a hotel for the night, despondent at having let us down.

We began moving back into Holland, where the officials, aware of our problems, were very helpful. I was just fetching Action when the chief came and indicated that I could leave the horse where he was. Behind him came the man with the gun, now carrying a large pail of water. I began to think they were not so bad after all. The morning would tell.

At 8 o'clock, as promised, the chief arrived with a vet, and they went straight up to Action. The vet pulled down his eyelids, lifted his hooves, peered up his nostrils and then asked me to walk him round. The only things he said was "horse documents". I knew I had virtually nothing in this line at all, certainly nothing relevant to German requirements. Instead, I rammed my folder of letters and cuttings into his hands. Another man was standing beside me and he said the vet wanted entry permits and a certificate for the Coggins test. There was no sense in bluffing. I admitted that I had none. I thought he passed this message to the vet.

For the next ten minutes, the chief and the vet looked at every letter and article. I never heard so many sighs, and puffs in my life.

"Come with us," said the English speaking official. "We would like to duplicate your documents back in the office."

Many officials were set to work on this task, each man putting one of the copies in his pocket to take home and show the family. Then the chief indicated that we could pass into Germany. His way of doing this was to turn his back on me, look down and point towards Germany, as if to say, "I have not seen you, but most of all I don't want to stop you." Johann now arrived and was delighted to hear what had been decided.

"Where are you going now?" he asked.

"Aachen," Max replied. "To try and find an institution or something."

"Let's see what we can do," Johann said, leading us back to the office. He spoke at length to the chief then said, "He knows a handicapped home in Aachen. He will telephone an introduction."

The chief made his call, meanwhile writing on a slip of paper, which he handed to me.

"Go and ask for Herr Kehrings, director of the Vinzenz-Heim in Aachen. He is expecting you," he said, signing the paper with his name.

So, the chief had come up trumps after all, and on two counts. We thanked him and Johann, grateful for his aggressive help, without which I doubt we should ever have got so far. My big regret is losing his address when some of our papers were stolen. I should like to have got in touch with him again, had that been possible.

We found the Vinzenz-Heim in a side street just outside the town, and Herr Kehrings was waiting for us. He was tall and slim, grey suited and with greying hair. He spoke little English and introduced Natalie, a young woman who translated for us. Within a few minutes, a reporter and photographer arrived and I began to tell my story.

Herr Kehrings was informed that we wanted to enter the centre of Aachen and get publicity for his home, also that we could make a street collection for it. Being Germany, all this required special permission, and Natalie spent the rest of the day between police and council officials trying to get the necessary documents. The council said we could collect in the main square, but they must seal the collecting boxes which could only be opened again in a bank, in the presence of ourselves and someone representing the

Vinzenz – Heim. Both we and the Heim's representative were to get receipts.

This was the formula used all over Germany, a country requiring many documents and having many laws, but with plenty of speed and enthusiasm. In the square in Aachen, we were continually surrounded by people while Natalie answered their questions and told our story.

Across the square from us two men sat on the pavement cleaning shoes. Occasionally, the younger man would stroll over and stroke Action before returning to his work. The older man had a cap sitting on the pavement beside him, and people sometimes threw coins into it even though not all wanted their shoes shined. While I watched them, these men came across to me, the younger man going up to Action and stroking him. The old man held out his cap with the morning's takings. He handed the money to Natalie and asked her to put it in the charity box, then talked to her for a while in German. She was standing in the doorway of the caravan, listening intently and surrounded by a group of elderly ladies.

I had not been taking much notice of this until I turned and saw one woman wiping tears from her eyes. I saw the old man leaning his head on Action's rump, his eyes also filled with tears. Looking to Natalie, she was also obviously upset, too. She gently put her hand on the old man's shoulders, speaking softly to him. The crowd was still standing silently, moved by what they had just heard. The old man pulled himself together and came to shake my hand, then he patted Action affectionately, spoke to his friend and then vanished into the crowd.

"I shall tell you what he said," Natalie began. "He said he was a Gipsy. He lived a life on the roads until Hitler came along. He well remembers horses and caravans, and travelling from town to town. Before the war he lived in a caravan with his family, and he has never forgotten them. Hitler decreed that all cripples and Gipsies must be exterminated. Millions, including the man's family, were killed; his parents, brothers and sister also. He was only spared because he was absent when the Gestapo came for them, but since that time he has never seen a real Gipsy caravan, and memories came flooding back. Nowadays he drinks to forget." As she spoke, Natalie was getting more upset, so I closed the conversation.

We returned to the home and had a guided tour of the building and its facilities, which included a games room and swimming pool. The furniture was better than many would expect to find at home.

That evening we headed towards Bonn, and Natalie, who lived on the road we were to take, offered to escort us out of Aachen. Along the way, she stopped at the roadside and introduced us to her mother and brother, who spoke good English. Natalie climbed down from the caravan and started to make a speech. She did not get far before tears took over and she choked on the words. She could say no more, but she handed me a present before turning away to hide her emotions. Her brother took over where she had left off. She wanted to say what a wonderful experience it had been to be with two such wonderful people, but she could not understand why two men from another country should put themselves out to help foreigners. It was a comment we would hear again and again.

He handed me a parcel saying, "For your journey. It is special. Enjoy it."

Max and I found it hard to leave Natalie, as we should find it hard to leave other friends on future occasions, when people had helped us in times of crisis or were very kind. Meeting Natalie had been a turning point for us. People of every country would appreciate that what we were doing was something special, and most would understand why, in the same way as she had. Sadly, her address was another that we lost when papers were stolen from us, and I have not been able to contact her again.

It was now dark and we needed a parking place. The only spot was on an airfield, so we came quietly through the gate and tethered Action where he was hidden by bushes. It had been a good day, the collection had been good and we had got some useful publicity, which we would be able to use during our stay in Germany, but most important was meeting a very special young woman, who showed us that people do care about others.

As we prepared for bed, Max and I shared the same thoughts. We opened the presents and found that Natalie had given us chopsticks, appropriate for our destination, China; her mother had given us a parcel of home-made cakes, so we tucked into them before going off to sleep.

Chapter Nine

The Rhine Valley and New Friendships

Travelling south along the Rhine towards Bonn, we entered wine growing country; vineyards cloaked every hillside. I had been looking forward to following the Rhine Valley almost as far as Austria.

I only knew one person in advance of leaving Great Britain, and this was Dr. Christine Schulz, whose home was in a small village just outside Bonn. We made straight there, hoping to surprise her, but when we arrived, at about 8 o'clock, she was out. Night was closing in and we had to look for a stopping place on the outskirts of the village.

Max guided us onto some open land divided into small allotments, but I could not put Action in the middle of this, so we tried again and, in the deepening darkness, came across an orchard where we parked among the trees. I tethered Action to a tree among plenty of grass. Max and I discovered that the trees bore blue plums, and as we had not yet eaten, we gorged ourselves on them. Action soon joined us, pulling at branches in his search for the fruit.

Next morning, I awoke to find Action standing motionless amid a pile of plums and twigs. He had tugged at the trees until all the plums had been shaken to the ground. It was a mess! I called to Max to hurry up and get away from the orchard before we were discovered. He, however, filled a bag with plums for later.

When we arrived at Christine's house, she was at home and happy to see us, but she had her leg in plaster, having broken it in a car accident. We sat talking about our trip and I asked her if she knew of any handicapped homes in Bonn we could visit. She immediately telephoned to a Dr. Schlack and arranged for us to arrive at his institute at 9 a.m. the following morning. As it lay on the other side of Bonn, we decided to move closer to it and drove easily across the town on wide, busy roads.

The large, modern hospital stood in its own grounds, and it was almost evening when we arrived, so I decided to park in the grounds, although I had not sought permission to do so. We found a piece of waste land that might once have been a railway embankment and where we thought we should be ought of sight. Then a girl aged about ten arrived and spent the evening chatting to us in German, her little fingers into everything. When it began to get dark, I had had enough of her company and tried to persuade her by signs that it was time for her to go, but she was reluctant to leave Action. At last, she went away.

At 9 o'clock in the morning we entered Gustav – Heinemann – Haus and were taken to the office of Professor Schlack. The Professor explained about the work they did there, most of which was caring for people suffering from epilepsy. He told us that this institute was one of the leading centres treating the complaint. The building was named after Gustav Heinemann, Germany's first postwar president and a man much admired for steering Germany towards its present prosperity.

We asked the professor for permission to make a collection, in the main square in Bonn, for the institute. It was all arranged in a short time, someone having been despatched to get the necessary documentation. Meanwhile, he guided us round the hospital.

I have to confess to being shocked by what I saw there. Although I had already seen many severely mentally and physically handicapped people, I was not prepared for this. The place was beautifully equipped and furnished, but the degree of illness increased as we went round from room to room. By the time we reached the last room, I felt shocked that such places existed. Before we went through the door, however, the Professor told me I had no need to go inside if I did not want to. Max, his face showing his feelings, and I went in.

We found ourselves in a small room. A young woman was sitting in the middle and cradling something in her arms. I thought she was holding a pallid child wrapped in a blanket. Two matchstick arms hung at its sides, and I felt too embarrassed to stare. Professor Schlack was talking, introducing us, saying names, telling me that what I took for a sickly, starving child was a man of 23. The young woman was gently kissing his gaunt, white face.

"Is this his sister?" I asked.

"No. She is one of our helpers," he replied. I realised what devotion these carers had, to find time to kiss something most of us would find so repulsive. "In this room are four patients and four women helpers," he continued. "They do twelve hour spells of duty, two of them on at a time, day and night." As he spoke, I could not tear my eyes away from the girl gently rocking the boy, and I wondered if I could pick him up and hold him close to me, or if I would be too disgusted.

Professor Schlack led us to a bed in one corner of the room. A blonde girl lay motionless under a white sheet, her eyes staring vacantly into space.

"This is Heidi; twelve years old, limbless and almost unable to comprehend anything. We try to stimulate her, and very occasionally she moves her lips in what might be a response, but we are not sure and it happens very seldom."

I moved towards her and touched her cheek gently.

"Hello, Heidi. I have come from Schottland to see you," I said, but this was only a nervous gesture on my part. Professor Schlack took me next to see the other two patients, both asleep in bed, and described their handicaps.

As we were about to follow the professor out of the room, we had to squeeze past the girl cradling the young man, and I wondered again if I could hold him. Unhesitatingly, I bent down and stroked his head, then his legs, as if to prove that I was not frightened or repelled. Once I had done it, I felt neither fear nor revulsion.

I turned once again to look at the face peering blankly from under the sheet. "Bye bye, Heidi," I called. Then something happened; so that if the whole of the rest of our journey had been uneventful, this would have made it worthwhile. Heidi's mouth opened. Not a smile, just a slight opening and a twisting of the lips. An ecstatic young helper hurried to her bed, talking, gesturing, trying to get another response, but the moment had gone.

Professor Schlack turned to me and said, "You got her to respond. That is the first time for ages." He went on to explain that she was cared for by women, and the sound of man's voice, albeit foreign, was undoubtedly the stimulus.

After this experience, Max and I became almost totally committed to visiting people with this sort of very severe handicap and those who never got out into the sunshine to watch the rest of the world. Max was very touched by this visit. He said his hearing problems would never worry him again after seeing the patients in Bonn. Max had been left with impaired hearing after a bad dose of mumps when he was only three. He had tried using hearing aids while still at school, but other children had made fun of him, so he learned to lip read. If I spoke to him from behind, he could pick up the sound, but not the words. Conversation with him could sometimes be frustrating, but he does not realise quite how impaired his hearing is and how much he misses of general conversation taking place around him. However, his loss of hearing has helped him develop other invaluable skills.

For some time, Max had been walking many miles each day, taking the horsebox on ahead and then making his way back to me. We took turns at walking with Action, so it was not surprising that he complained of sore feet, an affliction aggravated by the lack of time we had to wash out our socks. Sometimes I would suggest that Max let me take the horsebox ahead while he drove the horse, but he insisted that I was the horseman and he would stick to driving the horsebox and walking back. We did not argue. Sometimes we might disagree over minor matters, but I had made a good choice of companion for the journey.

When we left the Gustav-Heinemann-Haus, Professor Schlack handed us a letter of thanks for our visit: another page in our "passport". We spent the evening at Bonn's annual fair; the biggest funfair I have ever seen, and a spectacle indeed.

On the following morning, duly armed with documents from council and police, and ready to collect, we parked in Bonn's main square, the Münsterplatz, where stands a statue of Beethoven, who was born in Bonn in 1770. We had not been able to arrange for an interpreter, but were soon surrounded by a good crowd of people, all asking questions. We hit on the idea of pinning a selection of press cuttings, letters and leaflets from handicapped homes on the sides of the caravan, which seemed to be sufficient explanation for the public.

I noticed three men sat on a bench drinking beer interspersed with slugs of schnapps. They obviously had a drink problem, as it was only 10.30 a.m. One man came over. He was big and had long, curly hair, and he chattered away in German to Max, who nodded and smiled, although I knew he had no idea what was being said. Max asked me if I had understood, then a young man came up and translated.

"He is telling you that later he will do his act here in front of Beethoven. He eats fire and he worries about your horse being frightened. He wants to give the money he collects for his first performance to you for the handicapped people."

By one o'clock the square was full of shoppers, office workers and tourists, so the fire eater started his enthralling act. He swallowed gulps of fuel and then applied a lighted torch as he blew it from his mouth, sometimes creating a huge fireball twenty feet away that ignited with a bang. Action murmured at first, but soon got used to it, eating contentedly from his nosebag. When the act was finished, the man made a speech to the crowd. Our young translator told me he was telling them that the performance had been in aid of the handicapped and asking them to give generously. He offered to show them more if they did so. As his helper went round collecting, he continued his act by passing long needles in one cheek and out of the other.

When he had finished, he came to us and emptied all his takings into our collecting box. I shook his hand and thanked him.

I noticed two men dressed in black flared trousers, waistcoats, white shirts, black jackets and soft, black trilby hats with domed tops. Our translator friend explained that they were travelling carpenters from northern Germany, and there are many of them around, all good tradesmen. One of these men stood beside Action, stroking him. People kept coming up and giving him money, thinking he was with us. He stood holding the money in his hand, and I thought he would soon put it in the box. Suddenly he put it all in his pocket and made off in a hurry, leaving Max and me with our mouths hanging open.

A woman in the crowd invited us to visit her home at nearby Meckenheim and have a meal. She promised to try and organise a stopping place for us and Action, but when we got to the town we could not find her and we ended up on the station car park by a café. It was drizzling rain and very cold. I tied Action to some trees.

When we left Bonn, I had asked Christine to try and find out what documents we would need to enter Austria, as I wanted to avoid a repeat of the fracas at the German border. I had arranged to telephone her this evening. Max's feet were very sore and he was tired, so while he lay down in the caravan, I went to the café to have a coffee. I got into conversation with a handsome, grey-haired man who spoke excellent English with an Oxford twang.

"I have seen your caravan and read the articles displayed on the side. I am pleased to meet you. My name is Klaus Mangelsdorf."

We talked for a further two hours, he missed his train home, and as he departed he handed me his business card and told me to contact him if I needed any help at all.

I rang Christine, who had bad news for me. "I spoke to our Ministry and explained about you, but it misfired on me," she said. "An official said you would need to have an up to date Coggins test to enter Germany. I said you had not had the test done to get into Germany, and that was it. They told me you must leave Germany immediately, so it seems as if you have to go back to Holland, Bill."

I went back to break the news to Max. He asked me what we ought to do, but I had no better idea than to suggest we sleep on it. While I was undressing, I found the card given me by Major Klaus Mangelsdorf. I told Max about meeting him in the café.

"Right, then let's ask him if he can get us out of this mess."

Next morning I was up at six, checking on every passenger alighting from the Bonn trains. Major Mangelsdorf arrived just after 8 o'clock and I went up to him and asked if he remembered me.

"Yes, Bill. I've been telling my wife about you."

"You did offer to help me, if I needed it," I reminded him. "Well, I need help badly now." I then told him what Christine had told me.

"Come with me. I'll see if I can sort it out for you," he said.

He was dressed in civilian clothing, and I had no idea what job he held, if any. Max and I accompanied him on a fifteen minute walk to a building guarded by men in uniform. Max recognised them as German Air Force personnel. Klaus proffered his identity card and said something in German, then we were led into a small office and asked to wait. When he returned, Klaus was wearing a very smart uniform and had two men with him. He introduced one as his colonel and said he had told him our story and they would do all in their power to help us.

While we sat in the office for the next hour, Klaus and others were on the telephone, trying to sort things out. One call was to the Ministry of Agriculture in Bonn to ask what was needed. Klaus managed to avoid answering any tricky questions concerning our entry to Germany, as we did not wish to cause trouble for the border officials and the vet at Vaals. In the end it boiled down to Action having this Coggins test, which entailed a vet taking a blood sample and having it analysed, a procedure that would take 16 days.

The idea of hanging about for such a long time did not appeal, but Klaus explained that once the test had been done, and if it proved clear, it was valid for three months and we could enter any E.E.C. country on the strength of the certificate. Our problem was getting across the Alps before the onset of winter. The weather had already turned very cold. While Max and I debated, Klaus interrupted to say we had two choices. We could have the test done and wait 16 days for the result, or we could go back to Holland. He suggested we wait and have the test done.

Klaus telephoned the vet and told us we could expect him in fifteen minutes. We hurried back to where we had tethered the horse, but there was no sign of him. My heart missed a beat.

"There he is, Dad," said Max, pointing towards a small paddock where Action had been put by a woman with horses of her own. The vet arrived and headed for Action, who was in an awful state. He had the runs and his behind was sticky, he was muddy after rolling on the ground, and his leg hairs were full of burdock heads. It was not a good start for a vet about to inspect the horse on his general condition.

Once Action was free to run, there was no way that vet could catch him, and it took the three of us twenty minutes to chase him round the field before he stopped running and stood still, enabling me to grab his head collar. I led him over to the vet, but the horse was unimpressed by the man. As soon as the vet had hold of him, Action decided to leg it, the poor vet hanging on grimly, as they made for a barbed wire fence. I imagined the outcome with horror.

This vet knew how to handle horses, however, and soon brought Action under control, took the blood sample and gave him a thorough inspection; not that his fitness was in doubt after that exhibition of running round the field. When the vet left, Klaus asked us to meet him in the café at 5 o'clock that evening. He said he was going to try and get the sixteen days cut down.

"I have tried explaining to various officials that you want to get across the Alps quickly, but they will have none of it. I said it was Germany's own fault for letting you into the country, as you had official permission to enter. If you set off now and give me a ring in sixteen days, I will send you the result of the Coggins blood test. We have a special Air Force post that could even reach you on Mars."

We spent that night at the station. It was bitterly cold with a hard frost, and this was the first time I had felt cold in bed.

The following morning, Klaus arrived with a present for me, a book about Germany. He had warned me earlier that there was a parcel for me, and I had a bottle of gin from Hasselt, which I gave him. We said our farewells and began to make our way down the Rhine towards its tributary, the Mosel, and Cochem – Zell, where we found a parking place by the river. Here, Action was maddened by flies until I used a fly repellent on him, a product donated by one of our sponsors, Cooper, Pitman, Moore. It would really be tested when we came to Greece and Bulgaria.

Professor Schlack had arranged for us to visit two schools for the handicapped, both small places but very well equipped.

Later in the day, we took Action into the centre of Cochem and parked in a prominent position. It is a tourist town, with a castle set on a hill. On the river were many luxury craft. At lunch time, we had a visit from handicapped people from a home. The nurse decided they could all have an ice cream, so they went into the café, collected their ices and brought them outside to the open air tables and chairs. Some of the handicapped were in wheelchairs.

Sometimes the disabled, especially those with with mental disorders, can be noisy and boisterous, but Max and I felt disgusted by the attitude taken by the café manager, who came and asked them to move. He was happy to take their money, but not to leave them in peace. The helpers coolly moved them, but I certainly did not feel cool about it. The café attracted many coach loads of tourists, many of whom were elderly folk, touring the Rhine and the Black Forest. It was up to me to do something about the owner's behaviour.

Action is big, and it can be intimidating to have him at close quarters. I, therefore, pulled horse and caravan as close to the doors of the café as possible, so that customers had to squeeze past him to gain entry. As the crowd gathered, I told them what had happened and what I thought of the man's greed. The owner never showed his face and had no customers at all for the next two hours. In conversation with handicapped people and their helpers I was often told that this is a common problem when they go in groups to cafés, bars and restaurants. Owners did not want them, as their wheelchairs take up too much space, some of them are messy eaters and they cause embarrassment to other customers. Some owners will set one night aside just for the disabled, which saves upsetting other clients, but this separation is not the answer.

When I rang Klaus Mangelsdorf that night, to tell him our next destination, he asked me to telephone American Forces Radio, as they wanted to interview me. This interview I gave them by telephone.

The last two days had been warmer, but the weather was not going to hold. We handed the money collected in Cochem to the handicapped school we had visited. One home passed us on to the next, so that we visited many of them during the next few weeks. One was at Neuwied, where we were met by two sisters, who took all our dirty washing and did it for us in the home's washing machine. Then they took us to see round the town. With Action and the caravan we pulled into a small car park, where we left Action between the white lines. In front of him was a B.M.W. and a few yards away stood a café. I left Action with his nose in his food, knowing he would never move while he had this.

After having coffee, I went back to get Action to take him for a walk round town, but this was not to happen. Something got into him when I took his food away. He sunk his teeth into the boot of the new B.M.W., leaving awful scratches. We hurried back to the home and hid Action among the trees.

This was the first home where we let numbers of children sit on his back. He was tied to a tree and quite calm when I lifted a handicapped child onto him. She loved it, and soon they all wanted a turn.

Following the Rhine through vine covered hills with castles perched on their summits, we had a peaceful time on good, usually flat roads. We spent our nights beside the river, watching barges go past, and sometimes kind people would bring us food and wine and, of course, something for Action. The next home we went to was at Bad Kreuznach and had the usual excellent facilities. There were small children there with various handicaps. Our visit had been prearranged by the previous home we had seen, and we arrived just as the children were about to have a meal.

The home was part of *Lebenshilfe*, (Life Aid) a vast organisation with beautiful homes in Germany and Austria, financed by public subscriptions and state help, some of which comes in the form of fines paid for motoring offences. The judiciary in each area can decide how large a proportion of fines is handed over to homes for the handicapped. Most of the staff is female, but some of the male staff are men who opted to do this work in lieu of National Service. Anyone who gives a good enough reason can do 24 months of social work instead, and their strength is always useful where heavy patients have to be moved about.

Apart from visiting homes, I was paying attention to help for the disabled in the rest of the world, things like hand rails, ramp access to buildings, special toilets, availability of public transport and ease of access to buildings such as banks and cinemas for those in wheelchairs. The Germans have made great efforts in this direction, but it is not all perfect.

After we tethered Action, we were taken to eat with the children, who had been put into small, manageable groups of eight or ten. They asked if Max and I objected to being separated, me in one corner and he in another. We said, through our interpreter, that we did not mind. He told us that a speciality dish of the region had been prepared specially for our benefit. I sat down at one of the low tables surrounded by tiny chairs, and it reminded me of being at school. The women servers brought each table a large saucepan containing long sausages in brine. With these went mashed potatoes and white cabbage; of all the vegetables I like, white cabbage is my favourite and I had not tasted any since leaving Tywyn.

The helper asked me if I liked the cabbage when she saw my heaped plate. I told her it was my favourite, but when I dug my fork in and took a mouthful my eagerness vanished. It tasted vile, bitter and strong; sweet, earthy and smelly, all in one. I tried not show my disgust by mixing it with the potato, but every mouthful was torture. Since they told me it was a special food, I had not the heart to leave any. At last I got to the end, only to be asked if I would care for more. I tried to say no thanks, but another dollop landed on my plate.

"Good, yes?" asked a German voice.

"Yes," I said, wondering how the hell I was going to eat it without being sick. I looked to see if there was any more potato to help it down, but that had all gone. Down it went, slowly, with the help of sausage.

When I met up with Max again, I whispered, "Did you like that cabbage?"

"No," he said. "I refused. I don't like *Sauerkraut*." He laughed when I told him of my own experience. "It serves you right for being such a pig."

I would eat it again, later, but a much milder version of the dish. I was told that they always make it strong in this area, and when I eventually discovered how they make it, I made up my mind never to touch it.

We followed the wine route through lovely villages with beautiful, half-timbered houses, some of which had courtyards in which wine was made. Recently, I had seen grapes being gathered by hand and machine. Outside some houses people were selling new wine in white plastic bottles, and sometimes there was a kiosk by a vineyard where new wine was on sale. Buyers would drive up and down sampling the product and buying what they wanted.

We thought we would visit one of these vineyards at Edesheim. We drove Action along the drive and up to a large house with outbuildings. I knocked at the door, having been given to understand that it was quite common practice at vineyards for the owner to let prospective customers try a sample of the wine.

A young man opened the door and said, "I have seen your caravan and read all about you in our newspaper. Welcome to Weingut Werner Anselmann." He sat us down at a table and produced different bottles for us to try. He sat down with us and began to tell us the history of the vineyard and to explain how it operated.

I asked how the wine was actually made, and he took me through the process.

"All the grapes are taken to one farm to be mashed, pressed and screened to clear the juice. It takes 1.3 kilos of grapes to make one litre of wine. The clear juice is put into fermentation vats and fermentation usually begins on its own. We add special yeast which, with oxygen, starts up the natural fermentation process. It remains in the vats for about a year before being bottled."

He showed us over the farm, and I was surprised to see that the fermentation vats were not wood, which I had supposed, but stainless steel. He told me they were easier to keep clean. He explained that the juice sold by the roadside was called new wine, but although dark in colour, it was sweet and had little alcohol content. After tasting some more wines, he presented us with half a dozen bottles as present to help us on our way.

A little later, we crossed the Rhine on a ferry boat. The Captain and his mate could hardly believe their eyes as we trundled aboard, the steel rims of the caravan wheels crunching and clacking across the steel deck. Action thought nothing of it. Our destination was a home for the handicapped at Karlsruhe, where the director, a Herr Schafer, was expecting us.

There was little room at the home for Action, and Herr Schäfer said we should put him in the garden and let him loose. I explained that he would make a mess of it, but he told me that it did not matter.

We explained to him our wish to see round the home, give people rides on Action and collect money for them. We mentioned that he would have to apply for permission from the council and the police. He had already arranged an interpreter for us, a young man doing his social service, and this young man quickly set about organising our entry to the city centre to make a collection and get some publicity.

We looked round the building, finding it well equipped and home to adult disabled with mental and physical problems. The accommodation was made up of small rooms, each containing two patients cared for by staff. Many of the disabled worked in a nearby factory.

They were in groups of eight, each group having its own lounge and kitchen. They would help the staff prepare meals and lay the tables. We spent a few days with them. This grouping into small units, patients having their own room or sharing with one other, seems to be common throughout Germany and evidently works well because the homes were purpose built. Everything has been carefully thought out. We met a similar system in Italy, but because the buildings were older, it was more difficult to operate.

For the rest of our first day, we spoke to those of the staff who spoke English. We seemed to have been followed about all day by a young woman in an electric wheelchair. We could see that she had cerebral palsy, her legs were useless and she had great difficulty in controlling her head movements, often throwing her head back in a spasm. She had short, blonde hair, a pale, thin face and, considering her handicap, she was pretty.

Our interpreter returned to say that the council were quite happy about our plans, but the police chief wanted to talk to me personally in the morning. Then he left Max and me alone with the girl in the wheelchair, who had kept her distance until now, saying not a word.

"Hallo, Bill. Hallo, Max. My name is Nicola Mullard," she said. At first I paid her little attention, as her words were slurred and jerky.

"Dad," said Max, "She speaks English." He was right, and for the next hour she spoke to us using all the English she knew. Had she not been so handicapped, her English would have been very good. Max was managing to have a good conversation with Nicola, but it was time for her to go to bed.

"I must go to work in the factory tomorrow. I will be home at four o'clock. I will see you then," she explained.

Next morning, our interpreter arrived to take us to the police H.Q. to get our permission to collect in the city. Max, the interpreter and I went into an office holding two men, one in uniform, the other in a brown leather jacket. The interpreter told us the man in the jacket was Chief of the Karlsruhe Police. They chatted away in German, and I sensed something was wrong by the gestures and nods and the way the Chief kept taking letters and papers from our file and flicking through them.

"He will not let you enter the city," said the interpreter. "He does not believe you are genuine. He cannot understand why two men from England would do this for German handicapped people. He thinks it is a confidence trick."

I could not believe my ears. Max just stood and grinned sneeringly.

"Ask him what proof he needs," I said. I spent the next twenty minutes going through my major sponsors, my main patrons, the names of homes we had visited.

"He still does not believe you. He will not give permission," came the reply.

At this, I flew into a temper. The man in uniform stirred behind his desk, shaking his head and giving me a look that said he believed us and could not understand what his chief was playing at.

"He is calling us liars," I said angrily. "Frauds. Would you please ask the Chief to give us his reasons for this and get him to tell us what we have to do to convince him."

The interpreter translated my words to the Chief.

"Dad," Max whispered, "This chief understands English. I am sure. I can tell by the way he looks at you when you speak."

There followed another outburst from me. "I will give you our passports, and if you let me I shall give you all my cash and travellers' cheques to hold until we leave Karlsruhe."

The answer was still no. Max slumped into a chair and put his hands over his face, crying and saying, "I can't believe it. This Chief has been a policeman too long; he trusts no – one."

I could not bear seeing Max so upset. "Come on, Max. Let's go."

Max rose and followed me to the door. I was shouting, I cannot remember what, as I opened it. A hand caught me by the shoulder and a voice said, "Calm down, Bill." It was the interpreter. "Wait while I try once more."

He spoke quietly to the Chief for a few minutes then turned to us and said, "You have your permission. You can park in a small square and collect in the morning. In the afternoon you can collect in another place. Then the uniformed man gave us documents and wished us good luck. The Chief had vanished. I asked our interpreter what he had said to make the man change his mind, but he would not tell me, saying it was not important.

Max was probably near the mark when he said later that the Chief had probably had a bad experience with people claiming to help others and this had left him suspicious of everyone making similar claims.

It had been arranged for us to visit next the large engineering factory where the disabled people worked. As we walked round, we saw many of our friends from the home doing monotonous work on pressing machines. Nicola told us later that the work was unpopular with some who found it hard to concentrate or whose disabilities made them tire quickly. The walls on each of the several floors had been painted in different colours to enable those who cannot read to find their work place.

We were introduced to a Mrs. Robinson. She spoke perfect English and was married to an American serviceman. She agreed to accompany us to the city on the following day.

By 9 o'clock, we were at the square designated by the Police Chief. The place was almost deserted, and Mrs. Robinson, who knew about our ordeal with the Chief, seemed unhappy with our position there. She told us the square where we had to go in the afternoon was just as quiet. A newspaper reporter arrived at 10.30, and his first reaction was to ask why we were not in a busier spot. We told him what our reasons were.

"I want to know why the Chief put you here," he said. "I am going to telephone him." When he came back he said the Police Chief told him only that he had no wish to turn his town into a Turkish bazaar. He promised to report this in next day's edition of the newspaper. Mrs. Robinson looked shocked at his eagerness to criticise the Chief of Police.

In the afternoon we moved to the other site, finding it very quiet. I was struck by the fact that it was close by the Police Station, and I wondered if the Chief was keeping an eye on us from his office window.

Back at the home, Max and I talked at length with Nicola, who said her ambition in life was to come to England for a time to improve her English. We noticed how often she was troubled by cramp in her legs and had to shift them into a more comfortable position. She had been in the home for four years and she was only 23 years of age.

"I can also speak French as well as German. I find German more difficult than English to speak because of my disability. Did you realise," she continued," No – one here knew that I speak English and French, not even the helpers. I yearn to speak and I am thrilled that you came."

What she said made a lasting impression on me. So many handicapped people have an apparent mental problem that really amounts to their inability to communicate with staff. She told me she had been offered a chance to get further education, which would have taken her out of the monotony of factory work, but she chose instead to stay among her friends, who needed her and were her kind. I went to bed that night thinking about her unselfishness and bravery.

Before we fell asleep, Max suggested making an early departure before the newspaper article appeared on the streets. He reminded me that our insurance and M.O.T. on the horsebox had run out and we were still waiting for the veterinary certificate for the horse. I agreed with his proposal.

Next morning, when Max told Nicola we were leaving, it came as a surprise to her. She was getting ready for work and she said nothing, just turned her wheelchair and raced down the corridor towards the main exit. When we got there, nearly all the handicapped and helpers, including Nicola, were waiting to say goodbye. I went to Nicola and bent down to kiss her. At this she began to cry, howling almost hysterically. Helpers rushed over to calm her and Max and I walked away, knowing this was best. Action stood at the road side with the caravan. Max rushed past me and jumped aboard. Tears were streaming down his face, which made me cry also.

As we drove off, I could hear Nicola shouting our names. When we got a few yards down the road I turned back and saw a lone figure in a wheelchair on the pavement. In it was Nicola, making a great effort to wave goodbye. I waved back, turned the corner, and she was gone. We both felt downcast and talked about whether we might have done the girl more harm than good by our visit. Our conclusion was summed up by Max, who said,

"She had a burning ambition to talk more English, in particular to English people. We gave her that opportunity."

I am sure she will always remember us, as we shall remember her.

We travelled to Stuttgart and a Lebenshilfe factory for the handicapped. The Director, Herr Adler, showed us round, and we saw yet another work – place with the best of equipment, but, unfortunately, profit orientated. Handicapped people would find the work there hard and boring. There was a small yard, big enough to take the caravan, but not Action as well. Opposite the factory stood a row of houses with narrow gardens running down to the pavement. The horse went into one of these, and there was not much grass for him there, mainly weeds. Well tended vegetable gardens were on either side.

I mentioned to Herr Adler that the spokes on the caravan wheels were coming loose, which, in turn, made the blocks into which they sit also become loose[1], and we should soon have to mend them. I went to check on Action, and found him tucking into the grass. When I went back to the factory, I saw the caravan jacked up and all four wheels removed. Max was supervising some of the factory hands, showing them what had to be done by way of repairs. Metal brackets were already being welded to each joint to stop the blocks moving from side to side.

Council and Police permits for us to enter the pedestrian precinct in Stuttgart next day were soon arranged, but first, that night, we had to visit a house containing fifteen handicapped adults cared for by helpers. Many of the handicapped had Downs Syndrome, others had nervous complaints. The idea behind the home was to give them a measure of independence, and let them participate in the housework. There were many such places in Germany and Austria. We shared their evening meal, then went with them and some of the staff to the annual Stuttgart Fair.

We went there and back on the bus with them, holding their hands to stop them getting lost in the crowds. Many had rides, hot dogs and other treats and they soon came to accept our presence in the group. Holding hands and linking arms with these handicapped people was a rewarding experience for me. It showed their trust in us and helped Max and me to overcome our inhibitions about being touched by anyone deformed or ugly. I was not ashamed of these feelings, knowing that most people have them. In everyday life we have no communication with such people, most of whom had always been kept out of sight of ordinary society. Now, at last, in many countries, they are being brought back to their rightful place amongst the rest of us.

Next morning, I sent Max to get Action and prepare the caravan. He came running back to say the horse had gone. I went to the garden and found the fence flattened in one place. I looked into the next garden and saw hoof prints among the vegetables that Action had not eaten or trampled, and the fence was also down. I walked round the house into the back and saw him standing by the door with a bucket of water. A man came out and began to speak German to me in a friendly tone of voice. He pointed to Action's leg which had a small patch of blood on it. It was a small scratch from a wire in the broken fence.

The only way to get him out of his present situation was to go back the way he came, over the damaged vegetable gardens. Max tried to make good the fences behind us.

Soon after we arrived at the precinct, the police arrived to check our documents. We had the Stuttgart Chief of Lebenshilfe with us. The spot we had been allocated could not have been better for our purpose. A dense crowd, ten deep, quickly gathered round us asking questions. A young woman approached us and said she was from Bangor, North Wales, and spoke

---

1 See diagram on P89

German. She offered to tell the crowd about us. She spent many hours doing this. With her was a German friend who kept us fed with things she brought from shops and cafés. Action was fed continuously, with apples, carrots and sweets, but he was also to get a special treat. A boy eating a Big Mac burger came up to stroke him. Action lunged forward to get some of the burger, taking the boy by surprise. He just caught the food with his nose, the boy laughed and offered it to him. Action took the whole thing into his mouth at one go, and with lettuce and salad dressing dribbling down, he continued to chew. Then, to our amazement, out dropped the meat. Action had eaten everything else but that.

When Action had had enough of standing about in shopping centres, he would nudge me with his head and gently nibble my arm, as if to say, "If we don't move, I shall bite you." Usually this indicated that he wanted a pee. He would never do one while he was between the shafts, on Tarmac or concrete. He always preferred a bit of soft ground, so that he would not splash his own legs. I had to walk him to the nearest grass or garden, and round some precincts these were scarce commodities. He was not nearly so fussy about emptying his bowels, however, and it was left to Max to clear up after him whenever we left a shopping centre.

I think Action has left his mark in all the capitals and major cities of fourteen countries; a record indeed, and one never to be broken.

Stuttgart is an industrial city surrounded by tree covered hills. Apart from the motor industry, it is a centre for wine making, and all the shops had tasteful displays of expensive goods.

South of Stuttgart lies Tübingen, an ancient town, with a university founded in the fifteenth century, making it one of the oldest universities in Europe. To reach our prearranged parking spot on a camp site, I had to drive Action through the longest tunnel we had yet encountered, and I was a bit apprehensive. The roar of traffic echoed back off the walls, yet Action walked on unperturbed. When we had just about come half way through, there was another roar, like wind blowing. This made Action begin to bolt. I had difficulty trying to control him, and traffic was speeding towards me. As we drew away from what I assume was a fume extractor, the noise faded and he became quiet again.

Using Action's water bucket to make a street collection for the handicapped.

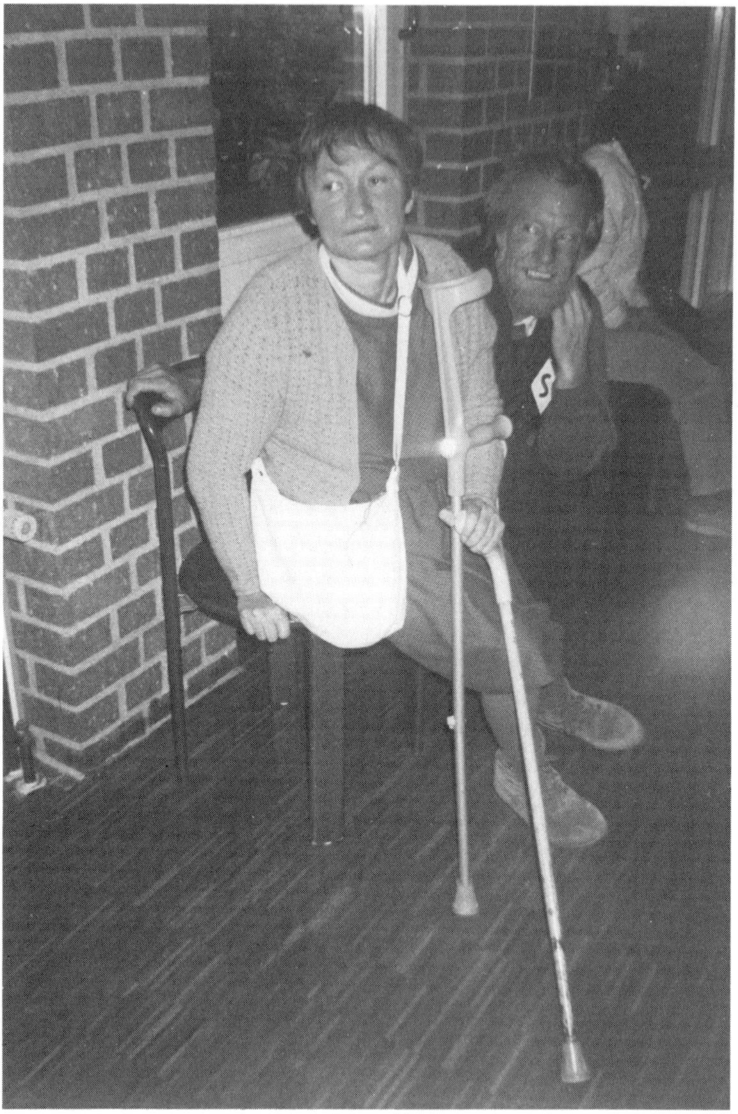

One of our German handicapped friends with the author.

Chapter Ten

Southern Germany and a Visit to the Blacksmith

In Tübingen, we met a group of handicapped people and their friends in a social centre, where they meet and enjoy evening activities. All the handicapped either lived in the home or in small units. That evening we went with some of them to a restaurant in the mountains where the owner set aside an occasional evening just for the disabled. One young man named Wenner, who had cerebral palsy, was something special to us. Although severely disabled and with impaired speech, he was determined to do what others did. After the meal, Max, Wenner and I went to a nightclub, and although he was in a wheelchair, Wenner's body was soon moving to the rhythm of disco music.

Then, without warning, he slid from his wheelchair, pulled himself up on the table and dragged himself, wobbling and shaking, towards the dance floor. I was riveted to my seat. Was this normal? He staggered forward, clutching at chairs for support, until he reached the dancers. When I looked for him, it was a relief to see that Max was with Wenner, holding him up to dance. He also enjoyed a pint. Unable to hold a glass, he drank beer, and plenty of it, through a straw.

We went to the main square in Tübingen to make a collection and publicise the home. Wenner, in his wheelchair, came with us. We were on a slight slope, and at one point Wenner let go of the brakes and started to roll forwards, pretending to be in trouble. Once, when Max was away, I wandered across the square, leaving Wenner alone with Action. When I looked back, the wheelchair was empty and someone was wobbling across the square shouting. Wenner's speech is non existent, so the noise he made sounded strange. He stopped wobbling and I could see he was in trouble, so I rushed over and grabbed him just as he was about to fall. I tried to get him back into his chair, but he wanted to go to the tobacconist. He crashed through the door, still shouting. The shop assistant could not understand what he wanted. He waved his arms about involuntarily, due to his complaint, trying to ask for a tin of tobacco. I understood and pointed to the one he required.

Wenner was happy to have got what he wanted, and Max and I loved the way he dealt with his disability. His brain was perfect, but most people, hearing him try to speak and seeing his actions, would suppose he was mentally backward. This is a common mistake to make.

During the afternoon, an Australian man spoke to us. He said he was touring Europe in a caravanette and, before he left home he had seen us on Australian television. I had not realised until this time that we were so famous.

October had come and we were still a long way from the Alps, which we had to get over before the snow fell. We decided to try and make quicker progress, which meant not visiting any more homes for a while. We did not keep to this, as we stopped at a couple of places in small towns. We reached Ravensburg, near Boden – See, by taking back roads through the hills and sleeping in lay – bys or car parks at night.

We had the address of the headquarters of a voluntary group for the handicapped. We found it in a narrow, one – way street that was awkward to park in, and there was nobody about. After we had waited for an hour, a young man who spoke English arrived, but he knew nothing about us coming, so he telephoned someone else. A group of young men and women arrived next. One of these was a tall boy with a ginger beard, *Lederhosen* (traditional, short leather trousers held up by braces) and bare feet. He spoke some English and said his name was Otto. Explaining that we could not stay where we were, he asked us to go with him to his family farm, some 12 kilometres away, in the village of Horgenzell. At the farm we were introduced to his two brothers, Bruni and Marus, two of his sisters, Margit and Sonje, and his parents, Herr and Frau Metzger. Later we met two more brothers, Ulrich and Sigbert, and another sister, Edith.

It was not long before we were sharing a meal of soup, various kinds of sausage and cheese with the family. Margit wanted to show us the district, and we soon discovered how religious she was, as she guided us to a place with many religious statues of Jesus, the disciples and Mary. Then we were taken to another shrine, in a cave.

We rose early next morning, as Margit and her mother had gone to church while the rest of the family were busy on the farm, the main income from which was derived from its apple orchards, but they also had store cattle and pigs in outbuildings. Otto took us into the cellar of the house and showed us a big wooden press and a barrel.

"Today," he said, "We make apple juice."

He emptied several boxes of apples into the barrel, placed some thick pieces of wood on the apples and screwed down the press. The juice passed through a gauze filter, emerging pure from a tap. The mother had prepared a huge and delicious lunch for us all on the verandah, and the family sat down to eat with us. Afterwards we went with Sonje and Edith to collect swedes from the fields to feed the cattle and pigs. Max and I were beginning to like this sort of lifestyle and the good company.

That evening, I decided to go for a drink at the local bar. When I invited Margit, she declined, saying she had never been in the bar and did not really drink. Through her, we asked her father if he would like to come. He agreed, although he had not been out for a long time. Margit came with us. Many beers later, when we returned home, Father was very merry and Margit quite merry!

many traffic lights; hence the impatience of German drivers. In the cities, traffic lights seem to occur every few yards, which makes drivers want to cross quickly and reach the next set before they change. When traffic queued up behind our slow moving caravan, drivers would often show their annoyance by pipping the horn or shaking a fist. I found that German bus drivers were the most impatient of all.

It was on the roads of Stuttgart that I learned something very special about Action. I was moving slowly towards the lights, which were on red, and I stopped just in front of them. The lights changed to green and Action moved off without me giving a command. I came to think that he could read the sequence of colours, and for a long time afterwards I would let him move off on his own.

It was in Bulgaria that I learned the secret. It was not the lights changing, but the cars on the opposite side of the crossing that gave him the clue. When they moved off towards him, he knew it was time to go.

There was something else I learned at road crossings with no traffic lights. When we stopped at the white line, Action would look left and then right. If there was nothing coming, he would go, but if a vehicle was close, he would wait for it to pass. He did not always get it right, but on most occasions he did.

We stopped to visit the Lebenshilfe home at Kempten, and found yet another immaculate, new establishment, divided into units containing six to eight handicapped people, all of whom helped with the daily running of their own part. The Director was Herr Lay and our organiser was called George. We were able to put the caravan on the home's car park and Action was tethered to a grassy bank adjacent to the building, during the two days we spent there.

On the first evening, I went to a bar for a drink while Max spent his time with the people at the home. I was sitting pondering the morrow, when we should begin our climb into the Alps, when a man arrived dressed in pyjamas and dressing gown. It was evident from their jeers and laughter that he was known to the people there.

A man turned to me and said, "I am pleased to meet you. I have read about you in the newspaper. That man there," He said, pointing to the man in pyjamas, "Has escaped from hospital to come here."

After I had made arrangements to meet the man on the next evening, I left.

Next morning, Max carried out maintenance on the horse box. The brakes had become soft and spongy, and when he removed one wheel to inspect them, he said they had been leaking brake fluid. This was a serious matter and it was a Saturday morning. Would it be possible to get spares for a Luton Bedford van in Kempten?

George took us round several motor spares shops and garages, but in vain. It was not the make of the van that was the trouble so much as the fact that it was of 1974 vintage. Having decided we were stuck, Max said he would put it all back together and we would have to chance it.

As the locals in the bar had shown interest in us, I took our folder of letters and articles to show them. We had our horse documents and vehicle papers in the same folder. The results of the Coggins test on Action, despatched by Klaus Mangelsdorf, had caught up with us in Kempten after being sent from home to home. My friend from the previous evening had brought some of his friends with him to the bar, and we all sat looking at the contents of the folder until about 10.30, when someone suggested that we go to another bar and meet more friends. After talking for a while longer, I said I had to get back as Max would be getting concerned about me, but I did not know my way back to the home. A young woman said she would drive me. In the dark, all I could see was that her car was a bright yellow Citroen 2CV. We were at the home within a few minutes, and I said good night and went to bed.

Next morning, I groomed Action and cleaned the caravan. At 10.30, George arrived with a letter of thanks for the money we had collected, and I went to put it with the others, but where was the book?

"Christ, Max, I've left it in the bar last night, but I can't remember which one."

"I told you not to take it, Dad. Now what do we do?"

George suggested that he take us to the bar. When we got there the owner was out, but there was a cleaner, and George explained our predicament. The cleaner telephoned the owner, but he said he had not seen a folder when he tidied up last night. George asked me where the second bar was, but I had no idea. He asked me to try and remember the names of the people I had been with, but all I could recall was the young woman bringing me home in her yellow 2CV.

George took us to the main police station in Kempten and related the story to a sergeant, but he did not get very far. The sergeant said he had read about us in the newspaper. He quickly understood how important the folder was to us, when George explained that it was better than a passport to get us into the countries we wanted to visit. George told him about the two bars and the young woman with the yellow Citroen. They chatted in German for some time.

"The sergeant has suggested he gets a newspaper reporter to come here and that I speak to the local radio station to ask for help," George said.

The reporter came and interviewed me while the sergeant was on the telephone to the radio station. The broadcasters agreed to make an appeal every hour, with particular mention of the girl with the yellow car and the long, blonde hair. I thanked the sergeant for all his help and returned to the home. Without the folder, we could not go forward or back, and I spent the rest of the day moping about, feeling guilty. Max said little to me after his initial outburst of anger. He could see how bad I felt. I lay in the caravan wondering what I was up to, putting us both through all this. I resolved to return home on the following day if the book was not returned by then. I felt as though I had had enough.

I began to think of Beth and how she felt. I had telephoned her often, but her attitude was that I was mad. I had been given the choice between keeping her or making the trip. I jumped from my bed, my mind made up. I would telephone her now and say we would be coming home. Unstoppable tears flowed from my eyes as I spoke to her.

"Don't give up," she told me. "You have overcome harder things than this to get so far. Being the lucky person you are, you will come up trumps."

I was still in tears when I said good bye. There was only one person I could talk to, and that was Max, but I did not want to let him see me in this state, so I headed straight for Action and put my arms round his neck. I stroked his ears and began to tell him that we were going to be on our way home tomorrow, when he gave a sudden jerk and I looked round to see a young, blonde woman emerging from a tan coloured 2CV. In her hand was our folder. When she gave it to me, I again burst into tears. I flung my arms round her, which took her by surprise, but she understood my feelings.

"I went to work this morning," she explained, "And I was on my home this evening, listening to the car radio. I realised whom they were trying to trace, looked round at my back seat and there was your book. I have come straight here."

Max had now joined us and we were both shedding tears as we thanked her, said good bye and watched her drive away in her yellow – no – in her tan coloured Citroen. Herr Lay telephoned the police station on our behalf, to thank everyone for their help.

Before we left the home, a man who had once been a patient and was now a caretaker and handyman whom Max had befriended, came up with blankets and clothes which he gave us. He said that if we had no use for them, we could give them to anyone in need whom we met along our way.

Chapter Eleven

Towards the Alps, Taking a Cold Wash

I could see the Alps towering in front of us as I climbed from the caravan. My sleep had been interrupted by Action pacing back and forth on his chain. I would find this a problem many times in stopping places where there was no tree or post on which to tether him. Action had been standing on hard ground and, as there was no dirt on him, I could see he had not been lying down in the night. On all mornings when we had camped on stony ground, I automatically looked for signs that Action had taken a good rest, and this night he had not. There was little green fodder or straw for him, and as well as lacking rest, he was hungry.

Max was stirring, and I said to him, "Max, I have decided something during the night. I think we ought to stop here most of the day and get organised to tackle that lot." I meant the mountains in front of us. "It will give Action a bit more rest, and we can groom him well and give him a good feed of Spillers. It won't do us any harm either, as we need to grease the caravan wheels and check all the bolts on the undercarriage."

"OK." replied Max. "I'll put on my old clothes."

I made a list of the jobs that needed doing, while Max collected firewood to make a cup of tea. A cup of tea in the morning was something I needed, and Max knew that without it I was not myself. There was no water in sight, nor any houses, but I felt that on this terrain of shallow hills and valleys there must be a stream or lake close by. Across a field I went and up a bank, to a cluster of trees, then down a track, until in front of me was a concrete bridge. Below the bridge ran a small river, its water as clear as crystal. As I lowered the container into the water, my mind wandered back to my home and life in Wales. The sea was uppermost in my thoughts. I could hear the lapping of waves on the sand and gulls calling high above me.

"What the hell am I doing here," I thought, "When I have everything at home? There is no need for all this." I felt sad for a moment, then I jerked the container from the water, in temper, and made my way back. Max was removing the wheels from the caravan for greasing.

"Dad!" Max shouted, "Look at this. Some of the spokes are loose in the outer rim." It was true enough. On the first wheel three spokes were worn; I could move them with my hand. On examining the rest of the wheels, all had one or several spokes well worn or loose.

"That was Antwerp, Dad." Max was right. The damage made by those cobblestones was now beginning to show.

"I know what we have to do, Max," I said. "We have to get the wheels submerged in water so that the wood will expand. The only place for that is where I've just been. They will have to stay in the river all day."

It was no easy task; the river was more than half a kilometre away and each wheel weighed around thirty kilos, but it was not only the weight; they were awkward to carry. So, one by one, we got them to the river. We submerged them, linked a rope through each one and tied the end to a tree, so that the current did not take them downstream. In all this time, Action was waiting to be fed and watered, so on our return I saw to his needs. The rest of the day was spent maintaining the caravan, cleaning the inside, and grooming Action, oiling his hooves, and clipping his tail and mane.

There were two other jobs to be done from time to time, and this day was as good as any. Because of the work Action had to do, it was important that his rectum was kept clean, as the tail harness runs across it, and it can become sore from his sweat and secretions. So I washed his backside with soap and water.

The other job was to clean the pouch in which his penis reposes, which entails putting your hand inside the pouch and removing any dead skin and bacteria. I was not too keen to do this, so Max got the job. When the pouch was clean, Max shoved some Vaseline inside so that any particles he had missed would come away as the Vaseline melted. Soaking the wheels in water, and cleaning Action's backside and pouch were among the many tips John Jackson had given me. All of them would be used as we were to get further into the journey.

In the late afternoon, I decided to do some washing. Both Max and I had run out of socks and pants, and we were down to our last clean shirts. But again, the closest water was the river, so off we set with two bin liners full of dirty clothes. It was not just the clothes that were dirty. After our cleaning up session, we needed a bath ourselves. The whole lot was accomplished by us getting into the water up to our knees and scrubbing away. The water was like ice, no doubt being fed from the Alps high above.

In the early evening we fetched the wheels from the river, put them on the caravan, and set off towards Reutte and the Austrian customs post. We were now climbing steadily, but progress, as I had anticipated, was slow. So far, we had been averaging about fifteen miles a day, but that would not be possible for the next week or so. I realised that the hard work would now fall on Action, who had coped well with hills before, but those ahead of us were a different matter.

That night, when we had parked on a scrap of land just north of Füssen, Max and I had a long chat about a couple of things. Firstly, we talked about our relationship. This trip had taken its toll of both of us and we were in low spirits. Visiting so many homes had been rewarding to all concerned, but it had put many pressures on us in trying to meet all our appointments. I told Max we would visit no more until we got to Innsbrück, about half way across Austria. All our efforts would, meanwhile, be devoted to getting us across the mountains.

Max listened eagerly, as I told him how I felt our relationship had strengthened, although, as we had become tired during the last week, we had also grown irritable with each other. We had to work together as a team now, as one mistake on the road ahead could end everything we had done so far. I spoke to him in this way to reassure him. It might have been unnecessary, as I had caught him discussing me with others and saying that his father is a good organiser, and if anyone can do it, he can.

Then we went on to talk about how we could tackle the road ahead, remembering all the advice we had been given by John Jackson. We would change our routine by having Max driving the horsebox as close behind the caravan as possible. It would make a long overtake for the heavy juggernauts trying to pass us on the steep, winding roads, but we had to play safe and not let ourselves be harried by impatient drivers into making mistakes. Action was the one that counted when the situation was dangerous.

We got out of Germany without difficulty and were met in Austria by looks of amazement from the immigration officers, who examined the caravan with great curiosity before officialdom prevailed and an officer came up to ask us where we were headed. I showed him the folder with our cuttings and the letter from the home in Kempten, as well as the address of the Lebenshilfe home in Innsbrück with the note of introduction from Herr Lay.

The man understood what we were telling him, but he kept trying to tell us something, of which I could only make out the word transit, which he used frequently.

"Dad, I think he's telling us we have to transport Action through Austria in the horse box. We are not allowed to let him walk. They have laws similar to Holland. They do not permit foreign horses to walk thorough unless they have special papers, which we don't have," Max explained.

I produced the certificate we had obtained for Germany and hoped I could bluff my way through, but the officer knew his stuff. He told us we must wait for the vet.

"Dad, our best bet is to put Action in the horse box and make it look as though we are going to transport him all the way in it. When he says transit, he means we must keep him in the box right through the country, from one side to the other, without letting him step outside it," Max said.

I went along with this idea, knowing the distance was far too long for Action to stay in the box all the time. We would get into the country first and sort things out later. The vet arrived, inspected Action and then took us into an office, where he started writing on sheets of bright green paper, while asking us questions about the horse. Then he came to the vehicle registration. After that, he handed us a green duplicate and told us it was a transit visa valid for no more than five days. Max and I both knew what he meant. We had to pay him 143 Schillings to cover his fee. I changed some Deutschmarks we had left over from Germany, and gave him his money.

We went into Austria in late afternoon. It was getting cold. We towed the caravan for a few miles, stopping on the verge to spend the night. I began to take Action out of the box and tether him to the caravan.

"Dad, we can't do this," Max protested.

"I know," I replied, "But he can't stay in the box all night. We'll just have to chance it."

We sat in the caravan, sharing a bottle of German wine and trying to decide how to get round the transit permit problem. Max tried to read it and understood that it gave us four to five days only. Our nervousness gave way to bravery by the time we had emptied the second bottle of wine.

"We'll walk him to Innsbrück and try to get help from the home when we get there," I said.

Still full of bravery from the previous night, I hitched Action to the caravan and, with Max in the horse box following close behind, we set off. There are two routes to Innsbrück, the northern route through the ski resort of Garmisch, or the southern, along Route 314 through Nassereith, and then continuing on Route 189. We were undecided at first which way to follow, but Garmisch meant crossing briefly back into Germany and then another entry into Austria. I was not having any of that, even though the other way was twisting and hilly and took us through the notorious Fern-Pass and numerous tunnels.

Making only a few miles progress each day, we came to the Fern-Pass. With its continuous hills and bends, it was the greatest challenge Action had yet faced. It is hard to describe the efforts he made, sometimes working himself to a standstill. When he could pull no more, Max would put the horse box close behind the caravan, taking the weight against it. Meanwhile, there was a build-up of traffic behind us, the roar almost deafening at times, until I could find a spot to pull into and let it all surge past. Some drivers were friendly, some tooted in annoyance, and I told Max to ignore the arrogant ones.

Occasionally, someone would stop and ask if we needed assistance. Others, travelling from Germany, would throw Deutschmark notes on the road and call out to us to buy food for the horse, or wishing us good luck. Many drivers would wave and shout encouragement.

When we were were nearly at the summit of the Fern-Pass, I began to hope there would be a parking place. Action's feet were slipping badly as he thrust his head down and pulled as hard as he could. Every strap and buckle was taut, his nostrils flared and his rib cage was going in and out as he sucked in air and exhaled. Sweat ran down his chest and his legs were soaking. Even the veins on his ears were exuding drops of moisture that ran down his bit and fell to the ground. I prayed that we should soon reach the top.

Then, as though the caravan had parted company from the horse, Action was almost sideways on and the caravan was rolling backwards, pulling him on his straps down the steep hill. The caravan was not in direct line with the horse, who was at an oblique angle to it. In that position, there was no chance of him holding it back. He tried, however, but his hind legs buckled and he sat down on his rump. I thought with horror that he must have injured himself. When he sat down, the caravan came to halt. I felt a slight bump as it came in contact with the horse box – not before time!

Action clambered clumsily to his feet, then stood looking as though nothing untoward had happened. I soon saw what had caused the trouble. One of the traces holding Action in the shafts had snapped, causing the caravan to go almost diagonally out of line with the horse. I wondered why Max had not acted quicker, since the whole purpose of him being behind us was to prevent just such an accident. When I went to ask him what he was thinking about, I found a man talking to him through the horsebox window while holding a crumpled bicycle in his hands.

"Sorry, Dad. The bicycle came untied from the caravan and fell on the bonnet. I pulled away and it got caught on the front. When I came forward to stop you rolling back, I crushed it."

I could hear a noise of horns sounding as the traffic built up behind us, then the man holding the damaged cycle began to direct the traffic round us as soon as there was a gap in the oncoming vehicles.

I made a temporary repair to the strap and we made our way slowly to the summit of the pass, where I changed the harness and checked every buckle and strap before continuing.

For mile after mile, we followed the twists and turns of the road, Max in the horsebox pushing the caravan to help Action uphill, or using a rope between the axle of the horsebox and the bumper of the caravan, to hold the weight when we were going downhill. There was already plenty of snow on some of the peaks, extending down the slopes.

Once or twice police in cars would stop us, but they would only ask questions out of curiosity. I felt nervous each time, for the M.O.T. and tax on the horsebox were out of date, and although I had made enquiries of the police in Kempten about how to put all this right, they could not help me, probably because these were problems not normally handled by them. Happily, we were not asked to produce the papers, so all was well.

Innsbrück is situated in a valley surrounded by lofty mountains, and I was glad when we caught sight of it in the distance, knowing that we could rest here and that we should find flat roads again. I had telephoned the home on the previous evening, to tell them we were coming. They were waiting to welcome us and took us at once to the kitchen for food. The Director was Mrs. Stefan Lami, and once we had explained what we wanted, she wasted no time in getting everything organised. I must say that she was the most elegant and understanding director we had met so far.

Action and the caravan were put into the home's small car park. The place was equal to any we had seen in Germany, with adult handicapped people living and working there. We had an interview with a newspaper reporter and with someone from Radio Innsbrück, after which, Mrs. Lami and another helper took us for a magnificent meal and we had drinks with some of the other helpers.

The following morning I telephoned Beth from Mrs. Lami's office. She was suffering from a bad chest complaint that always comes at this time of year. She was very miserable, and I put down the telephone and wondered what to do about her, as I was too far away to be of comfort. The only answer was to fly home. I went to the airport to make enquiries about a flight. It was going to be expensive and I should have to wait for seven days for a seat. Most flights into the town are charter flights and a few are domestic. I could take a flight to Munich and change there for London, but that was also expensive.

I decided to do it, and I rang Beth to tell her I was coming to see her. She told me not to be daft, that she would be alright.

"The time you spend travelling home and back will only add to the time you are away," she said, and so I did not go.

We had a pleasant time touring Innsbrück, capital of Tyrol, visiting first the old part with the famous Hofkirche and a monument to Emperor Maximilian 1, who often spent time here. There was the Fürstenburg castle to photograph and a wonderful botanical garden to explore, as well as the river Inn, from which the town derives its name. Many children came to help us hand round leaflets about the home for which we were collecting.

I told Mrs. Lami about our predicament with the five day transit visa for the horse, now out of date. We explained that this made us here illegally, but she gestured with her hand, telling us to carry on regardless.

We travelled south after leaving Innsbrück, to make the longest climb in Europe, ending at the Brenner Pass. To get there one can either use the motorway or take the old road which runs alongside it. Innsbrück stands 500 metres above sea – level, and the road climbs to Brenner, at 1,300 metres. The road is narrow and some stretches follow the railway line or the river. It dives in and out of tunnels and gives a spectacular view of the motorway soaring above on concrete stilts, spanning river and railway and minor roads. I was filled with admiration for the engineering skills it displayed.

With Action pulling the caravan along the old road, I compared our quiet old route with the autobahn above, packed with new cars and lorries. As before, Action pulled his guts out, apparently never tiring and only interested in food and water when we stopped. Mostly we stayed at night in lay – bys close to villages, cooking on our wood stove. Sticks were plentiful and we gathered them from the road sides by day and put them in sacks that hung on the caravan.

Brenner was not far away now, so we parked up early for the night and I thought it would a good opportunity to do some washing, although the atmosphere was damp and cold. I hung the wet things out to dry on a rope tied between a tree and the caravan, but this was too short to hold everything, so we put the rest wherever it could be hung on the outside of the caravan. Action was tied to the back, and I suggested to Max that we could lie down for an hour to rest, as we intended making an early start next morning.

Unfortunately, I overslept and so did Max. It was almost dark when I woke up, and Action had not been fed, as I never fed him after a hard pull, for it can make a horse seriously ill to eat or drink while sweating. I was thinking that he must be starving by now.

I climbed down from the caravan to waken Max. There was no sign of Action or the washing line. All the clothes were strewn around and had been trampled in the mud. Every single thing was filthy. I shouted to Max that Action had gone.

We knew by now to look for scuff marks on the road when the horse went missing, or for hoof prints on soft ground.

"He has to be somewhere on the road, Dad," Max said. Otherwise it is all fenced or walled by the rock on each side."

We had been asleep for about three hours, so even grazing the verges, he could have travelled three or four miles already.

"You head for Brenner, and I'll backtrack," I told Max.

We set off on foot. I looked carefully at the road for signs of his feet and scanned the grass verges for hoof prints, but after I had gone half a mile without seeing any traces, I turned and made my way back to the caravan. I ran all the way; it was dark and traffic streamed past me. I was remembering what the policeman had told me in England, that if someone is hurt on the road no–one reports it, but if a horse gets loose, it would only be a few minutes before it was known to the police. Surely, I reasoned, if Action was loose on the road, someone would stop and tell us. The caravan was clearly visible to all.

I wondered where the Austrian police were, although I dreaded them making an appearance because of the situation with our documents. I set off after Max, and saw him coming towards me, but without Action.

"He's gone this way, Dad. I followed his prints, then lost them. I decided not to go any further as I could see the customs post up ahead and thought it better not to get involved."

Max led me to where he last saw hoof prints, and we looked around. It was pitch black. I called out his name, "Action, Action," but there was no answering neigh. Wherever he was, he was tucking into some food. We walked as far as the customs post, keeping out of sight of the Austrian building. There was no way he could have got past that.

We went back to the caravan and searched the field as well as possible, but there was no sign of him. It had turned cold and drizzling rain was falling by this time.

"We have to contact the police now," I told Max.

"Not yet," he said. "I'll go looking again, on the bike."

He set off towards Brenner once more, while I sat in the caravan pondering what to do if he failed to find the horse. The police would never be able to find him in the dark, any more than we could.

Max returned at about three o'clock in the morning, soaked to the skin and cold, but without the horse.

"We'll wait until daylight and then I'll look. If we don't find him then, I'll go to the customs post and tell the police," Max said.

"You get some dry clothes on and then get some sleep," I replied.

I fell asleep, but I remember having a vivid dream. It recurred many times during the journey and I hated it. I am in some unknown town, walking by a red brick wall. The path is narrow, only about three feet wide, and on my right is a sheer drop into the unknown. I think it must be a salt mine. I can see water surrounded by banks of pure salt. Somchow, I am in the water and trying to reach the bank. I get to the bank and try to pull myself out, but the salt is like soft, shifting sand, and I cannot get a grip on it.

Suddenly, I came awake to the sound of a neigh. I did not know where I was. I saw through the window that it was already half light. When I sat up, the caravan moved slightly and I heard the neighing again and a scuffling sound. I looked out to see Action standing there, wet and miserable. He had come back to us.

I should never know where he had been nor how he came back. Maybe, it was luck, or maybe an instinct for his friends. No matter, I was so pleased to see him, even if it had stopped me drowning in my nightmare.

We hastened through the Austrian customs post and the 100 yards into Italy. I could see Italian customs men looking hard at us as we crossed no – mans – land. By the time we reached them, there were several men there, laughing, looking, standing back from Action. They walked round the caravan and horse box. One asked in English for our passports. He asked if we were English. I told him we were, placing our folder of credentials in his hand. The others gathered round him as he looked through the contents.

"Follow me," he said, and led us into an office. He spoke to a man sitting behind a desk. The man rose and went out, returning with a civilian who said we must see the veterinarian. He invited us into his office while he made a telephone call, speaking in Italian, but not asking us any questions.

"You have the Coggins test certificate?" he asked, still clutching the telephone in his hand.

I misunderstood, as his accent was unfamiliar, but Max got the question.

"The certificate for Action, Dad. The vet wants to know if we have one."

I said we had a certificate, so the civilian put the telephone down and told us to wait ten or fifteen minutes for the vet to come. True to his word, the vet was there in ten minutes. He looked at Action, glimpsed through our folder, and examined the Coggins test certificate, which he handed back saying we could go now.

I looked at Max and Max looked at me. We could hardly believe it. Out of courtesy, I asked how much I owed him.

"Nothing. It is my present to you," he said.

As I left the office, I thanked the civilian and his friends who had been holding our passports.

"Good luck," said the man at the desk. Up went the barrier and through we went. It had all taken less than one hour and had relieved me and Max of much anxiety.

As we moved off, the wind blew an almighty gust and down came the snow.

Chapter Twelve

Italy, The Country of Fantasy

I could not believe how quickly we were allowed in to Italy. Brenner is not the prettiest place we would visit, and its prime purpose is to check travellers travelling from north to south.

It was snowing as we passed a bar where, to our amazement, everyone came to the roadside and began cheering and shouting to us. This was in complete contrast to our reception in other countries. Then a woman in a shop window gave us a wave.

"It seems friendly enough," said Max, "But don't mention football, especially Liverpool. That disaster at the Belgian stadium was too recent."

I sent Max ahead to find our stopping place for the night, while I made the steady descent from Brenner, with Action trotting along in gently falling snow. This would be our pattern for the next few days until we reached Brixen (Bressanone). In this part of Southern Tyrol both German and Italian influence are felt in the names of both towns and people. We noticed many of the shops and businesses were owned by people with German sounding names.

We came to a steep, narrow section of road where Max was waiting with the horsebox, ready to tie a rope round its bumper and the axle of the caravan. This had become our way of taking the weight of the caravan when Action was descending a steep incline, for descent was far mare dangerous than ascent. On this occasion we were out of luck. The dodgy brakes on the horsebox were playing up, and although it was driveable, we considered it too risky to drive close behind the caravan, in case the brakes failed completely and Max rolled into the back of it.

"You'll never make this hill, Dad," Max said. "We have to stop and make an attempt to mend the brakes."

There was a lay-by ahead of us, so we pulled in there and Max jacked up the horsebox and began to do what he could to the brakes. Drivers of passing cars and lorries tooted their horns and waved, then an elderly man driving a pick-up truck pulled in behind us. He jabbered away in Italian while watching Max at work. By now he had the wheel off and was doing something to the brakes, but not being mechanically minded, I have no idea what. I tried to explain to the driver, who, to judge by the bits of hay and straw in the back of his vehicle, was obviously a local man, what we had been trying to do. I showed him the rope tied to the back axle and pointed to the bumper and the horse. He grasped the idea at once and, still talking, he got back in his pick – up and drove off down the hill. It was now late afternoon and growing colder by the minute.

The pick – up returned, this time with two men inside and a huge log hanging out of the back. They unloaded the log and carried it to the rear of the caravan. It must have weighed at least two hundredweights and one side was newly sawn into a flat surface. Bent spikes had been driven into each end, and the men produced two lengths of chain which they fixed onto the spikes and then to each side of the axle. I cottoned on to their idea, which was to drag the log behind the caravan to slow its rate of descent. I was sceptical about the theory behind this idea and tried to tell the men that I would rather wait for Max to finish. They were insistent that I set off down the hill, pointing at the dark sky as if to say there would be more snow that night and the sooner we were down the hill the better.

After all their efforts in preparing the log and bringing it to me, I felt obliged to try their method, as they had obviously done a lot of work. We descended after this fashion for about an hour and up to a point it was effective, apart from once or twice, when the log bounced up and let the caravan surge forward. Action always managed to control it. The two men walked all the way down this stretch of hill with me, helping and supporting, and it was almost dark when Max caught up with us. The brakes were now working, but not well.

The men left the log and chains with us and began to make their way back to the top. Max turned round and gave them a lift back to their pick – up truck. We kept that log with us all the way to Venice, as a safeguard against further brake failure.

Mrs. Lami of the Innsbrück home had arranged for us to visit a school in Brixen, where a woman called Maria was waiting for us at a prearranged spot on the edge of the town. Maria took us first to a small farm in a nearby village, where she had arranged for Action and the caravan to be accommodated. Max and I had had rooms booked for us in a small guest house in the same village. We saw Action settled into a barn before we were driven to a house some distance away. Here we met Hermi Assner, who had charge of six young handicapped girls with learning difficulties. There were two girl helpers at the home, Edith and Vali, who took turns to live in the home and teach the residents domestic science. During the day, Hermi taught them cookery at the school we were to visit. In this school they have many students and the handicapped girls form part of a team responsible for preparing all the food.

As yet, we had not learned any Italian. On our first evening, the girls at the house made us a meal and, together with Hermi and Edith, we ate a huge amount of spaghetti in sauce followed by sausages. This was the first of many meals of spaghetti and the last meal of sausages. During the meal, Hermi was trying to communicate with us, and I wanted to tell her something, too. She fetched a piece of paper and began to draw mountains, then a single tree with what seemed to be fruit hanging from it. Then she drew a pig, a knife, a fork and a plate. She wrote the next day's date underneath and a time: 8.30.

"I've got it," Max said. "She's trying to say she will take us into the mountains tomorrow night for a meal, and we shall eat fruit and pork there."

It was now my turn to draw. I had to explain that it was essential to submerge the caravan wheels in water to expand the wood and tighten them up. There was a river flowing through Brixen and I had seen a river in the village, near the farm where we had left Action. What I wanted to know was if there was anywhere we could leave the wheels in soak for a couple of days. I put the day's date followed by a picture of the caravan and horse, emphasising the wooden wheels. Then I drew a river with boats on it and an arrow leading from the wheels to the water. Hermi was quick to appreciate what I wanted.

She began to draw a river and, to my amazement, Action and the caravan standing in the water, its wheels covered. This was not quite what we wanted, and she could not understand that we needed to remove the wheels and submerge them. Alongside her picture of Action, I drew the pots, pans and clothing all floating off downstream, and she laughed loudly, having grasped the idea that we could not drive the whole thing into the river or it would float away. However, she knew of a suitable spot near the farm and she showed us on the following day.

Hermi used drawings to communicate with us whenever she wanted to explain something, and her uncanny knack of getting the message across never failed.

The owners of the home lived a few doors away, and one night we were taken to their house for a meal and a drink of home – made, strong, red wine, and I do mean STRONG. We also went to the mountains with Hermi, the two helpers and the girls, but the fruit on the tree was not actually fruit, rather it was roasted chestnuts, a traditional dish at this time of year in South Tyrol.

One afternoon, we met the director of Lebenshilfe for this area, and he presented us with a letter and the address of our next stopping place, in Trento.

These last few days had been enjoyable for Max, who had made some good friends, and when we left Brixen, he said he would return one day to renew his friendship with these kind people; and he was right, his return would be sooner rather than later. However, I was not in such good spirits myself as we made the climb uphill out of the town. My mind was filled with a multitude of matters which had to be resolved soon, but not while we were travelling.

Our vehicle had no valid tax disc, no insurance or M.O.T. certificate, and Max's one year passport had already run out when we reached Brixen. We had made tentative enquiries about obtaining a replacement passport for him and sorting out the vehicle documents while we were there, but as we were continually on the move the logistics of the exercise seemed insurmountable. In addition to these worries, my financial situation was causing concern. At home, I had certain assets: land and property against which I could borrow, but this could only be organised in Britain.

Lastly, my relationship with Beth was at a low ebb. She resented me being absent for so long, and whenever we spoke on the telephone the conversation would end unhappily for one or other of us. Often, it seemed as if what I was doing was done selfishly, although, deep down, I knew it was all worthwhile, but this was not enough to take away the feeling that I was doing it for my own glory. Something would have to be done about my relationship with Beth, and I could not do it here in the mountains.

It grew colder in the next few days as we followed the old Number 12 road down towards Bolzano, parking in lay–bys and car parks. We skirted round Bolzano and continued on the same road as far as Trento, driving along the valley floor with the motorway and river following us, on one side or the other, most of the way. To us the road seemed endless. Action went about his task, taking everything in his stride.

We stopped one night at a small town just north of Trento, and parked on a car park behind a factory. It was here that I made up my mind about going home to sort out some of my problems, and the event that made me take this decision occurred next morning. It was just growing light when I went to feed and groom Action. I bent down to lift his hoof, intending to clean his frog. His head was buried in his food bucket. As I lowered his hoof and it touched the ground, he adjusted his stance and accidentally landed one of his hooves on my toes. As I tried to ease my foot out from under his hoof, the pain was excruciating. All my strength seemed to drain from me when I tried to lift his leg. When that failed, I pushed his rump sideways and he moved at last. I had been wearing flimsy trainers that offered no protection.

In great pain, I hobbled back to the caravan and examined my foot. My toes were red and I had the imprint of the edge of his horseshoe on my instep. In a few seconds my whole foot had swollen up and the ache in my big toe was worst, although my whole foot was very painful. It was evident to Max and myself that the pain would not go away for several days, time in which I would not be of much use and most of the work would fall to my Max.

Hermi had given us the address of a handicapped home just outside Trento, and we visited it on the off–chance. We were made welcome by everybody there and after having a meal, the handicapped children came out to speak to Action. At this particular home, patients and staff make lovely, decorative articles which are sold in the shops. By now, the nail on my big toe was black and the pain had almost gone.

As we left the mountains behind, the valley widened and we saw on all sides apple trees laden with bright red apples. Action could hardly believe his eyes. When we reached Trento, our destination was the Piazza Duomo, the main square, which is surrounded by beautiful buildings, many decorated with historic frescos. Arrangements had been made by the previous home we had visited for us to contact a man called Peterlana Pompeo, who turned out to be a youngish man with a big, black moustache and with one of his legs disabled. He found us surrounded by a crowd of people asking questions which, with our lack of Italian, we were unable to answer. Peterlana, whose

English was fair, spoke to them and answered their questions. Many had already heard of us and our doings in Germany and northern Italy.

A newspaper reporter arrived, invited by Peterlana, and after we had spoken to him, we walked round the town with Action. The place had a Venetian air about its ornately decorated buildings. Then we were taken to a stables containing many horses, but before we were allowed to board Action there the director asked to see his documents. We produced the Coggins test certificate and this seemed to satisfy him.

Afterwards, Peterlana took us to the old part of the town, to a restaurant in a vaulted cellar under the ancient town walls. We sat at a table while waiters brought us dish after dish of exquisitely prepared food which we washed down with free flowing champagne. I tried to get our host to talk about what arrangements had been made for us for the following day, but he would only say,

"Tonight is for resting and enjoying yourselves. Eat well. We Italians do not discuss work when we are eating, particularly in my restaurant."

It was only then that I realised that he actually owned the place, and for the next three days, for breakfast, lunch and dinner, we would receive the same treatment: food, food, and more food.

The only information I gleaned from Peterlana on that first night was that he was president of a handicapped organisation in Trento and that on the next day we should be talking to the police authorities, and television and radio interviewers. He also instructed us to meet him in his restaurant at eight in the morning for breakfast. Peterlana began telephoning next morning, while we ate.

I took Action into the Piazza Duomo and presently two television crews turned up, one from a national TV company. This double TV appearance was to set off a chain reaction and lead to so many subsequent appearances that I lost count of them. After this, Peterlana took us to the police station, where Max was in dread of being asked to produce his passport. I had already expressed our fears to Peterlana, who told us not to worry. Within minutes of us arriving at the police station, he had made all the necessary arrangements for us to publicise his organisation, which was called HANDICAMP, and to make a collection for them. Peterlana was like a breath of fresh air to me. He was determined to make as much of our visit as possible, for us as well as for his organisation.

We set off to tour the town, accompanied by a police escort. Peterlana had told the police chief that we would be getting maximum media coverage, and he suggested that the police might also get some favourable publicity for themselves by taking care of us. That day we made the largest collection we had seen since leaving England. Peterlana arrived in the evening to count it. The following day he was tied up with a previous engagement, but he left a wad of money and a note for us. The note said he wanted us to have the money to use as we wished. If we felt we could not accept it, we could give it to those who need it most. There was also a letter thanking us for our visit.

On that same day, we made another collection in the main square, but, unfortunately, Peterlana had not returned by the next morning, and we wondered what to do with the money. In the letter he had left for us was the address of his friend who was to meet us in Rovereto, and we decided to keep the money and hand it to him when we got there.

Peterlana was a skilful operator, a generous person, a good organiser and kind. What he did for us in Trento was to set a pattern for the rest of Italy to follow.

We arrived at Rovereto, famous for its big bell, and Max asked some workmen laying curb stones if they could help us find the place we wanted. One immediately entered a nearby telephone kiosk, then he came back and asked us to wait a few minutes. Then a man arrived and introduced himself as Alex, an American living in Rovereto and dealing in antiques. He set about arranging for us to visit a workshop for the handicapped and finding us a police escort. After this we had to go to the Town Hall and meet the Mayor and town officials. First, however, Alex wanted to take us to a Halloween party.

Horse and caravan were parked in the grounds of a school, by arrangement with the police, and Action spent the evening contentedly, surrounded by children feeding him with tufts of grass. Alex lived in the old part of town, where the streets are very narrow, so I decided to take a walk round to try and plan a route for the next day.

We enjoyed the party, where there was plenty of food and drink, and we spent most of the time talking to people, trying to learn some Italian. At ten o'clock, I asked Alex if I could telephone Beth, as I had not spoken to her for some days. I offered to pay for the call, but Alex would not hear of it, saying I was his guest and could telephone anyone I wished.

Beth answered immediately, and I knew something was wrong. She still had a bad chest, which was a serious matter as she has only one lung. I told Max I was returning home after keeping our appointments tomorrow. I sat late into the night discussing it with Alex. I had no idea how to get from there to Tywyn, nor where Max, Action and the caravan could stay in my absence.

"Leave it to me," said Alex. "I'll sort something out tomorrow."

The police escort arrived at the school on the following morning and took us through the narrow streets to the town hall. We met the Mayor in his chamber and he presented us with a medal and a video tape containing the history of their famous bell. Then the police took us to the workshop for the handicapped. By the time we had finished it was already getting dark, so we tied an oil lamp on the rear off-side of the caravan and Max walked ahead, guiding me through the small back streets. I began to notice an odd smell – then it hit me. The caravan was on fire! I shouted to Max and we ran to the back of the caravan. Action's hay was alight. Max and I stood transfixed, caught by surprise and not knowing what to do.

A young man reacted quickly, caught hold of Action's water bucket, which hung on the outside, and threw water over the fire. If he had not been there and done what he did I shudder to think what the outcome might have been. The hay was still smouldering when Max cut the rope holding it and let it fall to the ground, where it flared up again. The road was covered in paraffin from the lamp, which had been jolted about by the movement of the caravan. The filler cap had become dislodged and the glass was broken. Other people came and helped us extinguish the flames.

Next morning Alex arrived to tell us that he had arranged with the police for our caravan to be lodged at the abattoir while I was away, but he had not found anywhere to put the horse. Max suggested taking him in the horsebox back to Brixen, where he had friends. I agreed. By the time I was ready to leave it was late afternoon. Someone had suggested that I go to the Dogama, a long distance lorry park, where international carriers have to stop and register their loads, as I might be able to hitch myself a lift home.

We made our way there with the caravan and Action, for I wanted to prove my credentials to the customs men and ask them to try and arrange a lift as far as Holland for me. When we got there we found the place strewn with heavy goods vehicles from all over Europe, including Great Britain. I drove Action right in front of the main customs building and officials emerged in droves and started to make a fuss of Action and to talk to us. One spoke good English, and I explained my desire to get a lift as far as Vlissingen, in Holland.

The customs officer came back with a driver and indicated to me to get into his lorry. I was on my way, leaving Max to his own devices. The lorry driver dropped me off in Stuttgart where I caught a train to Aachen. For some reason, when I arrived in the town, I made my way to the Vinzenz-Heim we had visited earlier. The Director, Herr Kehrings, was surprised to see me back there again, but I explained my need to get to Vlissingen. I was astonished when he at once volunteered to drive me there in his own car. Thus it was that I found myself at the ferry port in the early hours of the morning.

I knew that Paul Cramer would be arriving for work at 8 o'clock. He was also surprised to find me waiting, but he was able to arrange a ticket to Sheerness for me and I was off on the next boat. Then I went by train to London, on from there to Birmingham and thence to Tywyn. Beth was surprised to see me, but I am not sure if she was as pleased to see me as I was to see her. Perhaps she just could not show her feelings. Luckily, the chest complaint was clearing up, and I used the time to try and sort out some of the problems Max and I had.

First on the list was Max's passport. I rang the passport office, but they said that as he was away from the country, we should have to get the replacement issued in Milan. They asked me to send the forms and photographs to them and they promised to forward them to Milan. I had the photographs but not an application form signed by Max. I obtained a form from the post office and sent it to Max care of Hermi's home in Brixen. I asked him to return it to me immediately. When it came back I sent it off to the passport office in Liverpool and asked them to send the new passport to the British Embassy in Venice for us to collect.

Next, I had to tax and insure the van. Insurance was just a renewal and gave no problem, but I could not re-tax it without a valid MOT certificate, which could not be obtained while the vehicle was abroad. My solution was to do nothing. I travelled for a year, through twelve countries, without tax or MOT test certificate.

My other task was to replenish our money supply. Mr. Phillips, our newly appointed bank manager, was helpful and lent us £3,000 on the security of a piece of land I owned. He was enthusiastic for our cause, as he was also involved with helping handicapped people in Birmingham. I knew the £3,000 would not be enough to last to the end of our journey, but it would get us quite a way, perhaps even as far as the Russian borders. I would remain optimistic about getting the rest of the money we needed in one way or another. So far, including the expense of planning the trip and buying equipment, it had cost me about £22,000, and I sometimes wondered if it had all been worth so much.

My relationship with Beth had not improved during my visit. It was my own fault, for I had continued, as before, to be obsessed with my journey. When I was ready to depart for Brixen, she told me,

"I don't want you to come back to me when you return."

Chapter Thirteen

Continuing Where I left Off

I flew from London to Munich and continued by train to Brixen. Once there, I telephoned Edith to ask if she knew where Max was staying, and she said he was at the flat she shared with a friend. When I met him, Max said things had not gone well after I left.

"I managed to get to Brixen," he said, "And saw Hermi to ask if she could ask Maria, who had arranged the stabling and parking for us before, if she could help me find somewhere to keep Action for a few days. I think she got the idea that I wanted to spend the winter here, because, after three days, she said I must leave the area or she would call the police. I was scared and upset, what with not having a valid passport and Maria turning on me like this.

"Luckily, Hermi and Edith came to the rescue and arranged for Action to stay on a farm in another village. Edith said I could stay in this flat with them, but I was thinking about things and wondering if there was any point in waiting for you to come back. I couldn't understand why Maria wouldn't believe me. I'm glad you're back, Dad."

We thanked Hermi and Edith for their kindness and help, and next day Hermi gave us a load of good clothes, coats, trousers and such, saying that she had just lost her husband and had not yet had time to sort through his things. She felt it was right to give them all to us to hand out to those in need whom we met on our way.

With Action in the horsebox, we drove back to Rovereto to collect the caravan from the police compound. With Action again between the shafts, we set of for the Dogama lorry park to spend the night; it was already late in the afternoon. I was glad to be back with Max and Action and our caravan.

That night was bitterly cold and freezing hard. I was so cold in bed that I enjoyed little sleep and was up early next morning. Before we left, the customs officers brought us food, T-shirts and stickers with the name of the Dogama lorry park. They took many photographs of us.

The journey to Verona was pleasant. The rest had done Action good and he was feeling full of energy and glad to be on reasonably straight, level roads at last. I had bought myself a video camera while I was in England. Although each of the countries we had been through were different and interesting in their way, I felt that the parts most worth filming would come when we reached the Eastern Block. Maxell Tapes had given me 12 cassettes, which allowed me about five hours filming. Max had a good camera as well as our small Kodak, but I had not managed to get sponsored for many films, so we had limited our photography until now, in order to save on expenses. It is too easy to take pictures of everything on a trip such as this.

We arrived at the Emmaus Organisation's place just outside Verona and were met by Don Silvano, a young priest who escorted us to a beautiful monastery in a village at the foot of the hills encircling Verona. This was to be our stopping place for a couple of days. Don Silvano was a member of the monastic community there, one of ten priests dedicated to helping people with stress and other worries, social or religious. In some respects this monastery is like an hotel. One can come and go, stay for weeks or just weekends, help with the gardening or tending the vines, and pray with the brothers. People can relax here, sort out their problems in peace.

Action was tethered on the lawn and we were told that we could make as much noise as we wished outside and in some parts of the building, but there were places where talking was not allowed. We had to pass through such an area to get from our room to the refectory at 7.30, when dinner was served. I whispered to Max that I had doubts about how long I could keep up the silence. It was quite different when we entered the refectory and confronted the brothers, all soberly clad in their black habits, but laughing and chattering noisily. There was a television set in one corner, showing a football match, and many brothers were gathered round it, slumped in chairs, clapping and cheering.

A large table ran the length of the room, its surface covered with dishes filled with food. Every few feet down its length stood a large bottle of wine. We sat with the brothers to have our meal and were pleased to find some of them able to talk a little English. Every meal had here would be the same, plentiful and delicious. The wine was made on the premises and the vegetables grew in the monastery garden. What a contrast there was between the jovial atmosphere of refectory and some other parts of the building.

Don Silvano had made arrangements for us to visit Verona and meet the Mayor, *(il Sindaco)*. We trotted into the main square, a vast place with the municipal building on one side and a Roman amphitheatre, believed to be the second largest in Italy, on the other. The River Adige runs through the town and on its bank stands the Castellvecchio. The most famous item of interest is the balcony of Romeo and Juliet fame. Many people like me might have expected something grand, but it is small and plain like thousands of other balconies in Italy.

We soon drew a crowd of onlookers bursting with curiosity about us. We left Action outside while we were taken to meet the Mayor, Signor Pizzoli, in his chamber. With us were some handicapped people from a small private house in Verona known as *Gruppo Tutti Per Uno* (The All For One Group) as well as journalists and photographers. The Mayor presented us with a large bronze plaque of Romeo and Juliet, and his parting words to us, as we said our farewells were,

"No matter where you are on your journey, if you have difficulties and need help, contact me and Verona will help you."

During that day we collected money for the Gruppo Tutti per Uno, who needed it to support the handicapped children in their care.

The Emmaus Organisation is where Don Silvano works. It was founded by the French and cares for alcoholics, drug addicts, ex prisoners, social misfits and people with learning difficulties. The idea is that these people collect other people's discarded junk, electrical goods, clothing, books and anything else they can re-sell or recycle. The goods are sorted and the undamaged items are sold from a large warehouse. The rest is separated into rags, metals and other recyclable materials and sold for reprocessing. The income derived from this makes the community self-sufficient and enables them to give generously to other organisations. Sometimes they have quite valuable items donated to them, antiques for example. It takes a long time to walk round their warehouse, which is opened to the public every Wednesday and Saturday, and I found it extremely interesting to think that this was an idea of benefit to everyone. It provided employment for people and helped the environment by saving natural resources, while raising money to help others.

We had told Don Silvano that we could do with some help in repairing the horsebox and caravan. It was no sooner said than done, and a team of talented men was set to the task, with Max supervising. We were soon ready to go to Venice.

One night, we stopped in a village *cul-de-sac* and as all was quiet, we decided to go for a walk. We came to a door behind which was the noise of singing. We went inside and found ourselves in a small room full of men drinking wine. Bottles littered tables and shelves, and a man asked us in Italian what we wanted. I raised my hand to my mouth as if drinking. He said something else in Italian and Max said he was telling us that this was a private club. He pointed to photographs and emblems covering the walls. One man recognised us, however, and came over. I heard him say my name as he spoke with the others. Soon we found ourselves eating and drinking with them. They were veterans from the Italian Alpini, soldiers who fought to hold back the German advance through the Alps in the second World War.

Before we left, they gave us a letter of introduction and the address of another group based just outside Venice. When we reached them, they were expecting us, having been warned by telephone of our impending arrival. I was overwhelmed by the reception they gave us, with food and drink in abundance and songs of welcome. It was a moving night during which Max and I were treated like lords. It ended with them giving us a lovely letter wishing us good luck on our way. Sadly, like many other valuable papers, this was later stolen from us.

I was now preoccupied with thoughts of the winter ahead, with snow and ice. John Jackson had advised me to try and avoid as much of it as possible, since icy roads would be dangerous to Action, an animal used to a more temperate climate and unlikely to be happy in mountains where there were howling winds, driving snowstorms and no shelter. Beyond Venice lay

Yugoslavia and Romania. Yugoslavia held some of the largest mountains in Europe, where the wind blew and the temperature seldom went above zero, and we had to cross these to reach Romania. It was mid – December already, and even in Venice the nights were frosty. I had once hoped that we should already have crossed the Yugoslavian mountains by this time of the year, but the many visits we had made to homes for the handicapped had put us six weeks behind schedule. I had been told that I should need a green card for the vehicle and a current Coggins test certificate to enter Yugoslavia. Our Coggins test certificate was just about to expire, as it was only valid for three months from the date it was issued. There were other regulations to be observed concerning taking Action into that country, but before thinking too much about all those we had to sort out Max's passport, of which there had as yet been no sign.

Max and I talked it over and concluded that we should have to spend the next ten weeks of winter where we were, but where exactly was the real question.

I had carried to Venice one telephone number, that of a Scout called Sylvia Brentagarne, and I decided to ask her for guidance and help. She gave me directions to get to the main car park, where she arranged to meet up with us. The car park was on the right as we left the causeway joining Venice to the mainland. Trotting along, with the sea on both sides of us and traffic roaring past in both directions, horns hooting, hands waving, it felt good to be beside the sea again.

Max went ahead and parked the horsebox on the car park. He came back to me; the time was still only about ten o'clock in the morning, so we decided to go straight on into Venice. By following the main road, we found ourselves in a large square filled with buses and cars, coming and going on the same road as us, which ended in the square. Beyond this point one had to use a boat to get around.

I pulled up in the busy part of the square, beside the ferry boat entrance. Within seconds we were surrounded by people, drawn to us as if by a magnet. We plastered the canvas cover on the caravan with letters and newspaper articles, which the the ferry passengers crowded round to read. The ferries came and went every two or three minutes. Cars started to pull up round us, causing chaos. Action stood calmly as people fed him with sweets, cakes and apples and grapes. A building stood a few yards away, with police continually entering and leaving, and Max began to grow concerned as the crowds and the traffic jam grew. He was convinced that one officer had been keeping his eye on us from a vantage point by the wall. The man started to stroll slowly over to the caravan. He said nothing, but began to read the letters and articles on the canvas cover.

I also began to get nervous, tried to convince myself that we were not actually doing anything wrong, but knowing all the while that some of our documents were not in order, the most worrying among them being Max's passport. The policeman seemed to read for ever. When, at last, he moved towards me his face was stern, although he was holding out his right hand as if he wanted me to shake it. I found myself holding a 10,000 lire note.

"No," I exclaimed quickly. "I cannot take this. I have no permission to collect."

The crowd stood watching, waiting for something else to happen. The policeman understood English and insisted that I take his money, but I was having none of it, convinced it was some sort of trick. While I argued, a large, black car pulled up beside us and two high ranking police officers covered in gold braid and badges got out. My heart sank. These were the big guns come to sort us out. One of these men walked over.

"Can we help?" he asked.

I cannot recall what I replied, but within a very short time Max was inside the police station with the scrap of paper that Don Silvano had given us bearing Sylvia Brentagarne's name and telephone number. I remained with Action, talking to people with the assistance of an English speaking man from the crowd, who explained about us and what we had been doing. I looked inside the caravan and found on the floor the crumpled 10,000 lire note left by the first policeman. I lifted it up with a shrug, as if to say – what do I do with this? I do not know if the crowd misunderstood me, or what, but bank notes began to come from all directions, not into my hand, but thrown inside the caravan.

Max came back to say that the police had contacted Sylvia at work and arranged for her to meet us at 7 o'clock at the place where the horsebox was parked. She told the Police Chief that she knew nothing about us, and when he explained that we needed somewhere to keep the horse and caravan for a few days, she suggested we contact a Toni Mara, the Chief Scout for the Venice area. She thought he might have some ideas. The police had also telephoned the home of this man and left a message with his wife.

When Sylvia arrived at the car park, at 7 o'clock, she told us in good English that she had spoken to Toni Mara, who had given her an address in Mearne, a small town near Mestre, about 20 kilometres distant. It was now too late to travel so far, so we arranged to go on the following day, which left us with the problem of where to park tonight, as we could not stay on the car park. It was suggested that we ask the customs officials, so we drove up and discovered that they spoke English. They said it would be all right for us to leave a tired Action standing, tied to the caravan, between parked juggernauts and close to his hay bag.

Everything went wrong next morning. The horsebox engine would not start. Action had come loose and wandered off in search of grass. It had rained during the night and my bed was wet through, as were our clothes, which were stored underneath it. It was midday by the time we arrived at 113, via Frassimelli, in Mearne, the home of Luigino and Anna Nalessa and their two daughters, Frederica, who spoke English, and Sabrina. Luigino and his wife were scout leaders and the two daughters were scouts. Luigino and Frederica showed us their scout hut, a new wooden building close by. It stood in a small paddock with three sides fenced, the fourth flanked by a large ditch.

I unhitched Action and let him run free. He charged across the field, bucking and prancing with legs flying, enjoying his freedom. Then he stopped and started to sniff the ground, always a sign that a horse wants to have a roll. When he found a spot to suit, he lowered himself gently onto his side, then began to roll, grunting and snorting with the exertion. When he got back on his feet, he shook himself vigorously to shake off any rubbish he had gathered and then did his business to mark out the territory to himself. It is something all horses will do when arriving on new territory, as if they are saying – this is now my field.

Luigino and Frederica fetched camp beds and bedding for us, as we were to sleep in the scout hut. They also had hot food and a bottle of home-made wine. As we sat together, eating the food and telling our story, I kept thinking that we must soon find a stopping place for the winter.

Luigino arranged for Toni Mara to meet us on the following day, promising that Toni would arrange everything. When he arrived, Toni had with him Alessio, a young man who spoke good English. Toni was slim and dark haired, his complexion pale. He told us he was a chemist. Alessio was slim and had curly hair and glasses. He told us he was studying to be a lawyer and he also wrote articles for the local newspaper. We talked together and showed them our file of letters before going to Toni's flat, where Alessio telephoned various homes and institutions around Venice, and spoke to newspaper offices, television companies, to other scout groups in the district, and to police and council officials. He reminded me of our friend Peterlana, in Trento, in the way he grasped the essentials of our needs so quickly.

After about two hours on the telephone, he told us we were to stay in the hut as long as we were there, and the scouts would take care of us.

"I shall write out an itinerary of your appointments and make a list of what you will need, but first you must telephone home to your families," he said.

While I was telephoning, Toni's wife arrived with a small, pretty woman called Mariella, who was also a scout leader. We had more spaghetti in tomato sauce, which many Italians eat before their main meal of the day, which is eaten in the evening. We then had to meet the scouts of Mearne and talk to them of our exploits. I was surprised to find boys and girls in the same troupes and to see that they ranged in age from fifteen to thirty. It is apparently Italian policy to have mixed troupes.

Next day we were given our itinerary and list of appointments. It was going to be a busy week, with talks to scout troupes, interviews with the news media and visits to homes for the handicapped. We had also been granted permission to collect money in Mestre's main shopping centre and in Venice itself.

"I am also talking to our Minister for Health to get permission for you to take your horse and caravan on a special ferry to San Marco, in Venice," Toni said.

Our next few days were hectic, with visits to many homes, institutes and workshops for the disabled, including the Berni Institute. This was rather special for us, for it was here that Sylvia worked. It was a school run by A.N.F.F.A.S., an association for adults, children and families with disabilities. It is a vast organisation with places throughout Italy, many of which we were to visit during our stay in the country.

When we arrived at the Berni Institute, a crowd of several hundred youths awaited us. They all appeared physically fit, but many showed signs of being somewhat mentally retarded. They stood quietly in the playground while Alessio fetched a teacher to come and tell them about us. Suddenly, they all vanished and we were left with the teacher. A small, pretty woman wearing glasses was introduced to us as the Minister of Health. She was followed by Mrs. Pasqualetto, President of the Mestre, Venice, branch of A.N.F.F.A.S.

Alessio suggested that we take Action out of the shafts and tie him up.

"They would like you to come into the main hall and talk."

We found ourselves in a large hall with a table across the far end, on which were 2 microphones. The crowded seats were divided by a gangway down the centre. The audience consisted mainly of teenagers with a sprinkling of adults. I was directed to the centre seat at the table. On one side of me sat Alessio and Mrs. Pasqualetto, on the other side of Alessio sat Max and the Minister. Mrs. Pasqualetto introduced us and thanked us for coming to visit the homes for the handicapped. Then she handed over to the Minister of Health, who said more of the same. She also told us she was trying to get Action and the caravan in to San Marco. I was so choked with emotion at the massive kindness of all these people that I was not prepared when Alessio asked me to speak.

I spoke of our journey, the homes and places we had visited and the relationship between the handicapped and the ordinary public, and the facilities provided to help the disabled get out into the community. Then it was time to thank everyone who had been so kind and helpful. The words stopped as tears began to flow, and I turned to Alessio for help. He said a few words in Italian, then the audience began chanting. I have no idea what their words meant, but they were for Max and me.

A woman who had been seated in the front row stood up and began to talk in Italian. A handicapped boy had the seat beside her.

"What can we do to help others?" she asked, clasping the boy's hand.

"Many handicapped people only want what you and I take for granted; they want respect and independence. They don't want to be regarded as abnormal, as if they are not part of the human race," I said, using Alessio to translate my words.

Once again, I was overcome with emotion. I rose to my feet and the cheers from that audience of boys and parents was almost deafening.

I knew this emotional outburst signified that my nerves were frayed. It was time for both Max and me to take a rest, and here, amongst the wonderful people of Venice, was the very place for us.

When we got back in the evenings, two young girls, Valentina and Tamara, came to the scout hut. They were students, and Valentina would spend hours talking to Max. She could speak English, but was trying to teach him Italian, and he was soon able to understand a lot of what was said to him, although he had not reached the stage of being able to make conversation.

We followed the timetable set for us, and when Alessio was not available to act as translator he would arrange for a stand – in. Luigino and Anna saw to our every need, feeding us, doing our laundry and supplying us with logs for the fire and plenty of hot water. Luigino knew by now that I had decided to spend the winter in the area and he offered to let us stay on in the hut. However, I did not feel I could stay cooped up in the hut all the time, not because it was uncomfortable at all, but because I did not want to abuse his hospitality. I agreed to spend a few days there at Christmas.

We were disappointed in our hopes of getting to San Marco, when there was a change in the Government and our lady Minister of Health was replaced. There was nothing to be done now. With Christmas approaching, there was no time to make other arrangements, but Toni told us he had arranged for us to visit Don Orione, a Catholic institute for adult handicapped just outside Mestre. Don Orione was run by priests. The top man there was Don Severeno. The institute had a large estate where flowers and vegetables were grown for sale to the public. It also had stables with horses, some at livery, others for use by the handicapped, who cared for all the animals with help from the priests. There was a small school for handicapped youngsters in the gardens. We paid it a visit and gave the students rides round the garden in our caravan. We went afterwards to put Action into one of the stables and he began coughing. This was something I was always on the look out for. I gave him a few hours to settle, hoping the coughing would stop, but instead it grew worse until he was coughing every few minutes.

I told Don Severeno and he sent for the veterinarian, who said he thought it was due to dusty hay. I agreed that this was a strong possibility, as he had eaten dusty hay a few days previously. The vet injected Action with an antibiotic and gave me two more shots and a hypodermic syringe, saying I should inject him again later. He must have thought I had done it before, but when I explained that I had no idea how, he gave me a demonstration and told me to inject him again that night and on the following day.

Action needed new shoes, and again Don Severeno arranged things for me. While I stood watching the farrier at work, a tall, slim, ruddy featured, unshaven man arrived and gave his name as Franco Guerra. He invited us to go to his home for a drink that evening. When he added that he had a horse himself, we took up the invitation.

Franco had a wife, Elizabeth, and a son, Guido, and they lived on a smallholding somewhat off the beaten track. As we ate and drank together, we mentioned our desire to remain in this region for a while. Their generous response came at once.

"I have room for your horse in the stable and for your horsebox and caravan in the garden."

I could see that the idea of staying here appealed to Max, so I promised we would come back after Christmas.

As the evening wore on and I drank more, the idea occurred to me that I might be better employed back home, sorting out entry visas for Bulgaria and Romania and chasing Max's passport. Then a better idea came to me. I telephoned Beth and suggested she might come to Venice for two weeks for a holiday. I could then return with her and we could resume our journey on March the first, a date I had set myself anyway. When I told her my plans, Beth agreed to come to Venice, arriving on January 11th.

I spoke to Toni about Beth coming and he asked where we should stay. I suggested a hotel, saying I would make a booking tomorrow.

"It is too expensive to stay in Venice," he said. "Leave it with me." Later that day he told me that the village of Scorze wanted to help us. "The Council owns a flat above the police station and you can have the use of that free of charge."

I was thrilled at this news and accepted the offer at once.

We were fed well in the Institute, where we ate with the priests, and had one old priest to look after us. He never said a word, but watched out for anything we might require. When we left, a lady in the kitchens gave us food to take away. As we were driving towards Venice and our next handicapped home, I noticed a silver chain and crucifix hanging in the caravan. I had no idea who could have placed it there, but I saw it as a gesture of thanks.

Action now had to go on the ferry to get to the Lido, an island off Venice where the next home we were to visit was situated. This was a small house run by Amtiomella Bagagiolo, where eight young, handicapped men lived and took care of themselves. They were visited each evening at bedtime by a special assistant. Our interpreter was a black boy from Senegal, who gave his name as Osman, and he spoke perfect English, although he had arrived in Italy unable to speak anything but his native tongue. Working as a street guide in Venice, he had mastered eight languages, learned from the tourists.

There were now only four days to go until Christmas. Sharing a house with the handicapped boys was exciting. Each day, one boy who was deaf and dumb, would go to the town centre, dressed as Father Christmas, and hand out presents and good wishes.

Arrangements were made by Amtiomella for us to visit a school where they were holding a Christmas party. We put our handicapped people from the home into the caravan and drove there in style. On arrival we were welcomed warmly by teachers and pupils.

One handicapped boy from the house had been taking care of Action for the past few days, giving him his food and water and growing very fond of the animal. On our last night with them, the lads cooked us a dinner. While some of them had mental problems, some were highly intelligent, but confined to wheelchairs. A doctor and a priest shared the meal with us. There was a very affectionate mongoloid boy there, who followed me about by day, jabbering at me in Italian. At the meal he sat next to me.

I wanted to know how the handicapped perceived themselves and what life in general was like for them, and through a young woman who spoke English, a long discussion ensued, in which all those at table took part. I wanted to hear answers from the handicapped themselves, and they gave them freely. My overwhelming impression was their desire not to be regarded as freaks, but to be accepted as ordinary members of society. I then asked my mongoloid friend if he felt different.

"I feel the way I am. I was born like this. It is only normal people that make me feel different from them. I don't know why normal people fight when people like us help each other. I don't think God put us here to kill each other."

Next day was Christmas Eve, and Amtiomella told us we were to meet the Patriarch of Venice in his house. We took all the boys from the home with us, even those in wheelchairs.

We had no trouble getting the wheelchairs onto the ferry, but it was a different matter when it came to getting into San Marco. From whichever direction you come, it is necessary to use one of the bridges that cross the canals. I looked to see if any special facilities had been provided for handicapped people, but there was nothing, not even a hand rail on the bridges. There seemed to be nothing in the whole of Venice to make life easier for the disabled. This is a pity, as the town is beautiful and most people would like to visit it, but there is no way for the handicapped to get into the centre to see San Marco or the Doge's palace.

Northern Italy, near Verona.

Chapter Fourteen

Italian Winter and New Horizons

I spoke to Toni Mara about this lack of help for the disabled in Venice and he agreed with me that it was a great shame.

"Each year," he said, "We hold the Venice Marathon, and I always take part. It finishes in San Marco Square and many people in wheelchairs also take part, but they have to stop on the outskirts of the city, as they are unable to get further owing to this lack of aids for them. I feel sick, having run my guts out, knowing that they could not make it all the way.

"The facilities in northern Italy are sparse, but as we travel south they become almost nonexistent. I spoke about the matter to a leading architect, who told me that it is now a legal requirement in any new public building or block of flats that certain facilities for the handicapped must be incorporated, but I also know that builders and architects are often paid to overlook these requirements. Many laws for the protection of the handicapped are ignored. If you like, I will show you what I mean."

He took us to a building site where there was a building under construction. Where there should have been ramps there was none. Where rails should have been there was none. The extra width for the toilet, to enable wheelchairs to get inside, had been forgotten.

We managed to get our friends in wheelchairs over the bridge to the home of the Patriarch by carrying them over the bridges, with their owners sitting in them. Had Max and I not been present, the women helpers could not have managed this alone.

The Patriarch was waiting for us with our lady from the Ministry. His home adjoins the Doge's Palace, and he led us inside. Amtiomella told him all about us and the lady gave him our folder to read. He studied it eagerly.

"Very good. God bless you," he said. "God be with you." He handed me a cross. Meanwhile, television cameras were busily recording our audience with the Patriarch.

I felt honoured to have met him. Max and I are Protestants, but in Italy, which is almost universally Catholic, our lack of knowledge about their church made no difference to their attitude towards us. After this visit, however, I should regard the Catholics in a new light, as I came to appreciate how much good their priests and nuns were doing for the less fortunate in the population. I dread to think how these unfortunates would fare without them.

Christmas morning arrived; the first time in twelve years I had spent it without Beth, and I felt sad as I set about preparing Christmas dinner for Max and myself on the wood burning stove. Max was snoring peacefully, so I left him alone. We sat down at one o'clock to a meal of mashed potato, cabbage and sausages followed by cake given to us by our friends. I gave Action extra feeds during the day, as a special treat, and in the evening, I had a headache and went to bed.

I was in bed for three days with influenza. Max, Valentina and a newly acquired friend, Veronica, took care of me. Veronica is English and married to an Italian, Bruno, and she was to be of great help to us at a later date, when we ran into difficulties.

After Christmas, we visited more schools, homes and scout groups around Venice and we found time to do quite a lot of maintenance to the caravan in preparation for the rest of our journey. Then we met Beth on January 11th and took her from the airport out to Scorze where we were met by Graziano Pizzolato, who worked in the Municipality Building, and who had arranged everything for our stay in the flat. We also met another scout leader, Igimo Michelletto.

Beth and I spent many days wandering round Venice, but our relationship was still cool. She had a job to put up with my continuous talking about our experiences to date and worries for what lay ahead. In retrospect, I see that I must have bored her to tears. She had not come so far to listen to me. Even our sex life had gone, but with my head filled with thoughts of the journey, I could not see the harm I was doing to us both. Through my own indifference and selfishness, my devoted Beth, who had seen me through all the bad times, was now at arm's length. When we got home after Beth's holiday, I would still be busy making arrangements for getting into Romania and Bulgaria.

We resumed our journey in the first week of March, still without permits. In fact, the U.S.S.R. authorities said it was far too dangerous for us to travel alone there in this fashion. There was a lot of political unrest in some of the Russian border States that lay on our route, and troops with tanks were present in force to quell the uprisings. This did nothing to make me feel any happier about the future.

While I was away, Max and Action had been staying on Franco's farm. Max had made many friends in this time and Valentina had become more than just a friend. He felt that his religious beliefs might be a hindrance to him; although her parents were at ease with him, he suspected that they did not fully approve of his relationship with the girl.

I went back to the airport in Venice on March 6th, to collect a young man from Tywyn who's father had asked if he might travel with us for a month to broaden his experience, as he wanted to become a journalist. His name was James Williams, and I was happy to take him along and show him how man, horse and handicapped reacted with the public. He was to accompany us as far as Ravenna, along the flat, straight road that follows the Adriatic sea coast.

It was now time to bid farewell to all our friends. Max and I had bought a present for Franco and Elizabeth for looking after Max during my absence. It was a porcelain oil lamp. While I was carrying it towards the house, I let it slip and it smashed on the ground. Now I had nothing to give them. At almost every workshop we visited we had been given a memento of some sort, and the most precious thing I had was a rose bowl made by the handicapped people in Mestre. It was white and had a gold leaf rim, made more special because they had let me choose it from among their amazingly beautiful range of wares. I had selected it with Beth in mind. Without hesitation, I gave this bowl to Elizabeth. She was worthy of it. The tears were not far away when Max said goodbye to Valentina.

I walked, with caravan and horse, south towards Chióggia instead of east towards Yugoslavia, because so many people in Venice, scouts, handicapped organisations and others had arranged contacts for us, stopping places and people to see to our wants. If we took the ferry to Greece, they would try to get the ferry trip sponsored. After the good care that had been taken of us in Venice, I thought I could rely on further support.

While I was away, Max had finished attending to the caravan, touching up the paintwork and tightening the bolts. We had been given by the President of A.N.F.F.A.S. a list of the names of directors of handicapped homes still on our route, together with their telephone numbers and a letter of introduction. Toni had given us a similar letter for the scouts.

The sun shone on the road to Chióggia, and would continue to shine for days. The traffic was heavy, and I counted 291 lorries that passed us. James walked beside the caravan; Max went ahead to contact our scout man and came back to say we could park outside the town. The scout leader said arrangements had been made for us to collect on the following day for a handicapped group that was not part of A.N.F.F.A.S. and to get publicity for them.

When we entered the town centre and pulled up outside the Community Offices, the scout leader was waiting with councillors and journalists. He told us he had approached the council and been told we could not collect in the street. Meanwhile, a man in a black leather jacket had been standing at a distance watching us. A crowd began to gather round, and he came up and asked for our passports.

"Who are you?" Max asked.

A Welshman with a nightclub here told us the man was the Chief of Police and said we must hand over the passports. We did so and the police officer told us to bring the caravan and follow him. When we reached the police station, he ordered the three of us inside. I asked the Welshman to tell him I could not leave the horse. The police officer instructed me to leave town, and he took Max and James inside.

I was left wondering what to do. The crowd had melted away and I had the feeling the situation was serious. I went down the road, parked and waited anxiously for half an hour. Then Max and James appeared, with the Welshman, who told me we had to be out of Italy by Sunday night or go to prison. It was now Tuesday. The problem had been with Max's passport, the replacement for which had not arrived. We had asked for it to be sent on to

Venice from Milan, but it had not shown up yet.

"They asked for residence papers permitting us to stay in Italy, and when they discovered I had been here over five months without any, they went raving mad," Max said.

The Welshman told us that travelling tourists have to obtain, from a police station, a permit with a photograph if they intend to spend more than three days in the country. I said we had never been told this and I asked if we could obtain the permit now, but the man did not answer. Poor James was quite flummoxed by all this.

"I think the best thing is for you to leave quietly," the Welshman replied, shaking his head.

I was reluctantly sure he was right.

"That's brilliant," said James. "Travel with you and get thrown in prison. I was pleased to see you here. I wondered what had happened to you."

"There's no way we can be out of the country by Sunday," I said.

"This bastard means it, Dad," Max assured me. "Either we are out by Sunday or we go to prison."

"Did he put anything in writing?" I asked.

"No," Max confirmed.

"Right," said the Welshman. "Ring the Embassy in Venice and put them in the picture."

I did what he suggested and was told to ring again at 3 o'clock. When I rang back they said the Police Chief had overstepped his authority in ordering us out of the country without consulting the embassy. They advised me to get out of his area as soon as possible and to ask in the next town for a permit.

James and I decided to take the caravan on to Rovigo and let Max go back to see Valentina for a few days. It was warm and sunny, but James was as bad as Max about getting up in the mornings. Mr. Murruco, a director of A.N.F.F.A.S in Rovigo, settled us into a parking spot at his ceramics factory. Max arrived as planned with the horsebox, but he was cursing. He had had an accident on a car park in Chióggia, he said. I was horrified – Chióggia of all places, and us with no papers for the vehicle.

He had reversed into a car parked behind him, but the damage had fortunately been slight. Franco, who was with him at the time, sorted things out with the other driver, who wanted to call the police, and they then made a hasty departure.

Mr. Murruco took us to a school for handicapped children and we gave them rides. After this we went to a farm run by eight handicapped men. They gave us dinner and wine made on the premises. In the evening, we went home with Mr. Murruco and his two daughters, one of whom is handicapped, took us into the country to eat traditional Italian dishes. We tucked into a plateful of what I thought was beef stew. I asked him what meat we were eating, but his English was not up to answering me. Instead, he lifted his two fingers to his head and I thought he meant rabbit, but then he brayed like a donkey. We got the picture. I thought Max, who had a mouthful, was going to spit it out, but he controlled his instincts and began to chew slowly.

Max, James and I all thought it tasted nice. It was just the idea of it being donkey we could not quite take.

Mr. Murruco sorted out residence permits for James and myself, but Max still had no valid passport. However, he was able to sign papers and the documents could be forwarded to Mr. Murruco's address to be forwarded again to the home where we intended to spend Easter.

Our next destination was Ferrara, to a factory. The very person from whom we asked directions turned out to be our contact man. However, he knew nothing about us, although he was with A.N.F.F.A.S. It seemed that the letter from Rovigo had gone astray. He sent for a translator, listened to our story and, after confirming it with Mr. Murruco, declared himself satisfied.

He took us to an equestrian complex where there were trotting horses, breeding stallions and horses for handicapped people to ride. Action was given a stable and we parked nearby. We were hungry, as we had not eaten all day, so we lit our fire, intending to cook something, but we were told to put it out at once as there was so much straw and hay around.

Next day we took the caravan 10 kilometres to a very large handicapped centre, where able bodied people were also present. A new system was being introduced in Ferrara, and for the time being, residential institutions were closed and handicapped people would go home to their families at night. We also went to a school for severely handicapped children. While we sat talking to staff and doctors, Action destroyed their lawn. We were concerned about the damage, but they told us not to worry, as the children had enjoyed having him and that was more important. A small mongoloid girl and her mother took us to a sports centre for the handicapped, and in the evening we visited a scout troupe and spoke to them.

On our way to Ravenna we called at another school and did the usual things. Spring was showing in the flowers and trees. When we stopped in a village to brew tea, the people smiled in passing. Several times we were stopped by the police on this stretch of road, but they were merely curious about us. One day, we were stopped seven times. Every time, we suffered pangs of apprehension on account of our inadequate documentation.

One night, we stopped in the small town of Consándolo and parked on waste land on a housing estate. We tethered Action before starting to cook our evening meal. Many children gathered round, then a police car turned up and parked behind the caravan. I went over and gave them our folder to read. It was usually a reliable explanation for our presence and often got us out of tricky situations. They told us it was not permitted to park where we had, but this time they would overlook it, providing we were on our way be eight in the morning, before their chief came on duty.

The temperature rose to 29°C, making this the hottest day so far this year. We found waiting to meet us on the outskirts of Ravenna a female scout, who can speak six languages. Leaving Max and James behind with the caravan, I went with the lady scout to see the police, arrange our stay and to meet with Mr. Bergamasci, President of A.N.F.F.A.S. We were to visit three schools and a handicapped home. The police chief for this town had a handicapped son, so he gave us complete freedom of the place.

Later we met Patricia Inferrara, an English lady married to the Prefectura, the leading citizen and a scout leader. She took us to a farming holiday complex, catering for tourists interested in agriculture. The food they gave us there was exceptional, both quality and quantity, and we left with full bellies.

After a busy spell of visits, we were invited to a party given by some senior scouts. Romano, the man who issued the invitation, lived alone, in a state of chaos, in a house overrun by cats. We had appeared in the newspaper that day and the publicity drew the crowds to us when we were in the town. A Scottish woman watched Action drinking water.

"That is no Scottish horse," she said. "He just sips. A Scottish horse would drink it straight down like a Scotsman drinking whisky."

Mr. Burgamasci gave us a beautiful letter of thanks when we left Ravenna, and when we got back to the farming holiday complex we found Mrs. Murruco with Max's passport and residence permit. We went to Marina Romeo and met a man called Sante, who owned a restaurant to which he invited us. He said he had many horses running wild in a pine wood. He fed us that afternoon and then invited us to a party in his restaurant that same evening. We drank and ate well, so well, in fact, that Max fell off his bicycle on the way back to the caravan. He sustained a badly cut finger.

Next morning, Patricia arrived to take us to the radio station, but when she saw Max's hand, now swollen, she insisted on taking him to hospital, where he was given the red carpet treatment, as the doctors knew all about him.

Sante took us out on another occasion, to a party in a different restaurant, but the food and wine were just as good. The hospitality in this town was quite overwhelming.

We had been glad of the rest we had had in Marina Romeo with the Murruco family, and we were grateful to them for obtaining Max's passport. Their daughter Anna, who had been a brick, had to leave early one morning, before we could say goodbye. All we had left was a lovely letter tucked under the caravan door.

The old town of Rimini was next on the agenda.

Chapter Fifteen

Travelling South in the Italian Springtime

An old Roman bridge spans a dried up river bed in Rimini. We stopped just before this bridge to wait for our scouting contact, who had been told by Patricia to expect us. She arrived punctually, and as we stood together talking, a man emerged from a pizza restaurant and beckoned us to enter. He sat us down and produced salad and seafood, on which Max and I gorged ourselves. We were quite full when two large pizzas arrived with two bottles of beer followed by coffee. After we had eaten, I expected the scout girl to pay, but she said the meal was on the house and the owner of the place was inviting us to take all our meals with him while we were in Rimini.

There was a car park adjacent to parkland on the banks of the river bed. When the restaurateur said it would be possible for us to put Action and the caravan there, I tied the horse to a tree amidst lush grass and asked the scout girl to notify the police and council of our presence. When she returned it was to say that police and council already knew all about us, sent their good wishes and said they were pleased to see us. She said, too, that we would meet Don Queste Benti at his office in the morning. Don Queste Benti had been on television and at meeting in Venice that we attended, so I knew him for one of Italy's leading figures in work with the handicapped. It was a thrill to meet him and talk through an interpreter.

Rimini has one hospital set high on a hill and we called there for a visit. It is home to eight handicapped children, many of whom had rides round the grounds on Action's back. We also visited a hospital with all age groups, and here I met a disabled man who insisted on riding Action. He suffered from osteomyelitis and was virtually confined to a wheelchair. He was pleased for me that I had recovered from the same affliction as himself and he gave us 100,000 lire to use as we wished.

While we were touring the town, a man stopped his car and invited us to visit his bar in Cattolica. We found the bar and went inside for a coffee, leaving Action outside in the street. Unusually, he pissed on the hard ground, infuriating the shopkeeper in front of whose premises he did the deed. We knew all about it when the angry man rushed into the bar threatening to call the police. The bar owner helped us wash down the road with buckets of water, but when the police turned up they told us to leave town.

We were outside Pésaro and feeling lost, when a young girl arrived and told us, in good English, that she was a close friend of our scout contact's brother. The Pésaro scouts were waiting for us in a large church hall and arrangements had been made for us to park on the sports centre across the street. The scouts had tried to get permission for us to visit the main square and do our usual work of getting publicity for the local handicapped homes, but they had been thwarted by one man, the Community Chief of Public Affairs, who said that all the laws had been changed and it was no longer possible to take horses into the town centre. I had to submit to a detailed interrogation, which satisfied him and got me a chance to visit a day centre for the disabled and a public hospital.

In a small town to the south of Pésaro is a school and a workshop for the disabled, where we took 31 children and ten staff for rides along the seafront in the caravan. In the afternoon, another party arrived, with severely handicapped patients in wheelchairs, who had heard about the rides we were giving and wanted to try it themselves. With Action between the shafts it was impossible to lift the wheelchairs inside the caravan, so we unhitched him to load them aboard. It was the first time we had ever tried this, but the pleasure it gave was so manifest that we were to repeat it often in future.

The home had a lady director, who told me it was situated in a very narrow back street, which caused problems manoeuvring wheelchairs in and out of their minibus. She had informed the Community Officer and asked for a different location to be found for them.

We travelled along the old road, between the motorway and the sea, headed for Ancona. As we progressed we could see work being done on a length of sea defences. We pulled in on soft, golden sand to cook a meal on the wood stove. Max, meanwhile, had gone off somewhere. He came back with a smile on his face and a bag of mussels in his hand.

"You're too finicky to eat those things, " I said. "You've seen the amount of pollution there is in this Bay of Venice."

These can't be any worse than the pollution you intend to cook in," replied Max.

We ate them and suffered no ill effects. Afterwards, Max went to ride Action, who had been wandering about on the beach. He seemed interested in the sea water, sniffing at it and looking as if he would like a dip. Max sprang on his back and rode him up to his belly into the water. The delighted look on that horse's face was worth seeing.

When we moved on, Max drove ahead in the horsebox, checking for low bridges, of which a number can be found along the seafront. He was gone for two hours, and I was getting very concerned. I caught up with him at last, and found him cursing Italian drivers, and the horsebox up to its axles in soft sand. A car had come head on at him, making him swerve and landing him on the beach. He had been unable to get the vehicle free and it was to take us the next three hours to dig, pull and heave before we had it back on the road. When we set off again, one of Actions shoes began to flap with every step. It was coming loose. We stopped again while I nailed it back, and this was another first, because I had never fitted a horseshoe before.

We came to two long tunnels a little further down the road, and Max said we must have lights on the caravan if we wanted to go through them. I cursed and said I was going through as we were. At the end of the first tunnel a police car stopped us for questioning. They seemed unconvinced by our answers and began to rummage through our belongings. While they were inside the horsebox, Max proposed locking them inside. After they had searched the caravan, they asked us where we were going. I told them Ancona, where we were to meet with a scout troupe. I showed them the paper with our contact's name on – Alessandro Fucilli.

By the time they let us proceed, the Friday evening rush hour had begun and the road was thick with traffic. We could hardly have chosen a worse time. It was worse than the traffic in London. However, we met Alessandro as arranged and went with him to the old Cittadella overlooking Ancona. We entered through large wooden gates set into the outside wall of the fortress. A castle stands in the grounds. It is now a riding school run by Anna, an English lady who has many disabled children among her pupils. The rest of the grounds serve as a public park

Presently, more scouts arrived with a journalist in tow. They told us efforts had been made to get permission for us to tour Ancona with Action. What we had to do was take our folder of letters to the Municipal Building, where Alessandro would introduce us to the President of A.N.F.F.A.S. Thus, it was arranged for us to make our tour. In the evening, when we felt like taking a stroll and having a drink somewhere, we found ourselves firmly locked inside the castle grounds. The fence surrounding us was too high to climb, so we went to bed hungry and thirsty.

As soon as the gates were opened on the following morning, Max raced to the shops to buy spaghetti and tomato purée and made pasta to which he added curry powder, much to the disgust of our Italian friends.

Ancona had been badly damaged during earth tremors in 1972 and 1983. Some of the damaged buildings had not been demolished and we found the unrepaired road surfaces very rough. In the Piazza Cavoul we were joined by scouts and handicapped people to whom Alessandro told our story while children fed Action with sweets and other goodies.

That evening, Alessandro took us to dine with handicapped youths living in the community which he runs. When it was time for us to leave, he gave us a letter of thanks containing a 100,000 lire bank note to use as we wished and a photograph album with pictures of our visit signed by all the scouts and the handicapped. This was another of the treasured belongings stolen from us at a later date.

Alessandro and his sister accompanied us as far as Osimo where they took us to a hospital for deaf, dumb and blind patients. It was very moving to watch the blind children standing in front of Action while their nurses explained what he was. Action stood stock still and let them feel his soft coat; probably, for most of them, it was the first time they had ever touched a horse. The nurses gave constant reassurance and, after a time, I gave some of the patients a ride around the grounds. I wondered how it felt to be sightless and hearing the clop clop of hooves and the rumble of the wheels, and to sense the gentle rocking motion of the caravan. The children were clearly delighted. This hospital is the only one of its kind in Italy and there is a long waiting list of patients.

Alessandro gave us many bags containing clothing, before he departed. He said they were for distribution in Romania and Russia.

When we got to Porto di Potenza Picena we stopped at a large institute housing 400 adult patients. Our next stop, however, was unscheduled. Two nuns, in a small town we happened to be passing through, had read about us in the newspapers and invited us to visit their school, where they had 58 children aged between four and six. We lifted the children up, one at a time, and gave them rides on Action's back. One small child, bolder than the rest, persuaded the Mother Superior, seventy years old, if she was a day, to sit on the horse. Amidst much hilarity from children and nuns, she hoisted up her habit, exposing her bloomers, and climbed aboard. Amazingly and to resounding cheers, another plump nun also climbed on.

The next stretch of the coast road was a haunt of prostitutes and we saw many waiting by the roadside with their cars, hoping to pick up custom. We also saw police cars pull up and the officers inside speak to the women. At Silvi Marina a man stopped us. In his arms he carried a large bundle of fresh cut grass for Action. In good English, he told us his name was Franco, and that he wanted to help in any way he could. He explained that he was no longer able to hold down a job owing to schizophrenia and periodic bouts of severe depression. He asked if he might travel with us for a few days, as he hoped it might do him good. I told him that we could be glad of his company and his services as a translator owing to the number of times the police stopped and questioned us.

When I next telephoned Beth she had received a letter for me from the Bulgarian embassy. It refused us entry to Bulgaria.

Having come down to the south of Italy, we now had to go to Greece for the shortest route, via Bulgaria and Romania, through to the Russian border. Now we had been refused entry to Bulgaria, we would have to make a detour through Turkey to reach Russia. We contacted Patricia in Ravenna and she enquired at the British Embassy in Venice about this plan, only to be told that Action would not be allowed back into any other E.E.C. country, if he walked through Turkey, for fear of him spreading diseases. We asked her to see if the Embassy people could talk to the Bulgarian Embassy and try to get us an entry permit on diplomatic grounds, but they remained adamant.

This left us with a second option: we could go north from Greece into Yugoslavia and go via Romania into Russia. It would add a great deal to the distance we must travel and we were already way behind schedule, so there was no hope of reaching Russia before the winter returned and we had to reject the idea. I decided we would cross Greece, in the hopes of meeting someone with influence enough to persuade the Bulgarian authorities to change their minds. If not, we would chance our luck and see if we could get into the country without a permit. Having come so far, I would not give in, although Max was firmly against my proposal.

In Pescara we visited another Don Orione Institute, this one run by Don Guiseppe and some priests. We parked up behind the the institute and were warned to keep an eye on Action, as the place was a haunt of heroin addicts who left hypodermic needles lying about. That evening, leaving Max to mind the horse, I went for a stroll. I found myself in a large, run down housing estate that demonstrated clearly the vast gulf between prosperous northern Italy and the poverty stricken south. On the following morning we went down to the sea and looked for evidence of facilities for the disabled. We found not a single trace of anything.

When we returned to the institute, Don Guiseppe advised us to park everything inside the grounds as a horsebox had been broken into. There was a small courtyard and an equally small garden with shrubs. I tied Action to a bush. Next morning, we found him standing by a half–eaten tree. I was shocked, as it was a yew tree, highly poisonous to animals and humans alike. We gave him plenty of water and fresh cut grass to flush his insides through. So far as we could tell everything seemed to be in order, but I knew that the effects of ingesting the tree's taxin poison can take up to four weeks to manifest themselves. He had consumed some four or five kilos of the foliage.

Franco came inside when we toured the Institute and acted as our translator. Afterwards, he said he felt much better about himself after seeing the inmates in their suffering. Action, too, had made a friend during his stay in the courtyard. A stray cat had attached itself to him, and Don Guiseppe promised to find it a good home after we left, as we could not take it with us. Don Guiseppe had spent sixty years in institutions, studying religion. He had actually met Don Orione, founder of the chain of institutes bearing his name, before the latter's death in 1948.

We spent many hours discussing religion with Don Guiseppe and, before we left, he made us as a parting gift of the rosary and crucifix he had worn for many years. This was another treasured possession which was to be stolen from us in the days ahead. By the time we came to depart, the 104 children and youngsters, aged between six and twenty–five, had had a great time with Action.

Going towards Vasto, we had to pass through another tunnel, so Max went ahead to check it out. When he came back, he reported that it had a bend in and a downhill slope. It was also pitch dark inside.

"If you go through that, you are mad," he said.

"Action and I are going to do it," I rejoined sarcastically.

Max did not follow me closely this time, but stayed behind to slow the traffic. Just as we entered the darkness a police car emerged from the tunnel, but it was too late to stop me. I was already inside. I set Action to gallop and we came to the bend. Suddenly I heard the sound of metal clanking against the road. I thought for a minute that we had lost a wheel, but there was no way I could stop in the fume–filled tunnel. The noise of the traffic, Action's hooves and the steel tyres was deafening, and I wished I had not come this way. I looked behind me, hoping to see Max close at hand, but all I saw was a stream of cars piling up at the rear of the caravan.

When I emerged into daylight again and was able to pull in at the roadside, Max joined me. He climbed out of the horsebox with Action's badly dented water bucket in his hand. He threw it at me.

"You bloody idiot," he said. "This thing hit a car when it fell off the caravan. I had a hell of a row with the driver. He's going to report us."

"What about that police car we saw when I entered the tunnel, Max?" I asked.

"I don't know, Dad. I dived in the bushes and hid from sight."

"Let's get ourselves out of here quick," I said, although our top speed was usually about four miles an hour!

The ten kilometres of road to San Vito Chietino was full of twists and turns and we were glad to arrive and park on the seafront. That evening, a young man came up and gave us a bag of mussels which, Franco offered to cook for our breakfast. When I awoke in the morning, he had gone, but he came back with about twenty lemons. We lit a fire and began to clean the mussels. We cooked them with lemon juice, garlic, pepperone, green herbs, salt and water and a final dash of white wine. It was delicious. Franco spent the rest of the day sucking the remaining lemons.

The landscape changed as we neared Vasto, and Action perked up at the sight of hills after the boredom of so many miles of flat roads. The way in to Vasto was on a twisting road up a steep hill. I could not be sure of the terrain from below, and Max offered to go ahead in the horsebox to survey the route. Franco had been with us for a couple of days and this was his first sight of a hill. I explained that we would walk up it, to take the weight off Action, and that I wanted him to push the caravan from the rear.

The ascent was gradual at first, getting steeper as we progressed. Soon Action's muscles were rippling and I stopped to let him rest. I was inwardly begging Max to hurry back and help us in case Action's hooves began to slip and we had to chock the back wheels in a hurry. Once we set off again, we could not stop anywhere, as the traffic was already piling up. There was still no sign of Max and the queue of cars was considerable when I urged Action on again, with Franco pushing from behind. We ascended slowly and made it to the top in a state of exhaustion.

I suddenly saw Max running towards us. As he came closer I could see that he was angry and upset and blood was gushing from a cut above one eye. Shaking and pale, he threw his documents into the caravan.

"This is what the police have done," he said.

I calmed him down and listened to his story.

"I realised you would need help, Dad, so I parked the van on the side of the road. I knew it was not a good spot, only a small lay-by. I glanced in the cracked wing mirror and saw a police car behind me and two policemen climbing out. They came up to me, I wound down the window and they spoke to me in Italian. I asked them to speak more slowly and not in dialect, so I could understand them. It made no difference, they just went on in dialect, but I knew they wanted my driving licence and residence permit. They looked through them, still yapping away, then one told me to get out and open the horsebox. The second man covers me with a machine gun. I get the back half open when they tell me to close it. They said something about narcotics and bombs. I was confused and thought I had better not say too much in case I got it wrong. The younger man was getting angry.

"They seemed to be abusing me in the hope that I would be provoked into doing something wrong. I found the newspaper cuttings from Pésaro and a photo of the horse and caravan, as I realised they must have passed you on the way up the hill. I explained, in my best Italian that my father was with the caravan and he had a man with him who speaks Italian. I was met with more abuse, and they tore up the article and photo and threw them at me. Then they grabbed me, and one held me while the other punched my face. I didn't give them the satisfaction of retaliating. Instead, I asked again what they wanted. The officer with the machine gun was fiddling with it.

"They told me to go. I climbed into the van and asked for my documents back, as one was still holding them in his hand. They kept saying "go" at me, but I did not understand what they meant. Should I go 100 metres? I asked again and one of them hit me in the face. I felt very giddy. He caught me just above the jaw. I held my head as I walked away, so they could not see my face again. When I removed my hands, they were covered in blood. I got in the van and drove off. All the while, cars and lorries were driving past, slowing down for a better view.

"They still had my documents and my passport. I decided to pull in about 500 metres along the road, just off the SS16. There was no way I was going to go out of sight of other people. I sat in the van wondering what to do, when the same policemen stormed up to me. I had the door open and one thumped me in the chest, grabbed my arms and pulled me out of the van and onto the ground. Then he threw my documents in my face. When they left, I got up and ran back to you."

I told him to lie down in the grass and rest. Franco was speechless. Shortly after this we continued towards Vasto. Max said he would never lose sight of me again, and from then on he went back to following close behind us, still badly shaken by the experience.

When people stopped to talk to us now, after we had become famous from so much media exposure, we told about Max's experiences, and I was surprised when they all advised us to forget it. However, I was determined to report the incident as soon as we got to Vasto. If we could be treated with brutality, what about other tourists?

When we reached Vasto the scouts met us. The Chief Scout introduced himself, and Franco began to tell him about Max. Once again, we were advised to forget it.

"You have a long way to go yet. If you make a fuss it could cause you problems."

I got the feeling that Max agreed with him, but he said nothing and I made no further comment. His eye had blackened and his face was badly grazed down one side. I was still not prepared to to let the matter drop, but I had no idea what to do about it. The answer came that evening. The Chief Scout had arranged for us to stay at a youth centre called Salasiami, and

Franco had left us to find himself a hotel to stay in.

By arrangement with the Chief Scout, we were to meet the Bishop of Vasto that evening and have a meal with him in a restaurant. When the Bishop saw the state of Max's face, he asked how it happened. I told him, and his face registered disgust, although he said nothing. When I had finished speaking, he rose to his feet and left us with the scouts who were keeping us company. He came back after a few minutes and spoke in Italian to the Chief Scout, who told us the Bishop said he had spoken to the Chief of Police for the province and been assured that such a thing would never happen again and that the culprits would be found and dealt with. This gave Max and me some slight reassurance, but who could be sure about it never happening again?

Spring was almost over and my concern at reaching Russia before winter was growing, as we were now some two months behind schedule. I felt our slow progress through Italy had been worthwhile, and we had been able to visit many homes and institutions, but we might have been to too many places. There had been continuous media pressure, making us famous from one end of the country to the other, so that we were continuously being waved at, spoken to and showered with food and money. In all the rest of our travels, we were never to find a more enthusiastic reception than we had in Italy. When we were in Pésaro, I asked an Italian man in the crowd gathered round us what made us so popular, and he said it was for what we did through our journey to help the less fortunate. It was, he continued, something very special and no Italian would do it.

"Our people admire your strength and bravery. For the Italian his family comes first. It is difficult for us to understand you putting yourselves out to come abroad and visit handicapped people when you have a family of your own at home. They must miss you sorely, and it will be a long time before you see them again. We are proud to shake your hand and welcome you to Italy and share what we have to help you achieve your aim."

He took my hand as if to shake it, but instead pressed a 100,000 lire note into my palm.

"This is for you, to help feed your horse," he said, turning away to address the crowd.

We were not far out from Vasto Marina when the police stopped us. Remembering the thumping he had been given a few days earlier, Max began to shake like a jelly. He showed them our documents and began to explain what we were doing, speaking in Italian to them. They gave us a salute and let us go on our way. Soon after this, we were stopped by Guardia di Finanza and the same thing happened. The third time we were stopped it was by the Stradale Policia, boys from the same lot that had beaten Max up. Uncertain of what to expect, I handed over our passports without comment. We were amazed when they told us that their Chief gave the two officers responsible for injuring Max a thumping in front of all their colleagues. They seemed to find it amusing. We left them and continued on our way towards Térmoli.

We stopped in a lay-by just outside the town to meet up with

Antonio, our scout contact. A police car stopped to enquire if we were in trouble, then drove off again. When Antonio arrived, he told us that the police had been notified of our presence in the area and everything was O.K. with them. Then he found us a lovely parking spot on the beach. We took Action and the caravan into the old centre of Términoli and aroused considerable interest among the locals and tourists. A blind girl and her friend turned up and we led them to Action. They spent almost an hour running their hands over every inch of him.

We were escorted back to the parking place and assured by the police that our things would be safe there. Antonio took us home to have a meal with his family, and we discovered that he had a cousin from London visiting at the time, so we were able to talk freely of our adventures and explain more fully our purpose. Later in the evening, Max went for a walk along the beach. All along the coast the lights shone out and the sea, flat as glass, was silvered by the moonlight. The air was pungent with the strong smell of fish and seaweed, as the tidal rise and fall is slight here and what gets carried onto the beach often stays for a long time.

On the following day, Antonio telephoned Dr. Bozetti of Spillars in Venice to arrange a collection point for us to get some sacks of food for Action. There was a little confusion at first, but we sorted it out in the next couple of days. Antonio also contacted the scouts at San Severo, sixty kilometres away. Before we left, Antonio's father, who is a member of the Italian Blood Donors' Association, gave us a letter for our folder.

We headed inland and noticed how much greener the countryside looked only a short distance from the sea. The air was cooler and we saw thirty or more different species of wild flowers along the roadside verges. We stopped to pick a few to carry in the caravan with us. There were many grape vines to be seen, but there was also quite a lot of household rubbish dumped beside the road. The cars looked rather tattier than those we had seen further north, and many had been abandoned. There were numerous derelict buildings, too.

Max drove ahead to San Severo and found a parking place just outside the town, beside the SS16. He scouted round the streets on his cycle before coming back to find me. Meanwhile, Action and I had found our way to the meeting place with the scouts. When Max came back, he was unable to locate me, but a police car stopped and told him to follow it. The car led him to where we were, and the scouts already had everything well under control.

Many of the scouts present had brought parents along to hear us talk about what can be done to help handicapped people, and we mentioned the special parking places provided for them which the general public uses. We also named a couple of bars we had discovered that welcome disabled customers. We suggested they discuss the problems of being disabled with their local councillors and ask them to consider the provision of specially adapted toilets, better access to public buildings, subsidised riding schools and other facilities that would help.

At 8.30 next morning, some scouts arrived with a very good translator, an English teacher from the local high school, where we were taken to tell the pupils about our journey and pass on the same message as we had given the night before. During the hour or so we spent at the school, it was arranged for a police motor cycle escort to take us and the caravan to the Town Hall, in the centre of San Severo, to meet the Mayor and put some of our suggestions to him. The police found us a convenient parking spot close to the Town Hall and we were taken inside, to find radio and newspaper journalists there in force, as well as officials from various departments of the council. Our talk lasted for about three quarters of an hour, after which we were taken to a fine restaurant to eat a meal paid for by the Mayor.

In many of the southern towns in Italy roads are constructed from slabs of smooth volcanic stone which Action found rather slippery to walk on, and the small studs in his shoes wore down quickly, so we racked our brains to find a way of helping him keep his grip. Our next goal was Foggia, where we arrived in the late afternoon. Our instructions were to wait in a certain lay–by 3 kilometres outside the town and the police would come and escort us to a parking spot. No police appeared, but some scouts showed up and took charge of us. They had plans for us to spend a few busy days in Foggia, once again proving how much enthusiasm there is in the Italian Scouting movement.

When the police eventually came, it was already dark, at about ten o'clock at night, and they took us to a church hall where we spent that first night. The priests gave us breakfast and coffee in the morning, then a member of MASCHI, an adult scout group, arrived and introduced herself. She was Locea Fimamore, and she had at her fingertips every details of our stay in Foggia. First on her list was to take Action across town to the Regional Institute for the Breeding of Horses, where there was a blacksmith in attendance, to whom we explained our problems about slipping hooves. His solution was to fit rubber pads to the sole of the hoof before shoeing. He warned us to be scrupulously careful about keeping them clean, as neglect can cause the hoof to rot.

While he was there, Action was washed and groomed by the stable hands. When we were ready to leave, television crews arrived to film us setting off to visit a school for normal 5 to 11 year old children, but which also had twelve handicapped pupils. After the children had been given rides, we returned to the stables to meet its director, Vittorio Cocci. He told us the place was once a military establishment, built in the 1930s for horse breeding and containing 100 stables. Now it is used as a regional institute for breeding. It was being extensively renovated.

We made arrangements with Locea Fimamore for an address to which we could have our mail forwarded. In the evening we visited the Emmaus Community to talk to drug addicts, alcoholics and others about our journey. We learnt that Foggia translates as "Big Hole", and derives from a bygone age when grain was stored in holes dug in the city's squares. The Emmaus Community is partly financed from their agricultural products. Some are consumed by the members of the community, and the surplus is sold in the town. The title Emmaus comes from the Bible story in St. Luke's Gospel,

Chapter 24, that tells of two men walking towards the village of Emmaus and finding the risen Christ coming towards them, although, at the time, they do not recognise Him.

Locea and Vittorio told us next day that they had arranged for a place where we could stop in Otranto and had organised a veterinarian to check Action before we took the ferry to Greece. They had also contacted Dr. Bozzetti of Spillers about us getting a further supply of food for the horse. R – Line Ferries had also been contacted about our crossing to Greece. Before leaving Foggia, we were escorted by the police, as well as by Vittorio and Locea, to A.S.S.O.R.I. to meet handicapped children, parents and doctors. The two police officers came inside with us, and we had a chance to discuss things like parking for the disabled with them. They said they felt powerless as individuals to tackle the problem, which stemmed mainly from lack of public awareness of the problem, but they said they would take it up with their superiors. Vittorio promised to try and get the scouts involved in trying to persuade people to stop those who park on the areas designated for disabled drivers. When we mentioned horse riding for the handicapped, Vittorio said he would see if such a facility could be incorporated into the breeding centre. Our policemen helped us give the children rides, and said afterwards that they had enjoyed the visit.

When we were on our way back to the Institute, the two motorcycle police were in front of the caravan. We all stopped at some traffic lights and Action had his eye on the aerial of the second motorcycle, as if he was listening to the conversation coming over the police radio. Someone mentioned his name, at which he snatched the aerial between his teeth and bent it. The policemen looked shocked, but started to move off again when the lights changed, with Action still holding the aerial tightly between his teeth. They took it all in good spirits and wished us well in our efforts to improve the lot of the disabled, promising to talk about our suggestions with their bosses, and then they asked if they could act as our escorts again on the following day.

Our next visit was to a school, memorable for the good behaviour of the children, after which we returned for another talk with the Mayor, who seemed concerned to tackle some of the matters we had talked about previously. Vittorio took the opportunity to suggest using the facilities of his Institute for horse therapy. Finally, we were given a medal, an honour bestowed on those who have done something for the city. Back at the Institute, we had a session taking photographs with our police escorts, who had brought their own cameras along.

That same afternoon, we went to V.A.L., an organisation founded in 1984 with money donated by the public and caring for thirty – four people ranging in age from 20 to 80 years. The staff are volunteers and the patients have no relatives to care for them. Many had a ride in the caravan or sat on Action. In the evening we visited scouts at a sports and social centre on a large housing estate. The local lads were playing ball games when we arrived; some of them were a bit rough with Action and they wanted to climb all over the caravan. I resorted to grabbing one fellow by the hair and hauling him off. Most were interested in our journey, when Locea began to tell them about us. Then, after one lad had thumped Action quite hard on the neck, some of the older scouts suggested that it was time for us to leave. They telephoned for our police escorts, who came within ten minutes. Their appearance had a calming influence on the crowd.

We went next to visit the MASCHI Group, where someone made a very strong speech about the lack of facilities for the disabled in Italy.

We set off towards Margherita di Savóia, which took us back towards the coast. We were taken to the outskirts of Foggia by our police escort, our route covered by more wild poppies than I have ever seen in my life. After we had left the town we came upon an area of water covering several square kilometres. It was divided into half kilometre sections and the water was a brownish maroon colour. The water is drained away leaving a residue of salt which is then refined.

Picking a route through the town was not easy, for some streets are banned to horse – drawn traffic. Max was driving ahead in the horsebox when his bicycle fell off the back and landed on the street, which had heavy traffic flowing on it. Some bystanders snatched the bike and stood holding it while a police car raced past. When it was safely out of sight, they returned the bike to Max. They pointed out the best route through town to a construction site where we could park. Max came back to guide us in, our usual tracking method still proving satisfactory. The area in which we found ourselves seemed a little rough, so we decided to take turns at keeping guard on our belongings. However, the night passed uneventfully and the morning came with a promise of a hot day ahead, so we made an early start for Trani, where we had the name only of a scout contact.

We arrived in Trani in the early evening and asked our way to the railway station. We waited there for ten minutes and then a police car stopped alongside us and an important looking man in uniform stepped out and came over. He expressed an interest in what we were doing, and after a short chat, he came into the caravan and began to tell us about a friend he had in Scotland and his hopes of one day going to live in Scotland himself. He told us how to find the church in Trani where the scouts meet, assuring us that the priest would know the scout we wanted to find. A boy of about fifteen had been listening in to our conversation, and he promised to be our guide.

We were taken to a large church, and here the priest telephoned a scout, who arrived inside ten minutes. She said the name we had been given belonged to her leader. When the leader turned up he had brought the President of the local A.N.F.F.A.S. Group along. The President fixed it with the police that we could park overnight in the church courtyard. It was a fine, warm evening, and they decided to eat outdoors. The cutlery and food were lowered in a basket from a kitchen window in an apartment block. We ate the first oranges we had actually picked off a tree.

Later that evening, we went by car to Molfetta to arrange our programme in advance. That night was bad, as we were bitten all over by mosquitoes, and we were glad to make an early start for Molfetta in the morning. We had to pass through Biscéglie, which has a very large hospital.

Our scout friends were waiting to show us round, but there were far too many patients for us to be able to offer them all rides in the caravan. When we saw it there were 3,000 patients there, but it has the capacity to take 10,000. It has psychiatric patients, but none of them have been committed there. The doctor who was our guide said he felt that many people should stay here permanently, as the place had been built in an isolated spot deliberately, and the public's attitude to handicapped people was such that it deprived them of a chance to live with dignity and self respect in the community.

When we left the hospital, we went to see some ancient burial grounds dating back to prehistory. They are covered now by olive groves, also very old. Back on the road to Molfetta, we were met by scouts and taken to a western style ranch riding school where we were to spend the night. The owner, Gregorio, spent many years in the United States, studying horses and cattle ranching. He achieved a record in 1984 by riding an American horse from Canada to Mexico in 99 days. He had been writing a book about his experiences.

While here, Action was given his worming compound and the horsebox was disinfected and treated to a thorough cleaning.

The next morning we met the Bishop and the scouts of Molfetta and went with them to see 600 children coming out of a church. They gathered round to talk to us and some of the younger ones were given rides. We noticed that our public liability insurance was about to expire.

The scouts gave us an address in Lecce for having our post forwarded, then two of them took us to Casa de la Pace, a group run by volunteers and concerned with nuclear disarmament, third world poverty, homelessness and other social issues. The group owes allegiance to no religious organisation, and a lot of their funding comes from collecting paper for recycling. The bishop, who is also President of *Pace Christo*, Christ's Peace, in Italy, gave us a book. In the evening we went the the church of Santa Theresa and talked to more scouts.

We had to make a few telephone calls before we crossed to Greece. One was to Dr. Zara, the veterinarian in Venice who had updated Action's Coggins test certificate. He told us he was pretty sure that was sufficient for our entry to Greece, but suggested we ask the people in the ferry office. He said it was just possible we might need another export document. We decided to sort it out when we were ready to leave. Valentina had arranged for more horse food from Spillers to be collected at the ferry port or from a depot near by. However, Dr. Bozzetti, the Spillers representative, seemed reluctant to help us, so we decided not to bother him and instead we would contact John Stone when our departure was imminent.

Before leaving Gregorio's horse school, we checked the caravan wheels and saw that they needed another soaking.

The next part of Italy we went through was covered in olive groves and vineyards with other crops in between. The whole area was sprinkled with derelict houses. When a policeman stopped us, it was to give his address and ask us to send him a postcard from the Crimea. We found a car park and stopped. Swarms of children gathered round us and a mongoloid man of about thirty spent hours walking Action on a long halter and grooming him. Then a journalist turned up for a story about us.

We had two visits from the police during the night, but again, it was more from curiosity than anything else. They advised us to leave early in the morning. The weather had begun to get very hot, and fresh, green grass became scarce. The wild barley was bad for Action, irritating his mouth. The mongoloid lad saw Max trying to find good grass and he took him to a patch of good grass in the middle of a housing estate. Action looked so pleased to see it.

We walked Action through the town with the caravan and headed out towards Lecce. On the way we had to pass through a small village where we gave the children rides. The menfolk emerged from bars and began to give us their opinions on Action, the caravan and the harness. It was very difficult to get away from them all. We passed through another little town perched on top of a cliff and with breathtaking views of the sea. We could see that much reconstruction work had been done there. Although it had grown scorchingly hot, Action was still covering a good distance every day and showing no signs of being bothered by the heat.

One evening, we saw some young men who had got their car stuck on the beach. We put Action into his collar and used our chains attached to the car to let him pull it clear. He soon had the car back on the road. Before we got to Lecce, Max noticed that Action was salivating heavily and seemed to be trying to dislodge something stuck in his mouth. We gave him plenty of water to drink and that eased the problem temporarily. The flies had been annoying him again and we got out the Coopers Fly Repellent, which worked excellently.

Max drove into town ahead of me, to find out where the Salasiami Institute was located. It was a very impressive place, equipped with workshops, classrooms, sports centre and gardens. The Director welcomed us, and showed us where to park and where to put Action. Our scout contact, Franco, arrived at 6 p.m. and asked us what we intended doing in Lecce.

At the Salasiami Institute, the priest in charge asked his maintenance staff to overhaul our caravan wheels to the best of their ability. They welded metal strips across the wheels to the rims. We hoped this would reduce the flexing caused by wear in the mounting blocks at the ends of each spoke. As the next day was also very hot we made the best of it by doing all our washing and thinking about the route we should take through Greece. We were also making sure we had everything we should need.

We found time to take a walk through Lecce, which is very old and has some most attractive parts, and we managed to get ourselves lost. We stopped to ask two beautiful girls standing by an ancient monument if they could direct us back to the Salasiami Institute. Then we discovered that they were transvestites.

At 8.30 next morning, it was already sunny and warm. Max noticed Action behaving strangely towards some young boys standing near him. He was trying to nip them, which is something he only does when he can smell alcohol on anyone's breath. He did not want food or water either and was very touchy when we tried to groom him. I touched his stomach and he lashed out with his hoof, which took me quite by surprise. I wanted Max to send for a vet at once, but the priest said it would have to be a private vet, since the community vets always had Saturdays off work. He said it would be expensive, and I suspected that he thought Salasiami was going to get the bill. I assured him that I would meet all the expenses incurred.

Someone else said he had a veterinarian friend, a Doctor Pulito, whom he would ask to come out to us. Max wrote down all the symptoms we had noticed over the past few days, the way he had been salivating and the fact that he had not passed water during the previous night, and we consulted our veterinary books. When the veterinarian came and examined Action, he said we were to give him plenty of water and a little food. If he passed a motion, we were to leave it for him to examine when he came back next day. Our task now was to keep the children away from him.

We visited the Emmanuel Community and saw handicapped people, then took Action and the caravan to a school. It was in the centre of Lecce that we saw our first English people since leaving Ravenna. They were an elderly couple from Derby. When we got back to Salasiami, the two little girls who had befriended us came as usual and cleaned the caravan for us. Then they spoke gently to Action, telling him to get better soon, as Max and Bill were sad about him being ill.

On our last day in Lecce we took Action and the caravan to visit a small hospital in the town centre. It seemed as if Action had gone lame in his front right leg, and we took turns at driving just to make certain. Franco telephoned Doctor Pulito, who came quickly and advised us not to work him for ten days. This left us with the problem of how to get him to the ferry port in Otranto. We were getting more and more behind in our timetable, so we should just have to take him in the horsebox. The door lock was broken on the vehicle, and when we got to Otranto Max had to fix the door permanently closed. The window also had to be kept permanently shut.

The horse managed to pass some water, but he had not managed to pass a motion for 24 hours. We walked him to a hospital to let the children see him, but we could not give anyone a ride this time, as we wanted to let him rest. Later he managed to drink water and eat a little Spillers food for the first time in 40 hours, then he had a good piss and did his "business". In two days, the vet came to see him five times and had given him four injections. I was dreading the size of his bill, but when it came it was only for 30,000 lire (£15) to cover time and paperwork.

Franco and the vet had already notified a Ministry vet in Otranto to come and inspect the horse before we boarded the ferry.

By 5 o'clock that evening, Action seemed to be fully fit again, so we agreed to go on a caravan tour of the town in the company of five journalists and a band of scouts. Max, Action and I had to agree that Italy had proved to be a land of fantasy, yet amazingly well organised as far as providing us with assistance was concerned. We wondered what it would be like in Greece. What surprises would be in store for us there?

We had asked for 250 kg of Spillers food to be sent from England, but this was not possible, and we were advised to take plenty of barley, for which suitable additives could be provided. I was not too happy about this as the horse was finding it hard work pulling the caravan in the increasing heat, and needed proper nourishment.

After cruising a few bars on our last night, I suddenly discovered that I had lost our precious red telephone book. Max was incredulous at my stupidity, but he helped me retrace our steps and we found it where we had left it, in the telephone box from which I had called Beth.

We went to the customs office and showed our passports, residence permits and the vaccination certificates. They were quite happy with them, but asked us to get a local Ministry veterinarian to give us a stamped paper confirming that Action was fit. This presented no problems. The lame leg was evidently cured, and it was almost as if the horse knew he had to get fit by this particular day. In the afternoon, we took him down to the sea for a swim.

Max was annoyed when Action left a large deposit in the water in which a number of people were swimming, as he then had to swim round and collect all the floating lumps. I went and sat in a bar, out of sight, and howled with laughter as I watched Max cursing in a mixture of Italian and English.

We boarded the ferry in the evening, with a television crew to see us off. We both had tears in our eyes, and Max stayed on deck until the lights of Italy disappeared over the horizon.

"You'll see Valentina and Venice again, Max, when this journey is finished," I assured him.

"Yes, but when will that be?" he replied sharply.

During the crossing, I reflected upon my impressions of the two faces of Italy. The north had been prosperous, but about half way down towards the southern half of the country, conditions changed, as though the place had been cut with a knife, and we had seen poverty in housing, agriculture and in the peasants' way of life. To the Italian, family ties are all important, and the people found it hard to comprehend why two Englishmen should leave home to come and bring joy to handicapped people abroad. Many Italians had told me that it was something they themselves would never do, but it made them admire and help us with great generosity.

I had seen the Roman Catholic religion at work caring for the disadvantaged in society, and I dreaded to think what would happen to such people were the State to assume responsibility for them. It would be making a rod for their own backs.

In a country with some of the most elegant and beautiful buildings and works of art, it was disappointing to find such a great lack of facilities for handicapped people wishing to visit them. I loved it when we visited their handicapped homes. What showed most strongly was the family link outside and the pure and beautiful fantasy inside. Being adopted by the Italian scouting movement was a great help, for they made excellent arrangements in passing us from town to town.

Action had been on his best behaviour, in spite of being prodded, stroked and fed by crowds of strangers. Never once had he put a foot wrong. He seemed to know when handicapped people were around him and he showed his gentle side.

The Italian public had been kind and generous to us, and our stomachs had always been full. My only criticism lay with their police, who had stopped us continually, when we were doing no harm.

We saw the mountains of Albania, black as coal below the lightening dawn sky. The coastline was totally without a speck of light anywhere. The Greek coast, however, showed the welcoming flicker of lights, and Max pointed towards Albania.

"I don't fancy that dark looking place much. It looks abandoned," he said gloomily.

"I would actually like to try and visit Albania," I answered.

"If we get in there, no-one will ever hear of us again," he said thoughtfully. "Besides, what do we know about the place? Nothing! No thanks, Dad. Forget it."

SWEDEN
POLAND
U.S.S.R.
ZECHOSLOVAKIA
HUNGARY
Husi
U.S.S.R. Customs
Bacau
Odessa
Timisoara
ROMANIA
Tirgu
Beograd
Brasov
YUGOSLAVIA
Bucharest
Ruse
BULGARIA
Sofija
Gabrovo
Nesabar
Karlovo
Samokov
Kazanluk
Sliven
Tirana
Stobi
Plovdiv
ALBANIA
Thessaloniki
Kulata
Stavros
Krismata
Vera
Alexandria
Kosani
Konitsa
Joannina
Igumenitsa
GREECE

Chapter Sixteen

We Endure Hot Weather in Greece

When the ferry docked at Igumenitsa, in Greece, we were last off, after all the cars and lorries had disembarked. Although I had made several attempts to get information from the Greek Embassies about what papers we needed to take Action into the country, I was still none the wiser, so it was with considerable apprehension that we drove into the customs area with our horse in his horsebox and the caravan being towed behind. Three customs officials came up and one asked if we were English. When we answered in the affirmative, they asked us to open up the caravan and they commenced a search. One pulled out a scout neckerchief and asked me where I got hold of it. Meanwhile, I was aware of Max showing one of the men what we had at the back.

They then started to read through our passports and the folder containing the collection of cuttings and letters. They seemed impressed, but I was waiting for them to ask about the horse, who had his photograph in most of the press cuttings. I was certain they would insist on opening the horsebox next. However, one of the men took our passports and beckoned me to follow him to a hatch behind which sat yet another customs official. They spoke together in Greek, then the fourth man began to write in the passports, which he also stamped before handing them back to me.

"You can go now," he said.

I walked back to Max, who had seated himself behind the wheel of the horsebox. I slid in beside him.

"What about the horse, Dad?" he asked.

"I'm not sure they realised we've got one," I replied. "Let's get out of here quick."

We drove slowly past all the customs men, waving nonchalantly as we came by the hatch.

"Dad," began Max, as we left the dockside, "I was thinking about them not knowing we had Action. I suggest we stop within sight of them, let him out of the box and see what happens."

A few hundred yards beyond the customs point, between the road and the sea, was a rough piece of ground used as a car park. We pulled in, and in full view of the officials, took Action from the horsebox and attached him to the caravan, but nobody took any notice of us whatsoever.

The temperature was already 85°F and was the warmest weather Action had encountered so far. There was no shade on the road, and it would be interesting to see how he coped. That day we took a walk round Igumenitsa and then spent our time relaxing. In the evening we met a Greek man, who introduced himself as Johan Mitsos. His knowledge of English was not good, but we managed to communicate well. We spent the next three days with him, being fed in restaurants and having our shopping bought for us. He came early each morning and took us sightseeing with horse and caravan round the town. He seemed to know everyone and clearly carried much influence in Igumenitsa.

Johan came one morning when Max was still asleep. He took me to a café and gave his order. It was served in big bowls and resembled soup, but when I tasted it I thought it was foul. There was no meat to be found, but just great lumps of pure fat. More men came and the café was soon filled. Bowl after bowl arrived from the kitchen, and as I did not wish to give offence to my friend Johan, I did my best to get it down. When I returned to the caravan, I felt sick, having swallowed several large lumps of soggy, slimy fat.

In the afternoon, Johan took us to get some hay from a large farm with many hundreds of acres under cultivation. Max said the farm belonged to Johan. After this, we went with him to another farm where he kept goats that browsed the hillsides, tended from dawn to dusk by an old goatherd. It was at this farm that we got the hay, five large bales, enough to last Action for a few weeks. Johan was a very generous man, and although a bit of a lad, he certainly had plenty of money.

On the following day, he took us to a fishing village to buy some special fish, silver like salmon, but only ten or twelve inches long and possibly mullet. He bought them direct off the fishing boat, as fresh as possible. Before going back to Igumenitsa, we stopped at a beach with beautiful, silver sand and where the azure sea was clear as crystal. We all stripped down to our underpants and went into the water. A few well-tanned people occupied the beach, some of them topless females. Max found it hard to believe his eyes, never having been abroad before.

Johan spotted a young couple lighting a fire under the dry, grassy bank above the beach. He raced over and told them to extinguish it, as it was dangerous and could cause a brush fire. They were Germans, and he spoke to them in German. We heard raised voices. When Johan came back he was shaking his head.

"My beach. No fire. Here my beach," he said, making it clear to us that he owned the beach as well as the farms.

We came to a small village on the side of a hill, and Johan explained that we were not going to his home village to eat, but here instead. There was a small café, where several old ladies dressed in long black dresses and with black scarves over their heads sat chatting together. This was the Greece I knew. Johan took his parcel of fish and went inside, after exchanging pleasantries with everyone. There were some men seated inside and they all seemed to know him. He said a few words to them before going straight to the man behind the counter and giving him the fish. A spate of Greek talk followed, and Johan gestured towards us. We sat down and drank coffee and lemonade for a while until the café owner brought out the fish already cooked and in a large bowl. He also carried a plate containing large pieces of bread.

We were given a plate and a fork each and began to set about the fish. Max and I took one apiece and began to remove the heads. I tried next to remove the backbone, and saw Max doing the same with his. While Max and I had been using our best English manners to tackle the fish, Johan had been talking to the café owner. When he joined us and began on his own fish, we were amazed at what we witnessed. Using his fingers to remove a fish from the bowl, Johan put the head end in his mouth and began to suck. Next, still grasping the fish in his hand, he began to eat the flesh from the backbone. Having finished the prime meat, he did something even more unexpected. Holding the fish by the backbone, he put the head back in his mouth and crunched noisily on it for a time, chewing hard. I could see the look of disgust on Max's face and I know he has a sensitive stomach, but Johan had not finished with that fish yet. He now began to devour the backbone, which was gone in a trice, leaving him with just the tail in his hand. Max looked at me and I looked at Max, then we both burst out laughing.

Johan was perplexed at our hilarity until Max explained that we had never seen anyone eat a whole fish like that before.

"It is quite the thing to do in Greece," Johan said. "We are a poor country and this part of Greece has known famine in the past, so we eat most of everything."

Between the three of us, we managed to eat all the fish, but I could not bring myself to eat the heads with their large, fishy eyes looking at me.

Action had been enjoying a good rest and seemed unaffected by the heat of the day. As we toured round with Johan, he had shown us the road leading to the Albanian customs post. I had not yet broken the news to Max, but I thought I would try and get into Albania. Our immediate destination, however, was Joánnina and to reach it we would have to get over the mountains of north western Greece. The road wound round and round the steep sides of the mountains and there was a sheer drop on one side for most of the way. The steepness surprised me. We made slow progress as the temperatures soared to 100°F, even reaching 120° on some days.

Our Greek friend had suggested we stay by the lake at Joánnina and he promised to meet us there in three day's time, but our struggle to get across the mountains took us the better part of four days, as we contended with insect bites and unbearable heat. The drying heat of the sun was having a bad effect on the caravan's wooden wheels, causing gaps to appear where the spokes entered the hub and the wheel rim. Unless we could find some way of carrying out major repairs, they would not take us much further. In any other circumstances, we could have resorted to our old trick of soaking sacks and draping them over the wheels when we stopped at night, but the night temperatures never fell below 70°F.

Although we had been in Greece now for a few days, we had not yet made contact with any handicapped groups, but Toni Mara had told us, before we left Italy, that if we spotted any Greek scouts, to show the letter he had given us on headed notepaper with the internationally recognised Scouts' emblem, as he was sure it would prove helpful.

Joánnina is an isolated, ancient, walled town set high in the mountains and overlooking a large lake. Founded in the sixth century by Justinian, it was once a Greek seat of learning and is now the place where the language is spoken in its purest form. It has a maze of streets and shabby, untidy shops and workshops, many of them family run gold, silver and coppersmiths. Dotted among these are cafés and restaurants selling all manner of food and generally rather sparsely furnished. Others are take – away kebab shops, with the meat already prepared and sold on wooden skewers. We crossed the town and came to the lake, where we would stay for the next two days.

The spot we chose to park on was by the road adjacent to the lake and in the busiest part of town, and this proved to have been a good choice, for we soon drew a crowd. When we were asked questions, there was always someone who spoke English standing by to translate for us. We had our usual display of newspaper cuttings on the caravan and the crowds seemed entranced by us. A young man wearing a blue neckerchief stepped forward and told us he was a Greek scout and that he had seen a letter from the Italian Scouting movement asking Greek scouts to look out for us and offer what help they could.

We certainly needed help with the caravan wheels and we also wanted more hay for Action, but of the two, the wheels were going to prove more awkward to sort out. They would have to be taken to pieces and rebuilt, which required a workshop with welding equipment.

We chatted for a while with this scout, and the crowd grew ever larger. He told me we really ought to have a couple of large posters in Greek for the sides of the caravan, as most people only knew their native language. That would help us get our message across to people. At this point in the discussion, a young woman stepped forward and said she would be happy to make such posters, if we told her what to write. Max and I drafted a poster which said that we had travelled through Scotland, England, Belgium, Holland, Germany, Austria and Italy helping to raise money for, and visiting, homes for the handicapped, giving children rides in the caravan and on our horse, as well as observing the facilties provided for disabled people. Then we said we hoped to travel across Bulgaria, Romania and Russia in the same manner, but to reach those countries we needed as much help from the public as we had so far received in other countries.

The young woman and I went to a café a few yards away and sat down to write the two posters on paper I had given her. Then we came back and stuck them on the caravan. The plan worked well and the crowds quickly understood what we were doing there. The young woman told us she had links with a handicapped group and she would speak to its director and arrange for us to visit. She went off for a while and returned later to say the disabled people would come to us on the following morning and we could give them rides in the caravan.

While all this had been going on, a huge, strong looking youth with muscles bulging out all over, and with bare, grimy feet covered in hard skin, had been standing wordlessly by Action, stroking him and feeding him with hay which our scout friend had provided. All the while we were in Joánnina, this youth would be there; his devotion to our horse was something special.

An old lady, big and plump, arrived in a wheelchair, and our scout friend said she was the mother of Nico, the youth who had befriended Action. They were local characters and known to everybody. They spoke no English, but by signs and gestures we got to know them. Although they were obviously poor, their generosity was marvellous. Nico kept vanishing, only to reappear with chunks of bread and white, feta cheese made from ewes' milk. This cheese would plague me for the rest of our journey. I hated it. If Nico did not have bread and cheese when he returned, it would be ice cream or fruit. Whatever he brought us, Action was always included in the feast. Once someone starts to feed the horse, everyone else gets infected and starts to do the same.

That evening, we took the caravan and Action for a stroll round the town. Bars and cars seemed to be full, and every few yards along the way people stopped us and offered food and drink, as if the whole town knew of our arrival.

In the morning, our scout came back with the young woman who made the posters. Unfortunately, I cannot give her name, as it was among the papers stolen from us. The scout said we could immediately take our wheels to be repaired at a small workshop. The young woman said there would be a party of handicapped people coming on the following day, at 10 o'clock, expecting rides in the caravan, and there would also be national television and newspaper reporters present, so there was no time to lose.

Nico gave us a hand to get the wheels off. He was able to lift the caravan bodily, without the need for jacking, while we removed the wheels and blocked up the axles with wood and stones. We put the wheels in the horsebox and drove through narrow side streets to the workshop, where three men were waiting for us. Unable to speak English, we managed to indicate our wish to have the steel rims removed and cut down, and the blocks cut down enough to take up the slack when the wooden rims were replaced and the smaller steel rims put back.

We all worked steadily for three hours and thought we had made a fairly good job of it considering none of us was a wheelright and this was an engineering workshop. Max and I both felt that the rebuilt wheels would probably not last very long on Greek roads in Greek heat. When I offered to pay the men for their work, they refused to accept anything.

When we got back to the caravan, Nico was waiting there with his mother. Max said quietly,

"Dad, have you noticed how, when people walk past Nico and his mother, they give her money. I think people must know them."

He was right. On several occasions, I observed people giving money to the old lady, and I then knew this was the money that they were lavishing on us.

"Why don't we put the wheels in the lake for the rest of the day and tonight, Dad?" Max asked.

We lashed them together with a rope, suspended them in the lake and secured them to the post on which the ferry boat moored.

There was still no sign of Johan from Igumenitsa, so I telephoned his home to find out what had happened, and was told he had broken his leg and would be unable to join us after all. This was a disappointment, as he had been so helpful since our arrival in Greece. However, he had kept his promise to contact the police to notify them of our arrival. As far as they were concerned, we could do what we wanted without worrying about written permission.

Next morning, I woke with a start at the sound of Action's hooves on the road. Thinking he must have got loose, I struggled quickly into my trousers and jumped out of the caravan, but it was only Nico leading the horse down to the lake to get water. It was just daylight, and I woke Max hurriedly, telling him to get up as we had to recover the wheels and get them back on the caravan before people started to arrive.

I went over the road to where we had tied the rope securing the wheels and gave it a tug. It came up too easily over the edge of the quay wall. The end that should have been holding our wheels was empty and frayed. A bystander pointed at the departing ferry and made a churning motion with his hands, then pointed to where the wheels had been. The light dawned: the ferry had chopped through our rope when it set off across the lake. Peering into the dark water, I could not see any sign of the bright yellow wheels, and there was no way of guessing its depth, but it must have been considerable to allow the ferry to dock here.

I shouted at Max to tell him the wheels were gone, and he strolled slowly towards me in the irritating way he has. I always get annoyed with him first thing in the morning, when he does everything in slow motion. He looked down into the lake and then began to moan about things in general and ask why we did not just pack up and go home. I felt tempted to shove him in to stop his complaints, but there was no need. He stripped down to his underpants, dived into the water and began to swim around, searching for the wheels.

We knew that the rope tying them together was probably still intact, so unless the boat had hit them, they would have survived. If it had hit them, we could not imagine what damage they might have sustained. Max tried a few exploratory dives and found the wheels about six feet away from the quayside wall.

"We need a grappling hook," he said in triumph.

In the horsebox was the steel bar that restrained Action when he was inside. It was about right for the job. I attached one of his old horseshoes to the end to form a hook with which to grab the rope. It was not long before we had success, and with the help of some onlookers, we retrieved the wheels. By the time we got them back, Max had forgotten his moans. Perhaps a dip in the lake had been what he needed every morning, to wake him up properly.

After this, the morning went according to plan, with the handicapped people arriving and being given caravan rides along the lakeside. Afterwards, we went to visit their home and then, with our scout friend, we visited the Scout H.Q. and met the other scouts. Their Chief telephoned the troupe in Kosani and warned them to expect our arrival soon.

Our stay in the old town of Joánnina had been very interesting for me and I had been fascinated by all the small shops and local craftsmen. In a way it was reminiscent of Dickensian times.

At Kalpakion, to the north of Joánnina, is the turn-off to the Albanian border, and I sent Max ahead to park there and then come back to me, while Action and I made our way in sweltering heat through the mountains. Sweat was pouring from him, running down to his belly, dripping off his underparts and splashing the road. It was a lonely journey through sparsely populated terrain and with very light traffic. Cars and lorries sometimes came past, pipping their horns in salutation. Poor Action was frothing at the mouth from his massive exertions. When we got to the turn-off for Albania, I told Max of my intention to try and enter that country. He was most unhappy and told me,

"If we get in, we may never get out again." He was dead set against the plan.

I was determined to have a go, and with Max still grumbling about me being bloody mad, we prepared to set off towards the Albanian customs post some thirty kilometres away. Fate was waiting to play its part in the venture.

Action had been nibbling pony nuts while Max and I were debating, and as I walked towards him he shied away, as if ready to bolt. The chain securing him to the caravan went taut, halting him in his tracks, and he stood swishing his tail furiously, and obviously in some distress. I stroked him and tried to see what had happened. I found nothing until I looked at his penis pouch. Blood was running from it and the pouch swelled to the size of a football. Some insect or other, possibly a mosquito, had bitten him. I tried to wash away the blood with some cold water before more insects came to feed on it and irritated him further. He was, however, not prepared to let me touch him anywhere near his penis, and tried to kick me when I came too close. The only alternative was to get him to Konitsa, a small mountain town situated a day and a half's walk away. In the meanwhile, he could not pull the caravan any further until his penis was better, so we put him in the horsebox and drove him. This incident was the end of my plans to visit Albania. Action's welfare had to come first, and this now meant an urgent visit to a vet.

We found the small town of Konitsa perched in the hills and surrounded by rugged mountains and steep gorges. Dotted about are many small villages, some falling into dereliction. We entered the sloping town square and had an immediate impression of numerous small restaurants and bars, not all of them well kept. There were far too many for the population of 3,000, and we deduced that they must cater for tourists who come to explore the mountains and the famous Vikos Gorge, reckoned to be the second deepest in Europe, dropping some 1,000 feet. A lovely old, Turkish style, hump backed bridge spans the River Aoos here, and any lover of rugged mountains, old villages and peasant life – style, with all the cafés, could hardly find a better place than this.

No sooner had we pulled up than a crowd gathered to watch us unload Action from the horsebox. A policeman stood reading our Greek posters and I was waiting for him to come up and talk to us, but he exchanged a few words with some of the crowd and then walked away. Max went to try and find a parking spot and some grass for Action. When he came back he pointed towards the bottom of a hill where there was a car park. We stood in the square for a while and the locals brought us beer and food before we set off for the parking place.

I took another look at Action's penis and was pleased to see that much of the swelling had subsided. By next monring, all was well again, but it was once more time to get out the Coopers Fly Repellent we had been given by Coopers Animal Health Products. It was a new item we were field testing and it had to be applied to his coat with a sponge, being careful to avoid his eyes and other tender spots.

As we travelled on towards Kosani, the sun grew even hotter by day and the mountains loomed over us, swamping us and making me feel like a fly as we crawled our way, twisting and turning on hairpin bends of horrifying steepness, ever onwards. We had to use the horsebox to take the weight off Action as much as possible on any descending stretches, but even this was fraught with difficulties when the engine kept overheating, and the brake drums got so hot the linings began to burn, for the brakes were, anyway, still somewhat dodgy. It was a tense few days we spent before reaching Kosani.

Our horsebox was not the only item to suffer from the trip. Action, having had such a hard pull in intense heat, had been rubbed sore where his harness and collar came in contact with his coat. It was essential to rest him for a few days and give the sores time to heal. Among the chapter of disasters, however, was one bright spot; one thing that had gone well was the fly repellent, which had handled every possible variety of insect without exception. For the coming three months, we would apply it once every two days. Without it, Action would have been eaten alive.

Chapter Seventeen

Kosani, Sylvia, Sun and Scorched Grass

We arrived in Kosani in the evening and found a large patch of what looked like waste land covered by dry, parched grass that had horse droppings on and was surrounded by small cottages. A swarm of children came up and watched inquisitively as I tethered Action to the caravan by his chain. I took his bucket and went to the nearest cottage to ask for water. An old lady took the bucket from me and went back inside. She filled it and handed it back to me. I thanked her and she just nodded. By ten o'clock at night, when most of the children had gone, we felt it safe to leave Action alone, although there was still one small girl there, who had been standing beside him ever since we arrived.

We found a bar and got into conversation with some of the locals. It was important to find a blacksmith to attend to Action's shoes, which were very worn and had been slipping badly on the rough mountain roads. The men told us where to find the blacksmith. We also asked how to find the local scout troupe, and said we wanted to visit handicapped homes.

"A cockerel kept crowing outside the van this morning, at about five o'clock, and I couldn't sleep," Max said next day. "I threw water at him and scored a bull's-eye. I never heard another sound out of him."

I went again to ask the old lady for water, but this time she invited me into her kitchen to help myself. While the bucket was filling, she poured me a cup of coffee, and although she spoke no English, kindness showed in her manner. Action had lately been drinking twice as much water as usual, as there was no moisture left in the grass, which had turned brown under the blazing sun. By midday the temperature had climbed into the nineties and I worried that Action, with his black coat drawing the heat, might show signs of suffering. So far he had seemed able to stand it, but it was only mid-June. The summer would grow hotter yet.

At 10 o'clock, two of the lads from the bar arrived with nails for Action's shoes. They had misunderstood us, but when we explained again they took us in their car to find a blacksmith. We found him in an unkempt side street: an upright, slim, athletic 78 year old with hard hands, roughened from years of plying his trade. Using his fingers, he indicated that he had been shoeing horses for 68 years. We showed him the size of Action's feet and he came back to the caravan with us clutching a bag of tools and another bag of horseshoes.

His method of shoeing was new to us. He removed the old shoes and fitted new ones, cropping away any excess from around the edges. The appearance was rough, but he assured us the shoes would not fall off. His bill came to about £15, and I paid and thanked him.

While Action was being shod, a member of the local scout troupe arrived, proving that our two drinking companions had been in touch with them. The scout said he would be back next morning and take us to his scout leader. He also said he would help us in any way necessary. In the middle of this, the small child of yesterday arrived with a bag of food sent by her mother. We spent the remainder of the day carrying out maintenance work on the caravan. The wheels were again in a bad way and unless we got them back into some water, we would soon be in big trouble. They really needed at least two days soaking, but most streams had already dried up in the hot weather. We either had to find a big river or get to the sea.

All afternoon, the young girl attended to Action, grabbing handfuls of burnt grass with which to feed him and fetching water from the old lady. Her concern for our horse made me grow very fond of her.

Next morning, the Chief Scout took us to the Town Hall to meet the Mayor, who was also a scout. He had already notified the local police of our arrival and arranged for us to visit a handicapped home. We met a young lady called Olga in the Town Hall, and she said the handicapped people were due to go home to their families by this time, as they had been working in a special workshop making ceramic masks and pictures, but she would telephone the families and say everyone would be getting back home rather later than normal. In the next two hours, we trotted Action over to the workshop and gave the handicapped workers rides in the caravan. Once again, this treat was met with indescribable joy. I have never been able to find words to describe the happiness it brought to these people.

In the evening, we took Action and the caravan, plastered now with Greek posters written for us by the handicapped and their relatives, into the town centre. I wanted the public made aware of their needs and hopes. I remember one poster saying,

"We don't want to be looked on as though we are freaks. Look on us as you look on others." There were many other posters with similar sentiments.

That evening, we gave rides to many small children while Olga spoke to the crowds, mostly about conditions for the handicapped in the home in Kosani. The basic problem with the home was its size and location. It was too small and sited in a side street in the centre of town. The street was so narrow that it was difficult to manoeuvre a wheelchair and a car in the same street. We were just about to leave the square when the mayor showed up with a promise that he would try to relocate the home in a better position.

We were waving goodbye to the crowd and on our way out of the town centre, when one of the caravan wheels fell off. Each wheel has two nuts, one with a right hand thread, the other with a left hand thread. We soon found the right hand threaded nut, but not the other, without which it would have been dangerous to move. We were inspecting the pavement closely, searching for the missing item when a man came and beckoned to me to follow him. He took me to a small engineering workshop where, in one and a half hours, he made me a new nut. When I attempted to pay him, he shook his head and asked instead for an autographed photograph of us.

Action's hooves were still not gripping properly when we walked back to the waste ground, and I was growing concerned about how to effect a cure. The answer came to us in the morning, when we were sitting drinking coffee in a small bar. A horse pulling a heavily laden hay cart came round the corner and I noticed that its feet were wrapped in pieces of car tyre. It seemed like a coincidence when, later that same morning, we had to have a new tyre on the horsebox.

Outside the garage where we had the new tyre fitted, we started to cut up the old one with a borrowed hacksaw. Soon we had several men helping us cut through the steel reinforcing wires, which were very tough. While we were still at the garage, we had two metal strips bolted onto the shafts of the caravan to make them stronger. Two men carried them inside for us while others crawled underneath to tighten every bolt.

When the tyre had been cut into suitable sections, each about nine inches long, I used buckled straps to fix them to his rear hooves only and we tried them out on a small hill. Action reacted only by lifting his feet a fraction higher than formerly, but otherwise seemed quite happy, and his feet were no longer slipping on the road surface. We should find these pieces of tyre useful in future, whenever we came to steep hills.

Our next morning Max spent in the company of a scout, who took him to look round the local history museum. It was only two years old and had been equipped with many facilities for the disabled. I stayed behind with Action and his small girl friend. I discovered that her name is Sylvia and that the girl who came with her is her elder sister. I laid down on the ground to write home about our doings in the past few weeks, and when I next looked up, I saw all our belongings, pots and pans, clothes and ornaments spread out on the grass. The two girls had decided to give the caravan a spring clean. They fetched water from the old lady and washed everything, even the carpet, and I let them get on with it. They were such sweet girls.

Max and I went to a bar with some of the scouts in the evening, but I left early and Max stayed on.

Little Sylvia arrived next morning, with more food for us, and I tried to explain to her that we had to leave Kosani. I hitched up the horse and went to thank the old lady for all her help, then I indicated to Sylvia that she could drive Action for a while. I put the reins in her hands and stood behind her while she drove up the street leading from our camp site. Suddenly she stopped and started shouting to a lady standing in a house doorway. I realised this must be her mother, and I tried to explain to her that we are about to leave town for good, but Sylvia was welcome to come a little way with us, if that was allowed. The mother signified her approval.

Max had gone on ahead with the horsebox to check out the road through the mountains to Veria. With Sylvia still holding the reins, we found ourselves on the open road and I made another attempt to get her to leave, but she just kept on driving. When we had come a good kilometre away from the town, I stopped Action and told her firmly that it was time for her to return home. It suddenly dawned on me that she had not realised we were leaving for good, but thought we were simply taking a drive. When she finally understood, tears sprang from her eyes and she jumped down from the caravan, looked up at me, then turned and ran back towards Kosani, loud sobs racking her body at every step. Even after she had vanished from sight, I could still hear her and I sat for a minute or two contemplating her loyalty and devotion to Action, Max and me. I could feel my own emotions about to overcome me. It was time to take up the reins and drive on.

The heat of the day was becoming intolerable now, and all three of us were showing signs of tiredness. Action sweated profusely all the time he was pulling the caravan and Max would only take the horsebox a short distance ahead and either walk or cycle back to me in temperatures over 100°F and no shade anywhere. The roads through the mountainous countryside continually took us uphill or down, and Max could not ride in the caravan, as it would have made extra work for the horse, so he and I would have to walk. Even riding in the caravan to drive Action meant standing in the roasting sun and was almost as bad as walking. I had made up my mind that once we reached Veria we should alter our routine, make an early start in the mornings, rest at the hottest part of the day and resume our journey in late afternoon. Action, however, really needed something done to help him before then.

The answer to his problems lay in a large umbrella which the manager of the Beefeater Inn at Harlow had given us. We managed somehow to fix it between the shafts so that it gave shade to his head and back. In solving the first problem, we managed to create two more. At the beginning, Action was disturbed by the umbrella shaking and billowing when he was walking along under it. It also blocked my view when I was driving him from the caravan. I had to hang out sideways to watch for oncoming traffic: not the safest or most comfortable arrangement. Action soon grew accustomed to the umbrella and before long was walking under its shade as if it had always been there.

We had begun to make more use of the video camera and were also taking many still photographs, in black and white as well as colour, mostly in the handicapped homes we visited. Many of our video tapes and photographs were subsequently stolen from us, which is not to say that we had avoided having things stolen from us before this. We had lost, amongst other things, a tether chain, a bicycle, an oil lamp, a head collar and a radio already. Action sometimes had a chance to turn the tables in our favour by diving his head into women's shopping bags, having learnt that most of the titbits he was given by members of the public had been taken out of these. Occasionally, he would catch people unawares, particularly children with ice creams.

As we progressed, we observed a change in the type of agriculture practised and were amazed by the number of horse or donkey-drawn carts we came upon. We also saw more cattle, pigs, sheep and goats roaming the mountains. Men in trilby hats or caps, always with their bodies covered, worked as herdsmen or in the fields, cutting grass every night to feed the stock. There was very little agricultural machinery in evidence. Most of the elderly village women wore black, long dresses, and shawls which they either had wrapped round their shoulders or used as headscarves. The women in the villages walked about with covers on their heads, often made of newspaper, to shield them from the powerful sun. From one o'clock in the afternoon, the village streets would be deserted and every cottage would have its shutters closed to exclude the heat. Draught horses would be tethered in the shade of trees, their drivers asleep at their sides, waiting for the sun to lose its strength and they could return to their work in the fields in the evening.

I was surprised at the general air of untidiness I found in Greece, with its small, neglected gardens, semi derelict houses and pot – holed main roads. Lesser roads were little better than tracks covered with gravel or soil, and on the many occasions when we had to use them we found ourselves swaying in the caravan, which took a terrible pounding as the wheels cracked and crunched their way over the rough surfaces.

I had already spent some time asking myself why we had to have wooden wheels, since they gave so much trouble. Pneumatic tyres would have given us a softer ride and suffered no more than a puncture now and then. I always told myself that it was right and traditional to use wooden wheels, and something of a challenge, since so many wiseacres had told me they would never last all the way. I wanted to prove these people wrong. Besides all that, they do look nice, but I sincerely wished I had brought a spare set along. The things most people found intriguing about us were those wheels and Action. Greek men kept asking me what price I would take for the horse, and I know I could have sold him dozens of times and asked my own price – money or anything else I wanted.

All the time we had been in Greece, the only contact we had had with the police was a friendly wave when they drove past us.

In the old part of Veria, we found a small car park just off the main square; in one corner stood a large mulberry tree surrounded by burnt grass, and I tethered Action there and fed him with hay I had stolen from a haystack the night before. It is not my custom to steal hay, but I had come to the position where I had none and could not let the horse go hungry after a day of heavy pulling. I had taken no more than I really needed and I said my silent thanks to the unknown farmer from whose stack it came.

We had not been stopped long before we had a crowd of dark skinned, gaily clad children about us. I knew at once that they were Gipsy children with something of a Turkish touch about them. They seemed scared to come too close while there were other children in the vicinity, but once the others had thinned out they came up and stroked Action, feeding him with handfuls of what little grass there was. Then one Gipsy girl shinned up the mulberry tree with the agility of a monkey and began to pick the fruit, which she shared between her friends and us. They included Action in the share – out until I stopped them, afraid he would get diarrhoea.

The Gipsy girls were our helpers and companions for the next two days, helping us get food and water, giving us directions and showing us around. Everybody seemed to know them, and communication was easy in spite of their lack of English. One evening they treated us to a display of their traditional dancing, bodies swaying, fingers clicking, arms twisting. It was all beautiful and quite different from the formal shows they put on in hotels for the tourists. This was dancing just the way they performed it at their own camp fires, at night, after a day travelling. The only reward they would accept was a ride in the caravan. By pointing at my watch, I conveyed to the eldest girl that we would be in the main square at 6 o'clock and would be happy to give all her friends a ride.

We arrived at six to find dozens of children waiting for us. We toured the town square, which is surrounded by bars and restaurants with outside tables full of locals who wanted us to stop and eat with them, or drink ouzo, brandy, wine and beer. Most of the customers were poor agricultural or factory workers. At one bar, I happened to mention my need of hay. I offered to pay for it. Within a few minutes a pick – up containing six bales arrived. I was told it came fresh picked from the fields and the old farmer would take nothing for it. He simply wanted a photograph of us as a souvenir.

The incident set me thinking that I could have raised a lot of cash for handicapped homes if I had come equipped with postcards of Action and the caravan. Many people photographed us, but many others were not carrying cameras when they came to see us after watching us on television or hearing about us through the radio or newspapers. I decided to get fifty copies made of a good photograph and try selling these to see how I got on, and they sold out in no time.

The busiest street in Veria is a pedestrianised promenade, a straight street lined with trees and flowers and it was packed with people when we drove from the main square out through the town. I have never seen so many children. There were police to guard them and hold them back as we drove through. When we pulled up by the curb, a massive surge of children gathered round us to look at the posters on our caravan's canvas sides. We were kept busy for more than three and a half hours, giving rides up and down the promenade until after it had grown dark.

A man brought a sack of oats for Action and others brought us food. We were offered a great deal of money, but we refused to accept it for two reasons: we had no permit to collect and we had not yet made contact with the handicapped organisation in Veria.

We got back to our parking spot on the car park and discovered bags containing food and drink tied to the tailboard of the horsebox. There was nothing to say who had brought it, and when we looked at what we had been given we found fruit and vegetables, apples, peaches, cherries, lettuces, tomatoes, peppers, onions, cheese, bread and, most surprising to me, butter. If there was any one thing I missed while I was away from home, it was butter to put on my bread. I racked my brains to try and remember if I had mentioned this to anyone, but I could not think who it might have been.

I awoke to find the car park full, and it was going to be difficult to manoeuvre ourselves out. Action managed a delicate ten–point turn to get the caravan into the clear centre aisle of the car park, and I took him from the shafts, let them fall onto the ground and led him to his food. I heard a sudden bang and a crunch. A car had managed to stop, straddling the shafts. Max shouted to me about the idiot driver pulling forward and running over them. The driver got out of his car and examined it for damage. He could find nothing amiss, which is more than could be said for our caravan. One arm of the shafts was snapped through.

"Now we're in it, Dad," Max groaned.

I remained optimistic, however. We had had accidents in the past and always found some kind person to help us out of a mess, often without cost to ourselves. There were several lengths of wood scattered about the car park, and some lengths of discarded wire, so we made a splint from two pieces of wood and bound it to the sides of the shaft with wire tightened with a screwdriver, after the manner of a tourniquet. Then we bound it again with rope and found ourselves with a serviceable, if temporary repair that would keep us going until we could get a proper job made of it. While a crowd gathered to watch us at work, the errant and embarrassed driver had got back in his car and slunk away.

The Gipsy girls became sad when the time came for us to leave Veria. There was no more laughing and joking as they saw us making preparations to depart. Two of them stood stroking Action and one stood on the caravan steps. This girl called me to her, removed a gold chain from her neck and held it to me, pointing to my own neck and talking in rapid Greek. Tears spilled down her face, and I felt them wet against mine when she gave me a kiss on the cheek. Then she jumped lightly down from the step, ran to Action, buried her face in his neck and bade him a sorrowful farewell.

When Max and I pulled away, we experienced the now familiar anguish at parting from dear, kind people. In Veria, these kind people had been the children. My inner turmoil at departures would grow yet more painful when we travelled through Eastern Europe and met kind people who put themselves in physical danger on our account.

We now found ourselves going through roads busy with carts and lorries carrying fruit, peaches, melons and nectarines. We were on our way to Alexandria, famous as the birth place of Alexander the Great, where contact had been made by the Veria scouts. We had been told to make for the scout H.Q., which we found in a side street. A number of scouts were waiting with a welcome and food for us. Their Chief, Antoni Stylianidis, was a large man of middle age and with a delightful nature. After our visit, Antoni Stylianidis wrote out a letter of introduction for us in Greek, which an English speaking scout translated for me.[1] He also telephoned to the scouts in Thessaloniki, towards which we would soon be driving.

That evening, we met a man called Georgi, a teacher of English in

---

1 See end of chapter for text of the letter.

the local school, who fed us and, next day, took us along to meet some of his students.

As we approached Thessaloniki we came close to the sea again, leaving the mountains behind us, for which I was not sorry, for it had been such hard work crossing them. Worse than the mountains was the heat of the day, now 110°F and higher. Thessaloniki is Greece's second largest city, supporting a population of some 750,000. It has a university and many splendid buildings, broad streets, squares and monuments, and was founded in about 315 BC by King Cassander, who named it in honour of his wife. We arrived on a Sunday afternoon and found ourselves in a massive fresh food market in the town centre. The traders had already started to pack up, but seeing us appear they began to gather round. Soon Action was out of the shafts and being fed on a great variety of fruit and vegetables. One man took us into a café and treated us to meat balls, coffee and lemonade. The market was covered, and therefore cool, but also very smelly. We left Action to be looked after by one of the traders when we went to eat. When we returned, we found Action and the caravan being adorned with flowers by a woman flower-seller.

We asked the traders how we found the scout H.Q., and one of them drove ahead of us towards the sea, which we imagined would always be blue and clean around the Greek coastline. We came to the waterfront lined with bars, hotels and restaurants, but the sea was a dirty brown in colour, smelled of sewage and soapsuds and assailed the nostrils with a burning sensation. Small wonder is it that no-one swims here. The promenade is large and surrounded by lawns green and lush. Action's eyes lit up at the sight of it.

Two men, who spoke English, met us at the scout H.Q. and told us to put the horse and caravan in the back yard, which was surrounded by buildings and totally devoid of any greenery or shade except that provided by the caravan itself. This oven was to be our home for four days, during which the temperature soared to 120°F and there was just no air movement at all. We could not walk Action by day while the heat continued.

That first night, we were bitten all over by mosquitoes. I thought I was bad until I saw Max, who had forty-three bites on various parts of his body. He had to scratch them, the itching was so terrible, and he made them bleed. He began to look like a case of impetigo and was driven almost insane in bed at night, unable to get to sleep. Although I was also badly bitten, I managed to get some sleep and was not nearly as badly affected as he.

It was Action's neighing that woke me. The atmosphere inside the caravan was stifling and I was itching all over from insect bites. Action gave another neigh as I opened the caravan door, but this time it sounded a note of distress. I ran to him, but he had his eyes fixed on something or someone beyond me; the sound of running water and a man filling his bucket. I had left water for him the previous evening, but he had probably kicked the bucket over and was now very thirsty. When the man set the bucket down, he emptied it in no time, and also a second. The time was only eight o'clock and the temperature was already creeping into the nineties. The heat of midday was not to be contemplated.

Max got up slowly and painfully, his body now a mass of bites, and I wondered why it was that he always got more attention from the creatures than I did. The scouts arrived at nine – thirty and said radio and television people were waiting at the television studio and they wanted to film us walking towards it. The same studio also served the radio broadcasters, who wanted to do a live interview. Having satisfied the media, we went back to the Scout H.Q.

Action had run out of hay and the only available grass was in the verges and lawns along the seafront, which were watered regularly. Having no alternative, I took him to the nearest bit of lawn, where the grass stood three inches high, and let him get stuck into it. Several people passed on foot, some smiling, some displeased. A car driver pulled up and gesticulated angrily to me to remove myself and my horse and two workmen tried to pacify him. It looked as if things could turn nasty, so I gathered Action's rope and began to lead him away, when one of the workmen took the rope from my hand and led Action back to the grass. The car driver went away.

This situation did not last long, however, for two officious looking men arrived and told me to remove Action or the police would be called. I removed the horse. The problem of fodder was resolved in another way. In the early morning and again at night, for the rest of our time there, I would take a knife, go down on my knees and cut enough grass to fill a bag for him. Even in Greece, that summer was seeing record high temperatures, and travel was impossible.

It was arranged for us, escorted by police, to take the caravan onto the promenade, a pedestrianised area, at half past seven in the evening. Everyone was outdoors, and we attracted the largest crowd we would get. After the usual question and answer session and people flocking round to read the publicity posters, a woman came up and offered to arrange visits for us to two handicapped homes. We told her where to find us again. We were still out on the streets of Thessaloniki at 1.30 a.m. along with half the population. Bars and restaurants seemed to be open and busy.

A message came to confirm the visits to the homes, which lay close together on the outskirts of the town. They wanted us to take horse and caravan. The young scout who spoke English was delegated to escort us. At the first home a reporter was waiting for us. He said he syndicated to twelve newspapers from all parts of Greece. We gave him an interview before going into the impressive, newly built, well equipped home, which reminded me of some we had seen in Germany. However, this home was built by private subscriptions and the handicapped people paid to be there.

The next home was a few kilometres away, at the top of a winding hill road. It was a beautifully kept, large, older house, several stories high and in its own grounds. Our guide was the young doctor who met us on arrival. The ground floor had mostly wheelchair bound patients, and was clean but shabby. Staircases connected the floors, and as we went up and up, the degree of handicap we saw became more severe. The top storey was where we were shown a room with seventeen close packed beds containing limbless, deformed or mentally handicapped patients. As they could not understand our talk, the doctor was able to tell us about them. They were all adults, almost all incontinent and requiring constant attention. They had comfortable beds with spotless white sheets, and their room had a large window overlooking lovely gardens below, but a steel grid covered its glass.

Our young scout escort was upset at the sights he saw, but he had to act as interpreter for us when the doctor beckoned the two members of staff on duty in the room to come and speak to us. The youngish man was in a white coat and the elderly woman in a green smock. The doctor was wanted elsewhere in the hospital and had to leave us. I began to question the man in the white coat. He had served there for twelve years and the woman had worked at the place for many years, and these were the only two members of staff on duty at one time. There were two shifts: day and night. I have always tried to discover the patient : staff ratio in various institutions we visited, and now I asked why there were only two people on duty in a ward like this with so many patients. The answer was simple: it was a state run place and funds were inadequate to permit more staff to be employed.

I glanced through the steel clad window and down at the garden, before asking how often these patients were taken down to visit it. He told me they could not take them downstairs, with just the two to carry them, and the place had no lifts. He could have carried one at a time, on his back, but the woman would then be left alone with the rest of them. I was certain there were other things he wanted to tell me. He said that in order to bath the patients, they had to be carried downstairs to the nearest bathroom, and they required bathing once or twice daily, but under the circumstances they could only have a bath every three or four days, in rotation.

He was visibly upset by what he was telling us.

"Do any of them get visitors?" I asked.

"No. Their families are ashamed of them," the woman said.

The male nurse stood silent, his eyes fixed on me.

"It's a lovely day. Surely, such patients have as much right as we to feel the sun, hear the leaves rustling and birds singing."

"Yes," said the woman, "But if they were to go out there, they would not understand."

"But," I retorted quickly, that is no reason to deny them the rights of normal people. To do that is to impose a life sentence upon them."

At this, the male nurse broke down in tears and fled the room. I followed after him, aware that I had overstepped the mark. The scout was at my heels.

"Please, tell him I am not blaming him for anything," I begged.

"I believe he knows that," said the scout. "He is just ashamed that he cannot do more and he knows you are right."

We found the man slumped on a chair on a landing. He now had himself under control and I apologised for my outburst.

"You are right. I just don't know how to change things," he said.

Max had been lying down, trying to get relief from earache and mosquito bites. When I got back to the caravan, I woke him up and told him about what I had said to the nurse and his reaction. I deeply regretted being so insensitive with a man who was doing his best, and doing it with great humanity.

On my way back to the cauldron of heat at the Scout H.Q., a man had come up to me with a bundled handkerchief. He thrust it into my hand and darted away. When I opened the bundle, I found a wad of money, but I had no idea what it was for. Later, when I met the woman who had arranged our visits to the homes, I gave her the money to dispose of where it was most needed.

The time had come for us to leave Thessaloniki and make towards the Bulgarian border. The Scout Chief had suggested us going to the Bulgarian Embassy in the town, showing them all the letters and articles we had collected in Greece, and asking them to assist us in obtaining entry visas. He had arranged for us to take ourselves off to a horse farm at Litti, a village fifteen kilometres out of Thessaloniki. They had a stable for Action and a parking place sorted out for us. The owners of this farm, Georgi and Antheola made us very welcome. Max was rather poorly by now and needed rest. The daytime temperature in these early July days was punishing and still rising.

My face was already familiar to the Embassy staff, who had seen it on television, and they said we could have visas, but these would take some days to process. Not wishing to pass up this opportunity to get them, we had to hang around, almost passing out at times, under a roasting sun. Max was slow and lethargic, but he came with me each evening to visit a different village and give the children rides in the caravan.

The shops in Litti provided us with bread, cheese and salad vegetables, and we drank cold coffee shaken like a cocktail. There was a hose at the garage where we had parked, and its water, warmed by the sun, served us for washing ourselves. One night we saw flames, in the far distance, which grew bigger and bigger. The locals told us a piece of land 10 x 5 kilometres in extent was on fire and the fire was moving in our direction. This news had the farmers out with their ploughs, creating an eight feet wide firebreak around the edge of their fields. The fire had already left many farms and other buildings smouldering in its wake.

The villagers from the whole district worked for two days before the fire was brought under control, when it was less than a mile away from us.

Max went to collect our visas from the Bulgarian Embassy. The man we had met before was absent, but the visas were there. They wanted 5,400 drachma for them and Max paid with six 100 drachma notes. There was no change forthcoming. He just received a nod that said – "Get going, mate. We've done our bit".

While he was at the Embassy, I went to the bank to change £200 worth of traveller's cheques into drachma, for I had been told it was difficult to change big cheques in Bulgaria and there were only a few large hotels that could do it. I accepted a handful of 100,000 drachma notes and left the bank feeling happy. I still had a lot to learn about changing money abroad, however.

When we left Litti and made our way towards Bulgaria, we stopped on the first night at the roadside, somewhere in the country. Opposite us was a drive leading to some buildings. A car drove up and the driver got out and signalled for us to follow him along this drive, which led to a brickworks, of which he was the manager. He was living in a shack next to it. He let us park beside this shack and found a paddock for Action, then he shared his evening meal of salami, tomatoes, cucumber and onion with us.

In the morning, he took us to see round the brickyard, where most of the workers were women and young girls. Everyone knew about us, as they came from the surrounding villages, where we had given rides to the children.

The text of a letter, written in English, from the Committee of Greek Scouts, Mathias District, Alexandria, Naousis Street, N.9.

The local committee of Scouts of Alexandria congratulate Bill and his Son, Max, full of love for all the people and particularly for the problems of children all over the world, who set off on a very difficult indeed journey of love, showing that today the spirit of scouting lives all over the world.

Let them be bright examples of love to these young people in the difficult times we live in. Let the young people, our children, look at these simple people and see that there is always a bit of love for everybody today.

And again, "Well done", our brother Scout. Take with you our love and give it to other countries and tell them that the Greek heart beats for every man on the earth, with a hope for a better future.

My best wishes for your journey,

The Local Inspector,
Antoni Stylianidis.

Chapter Eighteen

A Farewell to Greece and a Welcome in Bulgaria[1]

Kilkis, a small northern town, was to be nothing more than a stopping place for the night, as we had made no arrangements to meet anyone there, but when we pulled up at an ice – cream shop a crowd quickly gathered, and a man and wife who spoke English entered into conversation with us. After they had read our publicity posters, they asked if we had anywhere to spend the night and offered to let us go to their place on the edge of town, where there was plenty of room for the vehicles and a paddock for our horse.

We followed their car out to the end of a *cul – de – sac* where they had the last bungalow in the row, a large place with a wonderful display of bright flowers and greenery. Stavros and his wife, Sula, lived here with their daughter, Effi. They helped us put Action into the paddock and then we were taken to shower, not indoors, but to a building with a large steel water tank on its roof. Stavros explained that for nine months of the year the water is heated by the sun, and he was quite right. Hot water cascaded from the shower head on our bodies that had become used to cold water from a a hose pipe. It was sheer luxury. After our ablutions, we were taken to eat. The table was laden with soup followed by salami, salad and cheeses.

Next morning I woke to hear the sound of horses galloping. From my bed I could see Action, pursued by another horse, chasing across a field of stubble. Two men were chasing after them, and I yelled for Max to come and help me. For an hour or more we chased the two horses from one corner of the field to the other. If one came close, the other romped away and the first followed. Action was evidently having a whale of a time and the only way to catch him was with food. I pinched two apples from Sula's fruit bowl and managed to tempt Action until I had him cornered. The second horse kept his distance, watching what was happening. There was no way he was going to let himself be caught, but knowing the way one horse will follow another, we led Action across to the bungalow and his friend dutifully tagged along behind. He was owned by a farmer from along the road, so I returned him to his barn by leading Action there and, once the horse was safely inside, getting Action away again as fast as I could. The farmer was very grateful to

---

1 Proper names have been omitted to protect our friends

us for this small service.

I told Stavros and Sula about my intention to enter Bulgaria, illegally if needs must, in spite of all the advice I had been given not to try and enter the Eastern European countries at all. One woman had told us we should meet nothing but thieves and villains. It is true that we were to meet our share, but there were other, decent people in the east as well.

Sula told us she could write in the Bulgarian language and offered to rewrite our posters, so that when we came to the border the immigration officers would understand our aims. Stavros sent his daughter to enquire about getting a supply of hay to carry Action through the next few days. She came back with a man who said he would take us in the horsebox to collect some that evening. He wanted to know, however, if we wanted fresh or old, said Stavros. Thinking he meant fresh cut hay, I said we wanted fresh.

The man called for us at 6 o'clock and sat beside Max, who was driving. We went on for miles along a road with clumps of trees at 20 yard intervals. As we came to each clump, the man glanced skywards, but I took little notice until he tapped my arm and asked us to stop beside a tall tree covered in big, green leaves. We were in the middle of nowhere, not a house to be seen. He jumped down from the horsebox, a bag in his hands. He took a chopper from the bag and set about climbing into the branches and chopping them off. When he climbed down again, the tree was devastated. He told us to open the horsebox and began to ram the bits of tree inside.

"This is your fresh feed, Dad," said Max with a wry smile. "Half a tree!"

I looked at Max and he shrugged his shoulders and began to help the man cram the horsebox with branches and leaves. The man was smiling contentedly, feeling that he had helped us. We all climbed into the vehicle and drove back towards the Stavros house. Before we got quite that far, the man asked to be set down. He shook me by the hand and walked off.

"What the bloody hell do we want with all this lot?" Max asked as soon as the man was out of earshot. "There's no way Action can eat it."

The matter was serious, but it had its funny side. When we got to the house and Stavros came out, I opened the tail-gate to show him what we had been given, intending to try and break gently to him the news that what we had was useless and we must have proper hay. As branches began spilling onto the ground, Stavros clapped a hand over his mouth to stop the laughter.

"That's food for goats, not horses," he chuckled, bent over the fence in hysterical laughter.

Bales of hay from another friend of Stavros arrived later that night. We took Action into town in the evening, and a man stopped us to invite me and Max into a bar to take a drink with him. He spoke good English and, in the course of our conversation, mentioned that his father had died recently and that he had an aunt living in Bulgaria. He told us where she was living, and asked if it lay on our route. I told him it certainly did, knowing that, true or not, it was worth getting hold of an address to give as our destination when we got to the border. I knew enough about entry requirements to all the Eastern European countries, to realise that an address was essential.

The man said his aunt had not been told of the death of her brother, and he had not written to tell her, since letters she had sent in the past had never arrived. He asked if we would be prepared to take a letter for her, and when I agreed, he promised to bring it to Stavros's house for me on the following day.

"If you have second thoughts about it, because it could be too dangerous, I shall understand," he said.

When he came with the letter, it was sealed in an envelope. Max was dubious about the whole thing.

"We don't know what's written in the letter, Dad," he said. "It might get us into trouble."

I suspected that he might be right, and I hid the letter behind the lining of the caravan door.

As we thought back over the kindness of the Greek people, people like Stavros and his friends, we wondered how we should fare once we were inside Bulgaria, assuming we ever got that far.

We got to the Greek border at 3 o'clock, after an uneventful drive, and found that it was, as usual, easy to leave a country. Within a few minutes we were out of Greece. Ahead lay Bulgaria, the country that had told us firmly we were not wanted.

Greece had tested our determination to reach our goal; the heat, flies, mosquitoes and bugs had made it misery to travel, and the real truth about Greece is that it is a dirty place, covered with litter and rubbish. The Greek people make up for all that by their kindness and gentle manners. Help was always just around the corner, and although the north, through which we journeyed, is poor, mountainous and rugged, we had freedom to travel anywhere, to visit homes and institutions without permits and paperwork. The Greek police gave us no bother; they left us well alone.

The handicapped homes were of rather a mixture. Those run by the state were not as good as those run privately. The people seemed to be a carefree lot, who enjoyed night life. The food was plentiful but plain.

My strongest memories concern Action, who exhibited his strength and character when he endured the searing heat and the lack of fresh grass and shade. He showed his quality by working even at those times when the native Greek horses were resting in the shade. He was great.

I halted Action at the border post in Kulata, shouting at the horse, trying to sound commanding and in charge of things. A customs officer sat on a stool, just watching wordlessly. A second man, in uniform and with lots of gold braid, soon joined the first. He looked like a police officer. I smiled at him and handed over our passports. He gave them a rapid glance before throwing them back.

"English, eh!" he grunted. "What do you want in Bulgaria?"

As he spoke such good English, I told him we wanted to cross Bulgaria to reach Romania. I hissed at Max to fetch the folder that had facilitated so many previous border crossings. The contents had been arranged in such a way that the message was got across in the first few pages. Both men began to scan the contents, then the uniformed man told us to wait where we were. The pair vanished inside a building with the folder. Ten minutes later they came back with some simple forms for us to complete with our names, vehicle details, our ages, addresses and such. While we wrote, the men wandered round the horsebox and caravan, stopping occasionally to read the posters.

I handed back the completed forms while one man explored the interior of the caravan, touching our souvenirs and personal belongings. Another man stood by Action's head. With so many officials around me I felt tense. It crossed my mind that they were not going to let us in.

"What is your destination?" one man asked.

"To this address," Max said, alert to the question and now producing a copy he had made behind my back of the address we had been given by the Greek man.

"You have thirty hours to cross Bulgaria," he said, echoing the words I had been longing to hear. I smiled my thanks. We had been given time limits before, for other countries, and found a way to circumvent them when necessary.

"Horse documents next," said the man.

I gave him the folder of papers we had accumulated in various countries, now quite a sizeable packet. I assumed he would be confused by seeing so much paperwork, the topmost page of which was from our own British Ministry of Agriculture, Fisheries and Food. He took it into the office, and when he came back it bore an official looking stamp. The bluff had worked yet again. None of the papers were of much use to anybody, had he but known it.

"Go to the visa office and get a 30 day visa," he said. When we went, they charged us about 30DM and the man issuing the visa said what sounded to us like 5 – day visa, as if it was only a transit visa to see us across the country. By this stage, Max and I knew when to keep our mouths shut. We went back to the caravan wondering what to do next. A soldier beckoned us to move forward and he began to lift the barrier.

"Let's go quickly, Dad, before they change their minds," Max said.

I urged Action to move and went through the barrier and up the road without a backward glance. We saw a long line of cars queuing up to leave Bulgaria, but there had been nobody apart from us making their way into the country. I wondered why that should be.

Action trotted steadily along until we were a few kilometres inside Bulgaria and a car pulled up in front of us. Five young men in their twenties emerged and came up to us.

"They're customs men," Max screamed. "Something's wrong."

However, they were just friendly and curious. When we discovered that one spoke English, we produced the folder and he read aloud a newspaper article in Greek. When he finished reading, two of the men ran off into a plantation of trees near the roadside. The others rubbed their bellies and pointed at their mouths. I thought at first that they were Greeks, but they were actually Bulgarians.

"They want us to eat with them," Max said.

The two men came back carrying a box of peaches which they thrust in through the door of the caravan before jumping back into their car and speeding off. It was a strange and unexpected encounter.

We were on a good, smooth road and making good progress when we came upon what appeared to be a primitive sort of restaurant. Next to this was a rough looking car park. Waiting here were our five friends with their car.

"We might as well park here for the night," I proposed, and we unhitched Action, gave him water and prepared to make ourselves a drink. The five men were hovering round the caravan. One of them took my arm suddenly and led me towards the restaurant, and Max followed with the others. They sat us down at a table and ordered beer and wine, followed by food consisting of cucumbers, tomatoes, onions and sliced meat. While we ate, we managed to convey to them our intention to visit handicapped homes in Bulgaria. In spite of their generosity towards us, Max and I kept remembering the warnings we had been given and we kept our wits about us, just in case they meant to harm or rob us.

One of the men drew a map of the road we were on, the E79 to Sofia, then he marked a turning off to somewhere called Stob, where he said there was a children's home. They left us soon afterwards, asking nothing of us in return for their hospitality.

"If all Bulgarians are as good as those," said Max, "It will be a doddle."

We got back to the caravan and, at 12.30, the police arrived and asked to see our passports. We handed them over, saying "British in transit from Scotland to China". While one man studied the passports, the other looked around the caravan. The first man said we could not park where we were. Tourists were only permitted to camp at proper sites or stay in hotels. We knew it was forbidden to park at the roadside in Bulgaria, especially if one was a tourist. There were two reasons for this rule: the first was for the safety of the tourist and the second was to part him from his western currency. When the second man returned from his tour of inspection, they conferred together for a moment, then one said we could stay the night where we were after all, but we must be on our way again by 7 o'clock next morning.

"We don't need this shit all the time," bawled Max, still with the courage of alcohol and not having heard anything of the conversation. Fortunately, the men did not understand him and let it pass.

We woke at 8 o'clock next morning to see two police cars parked beside us. One contained the officers we had met the night before. The two men in the second car walked over to Action, looked at us and laughed, then walked away. We wasted no time in packing up and setting off towards Sofija. Max noticed that some of our stickers were missing from the caravan and horsebox, and we remembered seeing a bunch of youths on scooters and motorcycles around the restaurant on the previous night. We assumed these youths had stolen the stickers. As we travelled through Bulgaria, Romania and

Russia, we quickly learnt how sought after this type of thing is and what lengths people would go to in order to obtain them.

Max told me that, after I had fallen asleep, these youths had come to talk to him, to ask for blue jeans, cigarettes, razors, after–shave, condoms and soap. To get rid of them he had given them some of our spare stickers and they had given him in exchange a bracelet: the rubber ring off an oil filter. It was the first of many souvenirs from Bulgaria.

The weather was not greatly improved, still up in the high nineties. We found the turning indicated on the map we had been given and saw a lay–by just beyond this point. As we pulled in we were met by a man and woman piled high with back packs and holdalls. They were evidently hikers. The woman dropped her luggage and ran towards us.

"Hello," she said. "We are from East Germany. I cannot believe what we see. Last week, before we came on holiday, we saw you on East German television. We live in Dresden."

The husband came up and joined us.

"It is not possible for you to have seen us on East German television," I told her. "We have not been to East Germany."

"We have certainly seen you on our television," the husband confirmed.

We spent time talking with them and they told us some facts about life in their homeland. They told us about the travel restrictions, the shortages and the low standard of living for most East Germans. We left them and continued on our way to Stob. I had already noticed that Bulgarian roads are free of litter and abandoned vehicles, unlike Greece with its mess everywhere.

We came to a small village and saw an old woman spreading tobacco leaves on the pavement to dry in the sun. Others were threading leaves on a string and hanging them up to dry in the air. Just beyond the village, where the road turns towards Stob, we came to a little bar, where we stopped. I took Action from the shafts and let him graze the roadside verges.

"Look out, Dad," said Max. "There's a lady coming."

I looked round and saw a short, plump woman bearing down on me. She unleashed a torrent of Bulgarian and I thought she was telling me off, but she had a kind face, though careworn and tired. She went to Action to make a fuss of him, before returning to the bar. I was uncertain what was going on, but presently the woman came back with a bag which she gave to Max. Inside it was a loaf, some chicken, salami, cheese and tomato. She thrust it into his hands and hurried back to the bar. Max and I wasted no time in tucking into the food.

The bar had a covered patio with tables and chairs where one could eat or drink outdoors.

"Let's have a glass of pop before we move on," I proposed.

We sat at one of the tables and waited to be served. Around us sat several men drinking bottled beer and eating small salads. There were no labels on the beer bottles, which puzzled me until I remembered that beer is a state monopoly, so there was no need to advertise it with a label. The brown glass of the bottle was enough to say what it contained. A large, strong, young man approached and told us his name. Pointing to the lady who had given us food, he told us she was his mother. He asked if we would like a drink, and fetched us two bottles of beer and two bottles of lime pop. Then he invited us to eat with himself and his mother. I was very surprised to get such a warm welcome from people who knew nothing at all about us.

Action had also drawn a crowd of admirers from among the local menfolk, one of whom had fetched hay from a stack and was feeding him. Several of them were carters and had their own horses and carts standing around. Their animals were very small in comparison with Action, on average about twelve hands high, with thin legs and small hooves, but well cared for. The V–shaped carts were painted yellow and had wooden wheels with steel rims, and wooden shafts. Their harnesses looked poor, well worn and frequently patched, some held together with string and rope.

"My mother and I run this bar," our young man said in careful, if broken, English. "We know where you want to go. It is a home for orphaned children, children with learning difficulties and children with problems at home. You will find it two kilometres away."

We thanked them for their help and set off again towards Stob.

"Why did they make us so welcome, and how did they know we wanted to visit the home in Stob?" Max asked.

"I think I know the answer, Max. The men we met last night must have called here and warned them we would be coming this way. They were the only people who knew our plans," I explained.

"And the police," Max reminded me.

We went a bit further along the road and were stopped by a small party of three adults and two children. It was an East German couple and their two children, who were being shown round Bulgaria by a Bulgarian woman guide with a very good command of English. After we had all spoken together for a time and I had showed her our folder, I felt confident enough to ask for help. I explained that we wanted to visit the children's home in Stob, but that no arrangements had been made for our visit, then I asked if the guide would kindly come with us and act as interpreter. After having a quick word with the German couple, she said they would all come.

We lifted the two children into the caravan and Max walked behind with the three adults.

We found in Stob a large square surrounded by big buildings, shops and a post office, just like any other village square, with the exception of an absence of motor vehicles. There were many horses and carts rumbling over the cobbled streets, however. Our Bulgarian guide began to ask for directions to the home, and was told it could be found up the hill on the right. We took the rough track filled with potholes that were hard on the caravan wheels. Suddenly, Max shouted that he had spotted the place. It was an old building standing fifty yards down an unmade dirt track.

"I can't get the caravan down there, Max," I groaned. "Just look at the size of those ruts and boulders. We'll park here, by the side of the road. You stay with Action and I'll go ahead with the lady and see what's what."

"Remember, Dad, we have no permission to visit homes and only a visa for five days, so be careful, and remember not to do any filming. It's too dangerous," Max warned.

As we approached the building, a handful of children ran towards us. They had already seen the horse and caravan and were shouting excitedly. Many had bare feet and all wore dirty clothes, tatty rather than in holes. Most of the boys and girls had dark Gipsy complexions. Two women came after them. They wore flowered frocks with plain green aprons tied over them. Our translator explained our presence and said we wanted to give the children rides in the caravan and visit the home. She turned to me and asked me to go and wait with Max. I went back and found Action surrounded by children and locals.

"Dad, you'll have to help me. I can't keep my eye on everything," Max said.

"Let's move him forward to that patch of grass, Max," I suggested, indicating a small patch of grass dried and brittle from the heat. It was no easy task to try and move the children back out of the way, as they were crawling all over the horse, three of them on his back and others between his legs. We managed to get most of the children away, apart from the three that were sitting on him, then I gently eased him forward. Max and I had been as patient with the little ones as possible, knowing that this was probably the first time any of them had ever seen so much as a foreigner, let alone a Westerner with horse and caravan.

Our translator came up with a neatly dressed woman in a black skirt and white blouse, whom she introduced as the director of the home. The woman spoke a few words to the children and they moved back from Action in a wave.

"She says you can come with us to the home, but you may not enter. She has to obtain permission from the authorities," explained the translator as, surrounded by a bunch of children, we all made our way towards the home. I studied the children as we walked. I could see that they had physical or domestic problems, but in general they all seemed to be happy.

There was a long table at the front of the building, with a wooden bench along either side. We were invited to sit down and have coffee. Hardly had we taken our places than a small boy aged about eight jumped onto my lap, his little bronzed body glistening in the sun. He put his arms round my neck and snuggled his face close to mine. His dirty little legs, grubby hands and black feet did nothing to put me off. I could feel his deep yearning for affection. Soon, a small girl tried to climb on me as well, so I shifted the lad to one knee and let her climb onto the other. Sitting like this, I chatted to the director and some of the staff by means of the interpreter.

I could see from the looks Max was giving me that he was touched by the sight of the little ones. Later, he told me he had been unable to decide whether I derived comfort from the children's touch, or if it had all been the other way round. I think he was probably right in both cases: I did need the love which the children gave me. Their trust gave me a great boost.

Max went to see that Action was all right, and when he came back he had the video camera with him. He could not resist the sight of those small children sitting on my lap, and although he knew the dangers of filming in Bulgaria without permission, he could not let the moment pass unrecorded.

The director and staff had been shown our folder by the guide. I could tell that they found it hard to grasp why we had come so far to visit a place like Stob. The director saw the value of the letters it contained, and she went off to write one in Bulgarian. The guide read it for me. It thanked us for our visit, wished us luck on the rest of our journey, and contained the hope that we would visit again on our return journey. It was the first such letter we had from anywhere in the Eastern Block, and I knew it would be of great assistance to us. Sadly, it was amongst the documents we had stolen from us.

Max and I had already made our minds up that the roads around the home were too rough to let us give rides, and we suggested taking everyone down to the village square. When we got there, several other children from Stob joined us. As usual, crowds quickly formed and one of the staff told them about us and our travels. The folder was displayed and the people listened attentively, even the children. Then a man who had been standing by Action also addressed them. At this point, the German family said goodbye and went off with our interpreter. Hardly had they gone when a man in a white coat came up and said in perfect English that he was the local doctor. He asked if he could help, so I explained that we wanted to give rides to the children, and we had to find a parking place for the night.

The next hour and a half saw us going round and round the square, down a slope on one side and Action twisting himself like a figure 8 to hold the caravan full of children on a steady course, a brisk trot along the bottom and a gallop uphill again. It was a great spot for the rides and caused enormous excitement among the children as the sound of the steel wheels echoed back from the enclosing buildings. The village adults helped to organise our small passengers and the doctor stood explaining what it said on the pages of our folder.

Unexpectedly, a woman came up to the doctor and told him she wanted to give us a little help on our way to China. She handed us bread, cucumbers, tomatoes, salami, apples, peaches and all manner of other food. There was no chance we could consume such a vast amount before it perished, but we accepted it gratefully, so as not to offend her. People tore whole loaves apart to feed Action and children gave him slices of ripe melons, and carters stopped their horses to give him bundles of hay. It was village hospitality of a very high order.

Action had been in the shafts for five hours now, so I unhitched him and led him towards a solitary tree. The villagers, however, had other ideas. The doctor told me to let him roam free, which I did. He wandered round the square, children running round pulling fresh grass and feeding him by hand. The sun was sinking and the air was still very warm. I watched the thinly clad children racing round enjoying themselves and reflected that it had been a good day for all of us. At last, Max suggested it was time we thought about somewhere to spend the night.

"You could stay in the square, but you would get no peace," said the doctor. "I will come back with you to the restaurant where you stopped before and ask if you can stay there again, but I would like to take you to my surgery to meet someone first."

"Dad, where are my trousers?" yelled Max from inside the caravan.

"Hanging on the hooks on the right," I told him.

"Then they've been nicked. There is no sign of them. I suppose it was those kids, when we gave them rides. I had three pairs hanging there and they've all gone."

The doctor had been absorbing this exchange and now he told the remaining onlookers what had happened. Then a commotion erupted in the crowd some feet from us. A man had a boy of about thirteen by the scruff of his neck and was pulling shirts and socks out from under his grubby T–shirt. He handed them back with an embarrassed look on his face, but there were no trousers to be seen. He cuffed the lad about the ears, and I recognised him as a lad from the home. I intervened to spare him further punishment and when the man released him, he ran sobbing back towards the home. How sad, I thought, that children should be in such need that they would steal clothes, even though they did not fit them.

Someone tapped me on the arm, and I looked down into a dirty little hand in which was one of the medals we had been given in Italy. I patted the little fellow on the head and thanked him. No word was needed. He knew he was wrong to have stolen and his guilt impelled him to hand back the loot. Not so happy was the story of Max's trousers. We never saw them again.

Two reporters awaited us in the surgery, one from a newspaper and one from a radio station. I gave interviews to both before the doctor took us back to the restaurant. The young man said we could stay there again, but we must stay round at the back, out of sight of the police, as he wanted no trouble with them. It was good for Action, who found the best grass here that he had eaten for a long time. Once again, Max and I were catered for, with the doctor as well, this time. I mentioned my need to get a fresh stock of hay.

We went to bed at half past eleven and were still awake when we heard the sound of voices and car doors. I opened the caravan door a crack and peered out into the night to see policemen standing by a car and talking with the restaurant owner. All sorts of uncomfortable thoughts crossed my mind in that instant, and I was immensely relieved when they got back in the car and drove off. I slept like a log for the rest of the night.

Next morning, I found eight bales of hay beside the caravan. Enquiries elicited nothing about the donor, simply that the hay was for us.

The restaurant owner told me he intended taking us by car to visit the Rela Monastery that morning. While he was talking, the police turned up again and Max and I felt our stomachs churning with apprehension. The restaurant owner continued by saying the policemen had arranged the visit for us and we should have our personal guide for the tour. When I looked across, they were both smiling at me.

The restaurant owner took us to the monastery by car. It was a beautiful place, built on a hillside, its interior decorated by lovely frescoes and religious texts. Max was enthralled by it, but I had other things on my mind at the time. We had to get to Sofija and sort out a few of our problems. The police had kept their promise to provide an interpreter to guide us round the monastery, and this service was free of charge.

When we got back to the restaurant, our Doctor friend was waiting for us. He said he had arranged with the administrator of a home for the elderly in another village for us to pay them a visit. When we got there we found large steel gates barring our way. We stopped Action close beside them. An old building stood some way down the drive. A woman in a blue smock saw us and came up and looked through the gates at us. Beyond her, I could see elderly people wandering about. When I tried to communicate with the woman at the gate, she withdrew.

Then a man and woman appeared and came towards us gesturing. Max said they looked none too pleased and wanted us to leave. By now we had the horse and caravan pulled across the entrance and ready to go inside, but this was not to be. The man slammed the big steel gates, making Action jump, and I thought the woman was going to faint when the horse scuffed his steel shoes on the Tarmac. She beat a hasty retreat back up the drive, closely followed by the man, who was still waving his arms and muttering. We left, thinking something had gone wrong with the doctor's arrangements.

The E79 road to Sofia had a good Tarmac surface and traversed a few low hills. It went through villages and small towns and was bounded by cultivated fields containing a variety of crops, but no hedges. Occasionally we came upon a building complex, regional communal farms, and, now and again, we saw a tractor or other farm machinery at work, but mostly there were the familiar yellow, horse – drawn carts, some with wooden wheels and some with pneumatic tyres. Parts of this road are banned to horse – drawn vehicles, which have to use instead the parallel dirt tracks which are rough and full of potholes.

The next night, when we stopped in a no – man's – land between towns and with no parking place, we were in something of a quandary. Our transit visa had expired and we had no wish to attract the attention of the Bulgarian police and be compelled to explain to them that we were heading for the British Embassy in Sofija for help. All we could do was press on. We decided to keep to the cart track and found the going better than we expected, but when it became quite dark we found ourselves in trouble. Action had already pulled for twenty miles in the hot sun and his only consolation now was the cooler air, for the temperature had fallen quite considerably since dusk. Cars pulled up sometimes and the drivers offered help. When we showed the folder it sufficed to explain our presence on the road.

Suddenly, there was a mighty crunch as the caravan's side hit against a tree. I was alert, luckily, and managed to control Action, who was ready to bolt, before he had the whole side ripped off. I jumped down and coaxed him backwards and then inspected the damage, which was not major; the wooden surround holding the canvas cover was broken in two places, allowing the cover to sag somewhat.

I wanted to stop where we were and wait for daylight, but Max insisted that we keep going in case of trouble if we were caught on the road. I reluctantly agreed and we plodded on, Max walking ahead with a torch. By 3 o'clock in the morning, we had come fourteen miles and were all tired. Then the rear end of the caravan gave a lurch and dropped. Action, thinking we had gone into a pothole, thrust forward. He was not frightened, however, and I soon had him under control. Max yelled to tell me the wheel had come off.

We hastily took Action from the shafts, as I did not want him making any more attempts to pull the caravan free while it was down on one corner. I tethered him to a tree and went back to inspect the damage. The heat and vibration had caused the steel shaft holding the wheel onto the wooden hub to come loose allowing the wheel to come off. The undercarriage was undamaged.

"Come on Max," I said, "Let's get some sleep."

We were up again by six o'clock and began working on the wheel. We used rag from my oldest shirt to pack round the shaft, which we intended to hammer home with the sledge hammer to make it firm. When Max went to fetch the hammer, it had gone. All we had left was a cast iron chock weighing about 15lbs that we used when stopping the caravan on a hill. It was an awkward shape to handle.and we took it in turns to hammer the shaft into the hub. Then we went on our way to Sofija, making regular checks on the wheels.

We walked for two days, our caravan causing extraordinary interest with the public, who found it astonishing that we could travel Bulgaria with a caravan smothered in publicity material from all the companies that had sponsored us. It would not normally be permitted over there. Many people tried to buy things from us, anything from razors to stickers.

We arrived in Sofija at lunchtime on Sunday, August 13th, and found a clean town devoid of litter. On the way in, we had been stopped by a man from the Austrian Embassy there, who was very impressed by what we were doing. He said he would approach the television company and get some publicity for us. He told us where it was and then left. I knew the value of this sort of publicity for our work for the handicapped, but against this I had the knowledge that our visa had expired, something that brought me out in a cold sweat every time a police car came near, even though the officers were only interested and curious in a friendly way.

The television studio was just outside the centre of Sofija and two policemen guarded its door. Three young men came up and asked what we wanted, and two of the three spoke English. Max said we would like to go on television, and one of the men told the policemen and ushered us inside. Within a few minutes, we were being filmed in the street, walking with Action and then we gave an interview in English, during which we described our journey. The television people assured us it would be shown on national TV news that same night.

The doctor we met in Stob had given us the address of his parents' home in Sofija, and we went off to find it. They lived in a block of flats on a housing estate. The blocks were all very plain and their block had the number 54 over the main entrance. All the East European countries numbered their housing blocks like this. Between the blocks of flats were small patches of grass with a few shrubs and trees, but no flower beds to add colour. I was to conclude, after seeing Romania and Russia, that one architect had drawn the plans for these estates and his plans had been sent to all the communist countries, who had built according to them.

A lady in a nightdress opened the door and recognised us on sight. She spoke fair English, which I suspect she had been rehearsing carefully for our benefit. She took us inside to her sitting room furnished with a settee and some easy chairs. A long, modern looking, utility wall unit stood against one wall, and in the centre of the room was a small wooden table holding a pretty little tea set. She said her son had telephoned the previous day to warn her of our arrival. We sat drinking tea and her husband came in. He invited us to come to their holiday home on the lake with them. Max looked at me in amazement. Surely, he thought, they don't have such things in a communist country like Bulgaria.

Their son, the doctor, arrived at 6 o'clock in the evening and we all set off to their holiday home, a few miles out of town. The lake had a good road running round its perimeter, reminiscent of places in Great Britain. We found the cottage standing in its own grounds just off a quiet side road. The path leading up to it was too narrow to admit the caravan, but the doctor said we could leave it on the roadside and Action could come into their garden.

The interior was sparsely furnished. The walls were white, the ceilings blue, and the wooden floor had a scattering of hand–made rugs. There was a small, pleasant garden with trees and bushes. I found it a very peaceful spot for a holiday. A young woman with her two children arrived at 8 o'clock and she sat down to dine with us. The doctor's mother fetched each course to the table, and we had chicken, potatoes and salad, followed by fresh fruit salad. We had not expected to find Bulgarians living like this.

The parents went off afterwards to wash up, leaving us with the young woman and the doctor, who told us that both his parents were doctors in Sofija. The young woman also spoke a few words of English, but it was what the young doctor said that surprised me.

"Bill, I want to ask if you can help this young woman," he began. "Her son has infantile insulin deficiency; he has diabetes and unless he gets help soon he will die." Regardless of the mother's knowledge of English, the young doctor did not mince his words. "I have tried everything I can to get help for him. Our specialists and our Health Ministry have told her that there is no treatment available for him in Bulgaria and she must accept that her son's end is inevitable. She refused to accept this answer and asked them to have him sent to the west. They cannot or will not do it."

I looked at the young woman. She had understood perfectly, as the tears on her cheek showed me.

"About a year ago," continued the young doctor, "I found out about a place in America that could treat him. She wrote at once to ask for details, but you can imagine how she felt when they wrote back to say it could be possible to treat him, but it would cost $20,000. It is impossible to amass that sort of sum over here. It would be the income for several years for a worker in Bulgaria."

"I will do anything," the woman said. "I would go to England and work for nothing, but I am not allowed to leave Bulgaria. It is a prison in this country. I considered leaving secretly with my children, but if I am caught I might never be seen again."

She continued by telling us that soon after receiving the reply from America, she had a visit from two men in dark suits, who pushed their way into the house and made a systematic and detailed search of all her belongings. She knew they were from the Secret Police and she was terrified. One of them accused her of receiving a letter from the U.S.A. concerning her child. He said that she had been told by the Bulgarian Health Ministry that the child was doomed, and that if anything like that happened again, she was in serious trouble. They left her standing in the hall trembling from head to foot. One of them turned in the doorway and asked if she understood that if such a thing were to happen again, she and her children would disappear for good. Then he slammed the door behind him.

"I knew what he meant all right. Many people go missing after they cross the authorities, but what can I do?" she asked helplessly.

"Bill, we don't want to endanger you, but with your contacts with hospitals and homes in Britain and all over Europe, could you please try and find out if there is anywhere besides America where he could receive treatment?" the doctor pleaded.

I said I would telephone a friend in Britain right away and also write to some hospitals in Europe, but the woman warned me not to do that, as all calls and all mail to the west are monitored.

"But I won't be going home for a long time yet," I explained.

"That cannot be helped," the woman said. "If we find out where such treatment is available and it is too late for my son, at least it can help other children with the same complaint."

"Mother and I have to return to work tomorrow, Bill, but if you would like to stay on here for a few days, it is fine by us," said the young doctor, breaking into my thoughts about the bravery of that young mother.

Max had been sitting quietly, head in hands, for a long time.

"Dad, I feel awful. I'm sick and giddy. I will have to go to bed," he said.

The doctor's mother made up a bed for him, as by now he was in some distress.

When the young mother and her children said goodbye, I found it hard to tear my eyes from the sick boy. I kept thinking that he would be dead by the time I reached home again. I took the woman by the hand and promised to do something for her. These words I would say again and again, in the emotion of the moment, when I heard cries for help in Romania and Russia. They would be promises I could not keep, though at the time they were well intentioned.

I was unable to get to sleep for thinking of that small boy and wondering if there really was nothing I could do to help him. Could I send a message home in code, or should I catch a plane home and then come back? As sleep overcame me at last, my thoughts became more preposterous.

I was awakened by someone tapping on the door of the caravan, and still not quite awake, I opened the door and saw a man in a grey uniform and a peaked cap with a large badge on.

"Passport. Visa," he said.

I fumbled around in the caravan, not sure where I had put the documents he wanted. He grew impatient. At last, I found them and passed them to him. He spent a long time studying both before handing them back to me. I falsely assumed that he had not spotted our visas were out of date.

"Come with me," he said, with a wave of his arm.

He led me back to the doctor's house, where the father was fetching water from the garden. The two men spent a long time in conversation, and I could see things were not going well. The doctor looked grim and nervous, and the policeman brusque and authoritarian.

"Bill, your visa is expired. You must leave this country immediately. I should not have let you stay here at my home. You must leave at once, but first we must go to the local police station to inform them which route you will take. I am very sorry." His voice betrayed the fear he felt.

I went to rouse Max, who was still feeling lousy. I explained the turn of events, and he understood that we had no choice but to obey orders. We were starting to feel the pressures of life in a communist state for the first time, but not for the last.

At the police station, the doctor did the talking for us. At length he said we must leave the country, but could stay the night on a camp site on the outskirts of Sofija, to which he would escort us. I was sorry to have given him so much worry from his association with us, and I was not surprised when he left the moment we got to the gates of the camp, as I knew he expected trouble from the authorities.

The after effects of a night collision with a tree on the unlit roads of Bulgaria.

Children of Sofija, Bulgaria, enjoying rides in the caravan.

Chapter Nineteen

Sofija and a Famous General

Once the doctor was out of sight, I turned Action around and headed off towards Sofija.

"Where are you going, Dad?" asked Max in consternation, as we left the camp site behind.

"To the British Embassy in Sofija," I said.

"But, Dad, we ought to go on the camp site first. If we wander about Sofija, we're going to end up in prison," he protested.

"I don't think so, Max," I said. "We just need to take Action and the caravan to show them what we are doing."

It had become almost instinctive with me now to take the horse and caravan to Embassies, police stations and other authorities, in place of any missing or suspect documents, for the posters and our folder of letters and cuttings always worked the trick. We found ourselves outside the British Embassy, without having been bothered by the police, and pulled up at the front door, which opened onto the pavement. Next door was a rather grand, white house of a type seldom seen anywhere in Bulgaria. Leaving Action to stand and wait, Max and I entered, although most of the staff had already come out and gathered round the horse and caravan

A young woman, speaking perfect English, asked if she could help. I hastily explained about the expired transit visa and began to tell what we had been doing in Bulgaria, when she broke in to say she knew all about us, having just seen us on television. She took us to the office of the Vice Consul, Mr. Cobden, a tall, slender man in his forties. I had with me a list of things with which we needed his help: a visa to allow us to stay in Bulgaria; permission to visit handicapped homes; permission to travel freely in the country; to get relief from the requirement to stay on official camp sites or in hotels; and to get permission from Russia for us to enter there from Romania. Time was running out on us, if we were to visit the U.S.S.R. in decent weather for travelling.

Mr. Cobden sent a telex to the British Embassy in Moscow asking them to try and sort out special entry permits enabling us to travel the country with horse and caravan. Then he made arrangements for us to call on his opposite number in the Russian Embassy in Sofija, to see if pressure could be put on the Kremlin from there, and although we were taken in a staff car, our pleading cut no ice. We were told it would have to be sorted out between the British Embassy in Moscow and Mr. Cobden in Sofija.

We got back to our own Embassy in mid-afternoon and I had not yet found an overnight parking place. Mr. Cobden said it was in order for us to take Action into the Ambassador's back garden, at the grand house next door, where there was a beautifully tended lawn. When I protested about this because of what the horse would do to the grass, Mr. Cobden said I need not worry as the Ambassador was away. So there was Action, on English grass in the centre of Sofija.

Next day, I was taken by car to meet the Chief of Police for Sofija, and once I had showed him our folder he issued a permit allowing us to tour the town, all except for three streets in the diplomatic quarter.

Mr. Cobden had also arranged for us to meet Miki, a Bulgarian holding the post of Commercial Trade Attaché, who was to help us sort out our other business. In his office, we went through the list, starting with the restrictions on choosing an overnight camping site.

"I think I know who might be able to help you," he said. "The director of the Bulgarian State Tourist Organisation, known to us as Mr. Fix-it, officially known as Vili Sabev."

Mr. Sabev was a handsome, sun tanned man with wavy hair greying at the temples. His solution was to arrange for us to use official sites, but to do so free of charge. A television crew turned up to film us outside the Embassy, and radio and newspaper reporters interviewed us, and after this Mr. Sabev began to organise our itinerary through Bulgaria, fixing with Balkantourist's State run hotels to feed us and, at night, find parking for us and Action. Having seen to all this, Mr. Sabev invited Yanka Rypkiner, a leading Bulgarian folk singer, to come and sing to the crowd from the caravan steps. He also fixed trips to monasteries and other places of interest for us.

Next day, Mr. Sabev came to give us our itinerary, which was very detailed and contained dates and addresses of camp sites, hotels, places of interest to visit, people to contact and handicapped homes for us to call on. He said everyone had been notified to expect us on the dates shown. Our first visit would be to the Union of the Blind in Sofija, where our contact was the Foreign Public Relations Officer, Morfi Scarlotov.

Mr. Scarlotov spoke good English and we found the Union of the Blind a very impressive establishment. After our visit, we were given a letter of thanks and a promise that he would make advance arrangements for us to see three other Institutes for the Blind, in Plovdiv, Russe and Varna. Mr. Sabev certainly deserved his nickname – Mr. Fix-it.

Miki, our Bulgarian friend from the Embassy, took us to lunch after we left the Union of the Blind. We went to a restaurant in the town centre and had with us also members of the British staff, some of whom we took the half mile from the Embassy to the restaurant in our caravan.

A large crowd gathered outside the restaurant to look at us and offer money, for they had already seen us on television. After the meal, the manager of the place gave us a sum equivalent to £50 to help us on our way.

We could not refuse to accept it.

There was a group of Libyans at our first camp site, and they took care of us for the next four days, gave us food and drink and let us pay for nothing. They showed no hostility towards us, in spite of the fact that our allies had bombed their country a few months previously. They even went so far as to prepare a poster in Arabic for us, which they presented to us on the morning we were leaving. Their message was touching in its sentiments and beautifully executed. It said in short:

"Good Luck on your journey, brave men. Perhaps, one day you can come to our home and sit round our fire, and one day we can visit you in your home. We hope that day will not be long in coming."

On our second day at the camp site I left Action tethered to a tree on an adjacent patch of land through which ran a stream. When I returned, there was no sign of the horse. I ran back to the camp to tell Max. A number of Poles, East Germans, Czechoslovakians and Russians, besides our Libyan friends, were staying there and several of them spoke English. When I explained that Action was missing, a full scale search was quickly mounted. The camp lay four miles out of Sofija, in open countryside with only occasional factories or houses to be seen. The first thing we did was look for footprints, but the dried ground gave us no clues to the route he had taken.

We split into small parties and went in different directions, checking roads and fields. He could have been on the run for anything up to three hours, depending on when he got loose. Searchers began to drift back as dusk fell, but there had been no sign of him to the north, which was a vast expanse of open, hedgeless country and small, scattered villages. If he had taken that direction it would be like searching for a needle in a haystack. He could have wandered miles.

When we were all gathered again at the campsite and Action had still not been sited, I said I would notify the police and ask if they could get a helicopter to search for him. While waiting for them to arrive, I walked across the fields to what looked like factories. We had avoided searching built–up areas, as they contained no grass and it seemed useless to bother looking for him there. It was nearly dark when I came to the jumble of brickwork and began running from building to building. An old man came and shouted at me. I thought he was telling me to get off the site, but that was not it. He pointed through a gap between some derelict buildings, and I felt certain he had seen my horse. Charging through the gap, I came across Action busy nibbling at some sparse grass, his rope in the hands of a small boy, who was surrounded by several other children. They knew he was my horse as soon as they saw me and they accompanied me to the campsite, where the police had been questioning Max. They laughed to see us and then left.

Later, two coachloads of Russians arrived at the site and they came over to read our publicity. One man with some English asked when we were expecting to be in Russia. I told him we should be there in two months and he asked our destination. When I told him Odessa, he said they had come from there, so I told him of our problems in getting permission to enter the

U.S.S.R.

"I shall come and see you later. It is possible we might be able to help," he said.

When he came back, he had another man with him. He explained that they were a party of Marathon runners on a trip to Bulgaria and the other man was their team President. They gave me a flag from their group and said they would like to help us. I said we had hoped to spend the Russian winter in Odessa, if we ever got into Russia.

"My team President has asked me to tell you to telephone us when you reach the customs post at Albeata, and we shall meet you. Your horse can stay in the Hippodrome and you will be put into an hotel and looked after during the winter, and when you resume your journey, we shall contact organisations along your route to care for you as far as the China border. If you have problems at the border crossing, ring this number. Our President will speak to the authorities and you will get in. Don't worry."

I could hardly believe my ears. I asked him if he could really do all this for us.

"Our President is Secretary of the Odessa Communist Party and Odessa has a population of one million. He can do all this for you," he said and then began writing something on a sheet of paper, which he handed to me. "This is your invitation to Russia and it says what we shall do for you. You will not get in without one."

The President appended his signature and then they left me, saying they must be on the road at six in the morning, but would see us again in Odessa. What a stroke of luck!

We went into Sofija's main shopping centre next day, and caused complete chaos when the crowds round us managed to jam traffic in the main roads. The police turned up and tried to move us on, but the crowds jeered their efforts, so they resorted to diverting the traffic instead.

We were making our way back to the campsite along the main highway, teeming with traffic, when disaster struck. Action was trotting along in the darkness when the caravan lurched horribly and there was a crunching sound that scared the poor horse half out of his wits. He stopped abruptly and Max began to yell something about the wheel being smashed. Inspection showed that his diagnosis was something short of the facts. There was almost nothing but debris left of one wheel, even the steel rim had cracked in half at the welded joint and bits of wood were scattered all over the road. We were blocking half the carriageway and forcing the traffic to squeeze past. The campsite was still about a kilometre away and we had nothing with which to tow the caravan. Max and I could not move it and Action would have been too terrified at the sound of it dragging against the road for us to use his muscle on it.

"I'll run and get help from the camp site," Max offered.

Max ran off and left me to direct the traffic by means of a torch. It seemed an eternity before Max returned with help. There were two cars with him, containing between them eight men. Many were only half dressed, as they had been in bed when Max came bursting in on them. They managed to drag the caravan back to the camp site for us. What good friends these Libyans and Eastern Block people proved to be.

Now we had to face the problem of how to get the wheel mended, and one name came immediately to mind: Mr. Fix – it, our man Vili Sabev. Within two minutes of our telephone call to him, a taxi arrived to take us to a wheelwright in a village. Mr. Sabev said the man would charge us, but if we paid in dollars it would not be expensive. We put the remains of the wheel in the taxi's boot and set off. It took us twenty minutes to reach the wheelwright, an old man working in the yard of his home. He looked at the the job and said it would be ready next day, new spokes, new blocks, new rim, the lot. The taxi took us back to the campsite and the driver asked for the equivalent to £30 for the fare. This was a considerable sum, but I paid up rather than make a fuss, although I knew we had been swindled.

Next morning, we fetched the wheel and paid our East German friend, who owned a car, a much more reasonable amount for his trouble in driving us there and back.

The time came for us to leave the camp site, but before setting off, we telephoned the Embassy to ask if there had been any answer from Moscow concerning our entry permits. Mr. Cobden said Vili would contact us about it, when news came through. Vili came to see us off and begged us not to enter Romania, where, according to him, we should be robbed of everything by people who have nothing. He asked to take our passports and said he would arrange a ferry for us from Varna, on the Black Sea coast of Bulgaria, to Odessa.

"We can't travel without passports," I objected.

"If you get stopped, show this," he said, scribbing something on a sheet of paper and handing it to me. "I shall meet you in Sliven on the 17th of October."

Reluctantly, we surrendered our passports, something one should never do, but I trusted Vili to return them in due course, with the ferry tickets. His last act was to take us to visit General Stoichev, the world's oldest living general, aged 94. He had stood with Stalin to welcome home the Russian Army after the second world war and had been a friend of Charles de Gaulle, Marshal Tito, the Duke of Edinburgh and many other illustrious characters. He spoke twelve langauges and had an Olympic gold medal for wrestling, which he won in his youth. He had also been one of the world's greatest horsemen and won the European Equestrian Grand Prix in 1927. His political beliefs and activities had led to several brushes with the police and spells in prison. In 1944, it was he who ousted the occupying German forces from Sofija; one of many similar acts of heroism in his long life. He had a distinguished diplomatic career in later years, with a spell as Military Attaché in post – war Paris, and was the first Bulgarian Amabssador to the United States of America, in 1957. He was founder of the Olympic Committee in Sofija; the list of his achievements seemed endless.

He inhabited a flat in one of Sofija's side streets, not at all in the sort of style we imagined such a famous general should enjoy. The place was cluttered with souvenirs, photographs, medals, firearms and trophies. He was very frail by this time, but still had a wonderful command of English. He had many questions to put to me about Action. As we chatted, the telephone rang and Vili answered it.

"It's for you, Bill," he said.

A man was on the line, Bulgarian from his accent, but talking to me in English.

"Welcome to Bulgaria. I hope your stay is good. If there is anything I can do, let me know. Goodbye," he said and then hung up.

"Who was that?" I asked in astonishment.

"The son of our President," Vili answered.

It had been a great honour to meet the General. As I was about to leave the room, he pushed two photographs at me.

"You know these people," he said.

One was a picture of Pat Smythe, the other of my Father's neighbour, Nick Skelton, the Olympic show jumper. I was amazed at the coincidence of seeing a photograph of my father's neighbour in this tiny Bulgarian flat in far away Sofija.

According to our timetable, we were to visit next the convent at Samocov, which turned out to be a lovely, half-timbered house set behind a wall and housing six nuns. Sisters Gabriella and Magdalena made us welcome. They were both probably in their sixties and a real pair of cards they turned out to be. There was no room in their small yard for our caravan and it had been arranged for it to be parked in a drive opposite. Action was brought into the convent garden. Both seemed safe enough. A bunch of youths had watched our arrival and remained milling around. They all knew the nuns.

The nuns insisted that Max and I sleep in proper beds for a change, but before it was time to sleep, they took us into the mountains for a meal and a few drinks. Between them they only had a few words of English, but they ate and drank with us very companionably. As they were driving us back to the convent, they began to sing some Beatles songs. They were a very jolly crowd.

Next morning, Max was feeling unwell, so I told him to stay in bed while I had breakfast and inspected the caravan. I discovered that the doors had been forçed; most of the scout neckerchiefs had been taken and almost all the souvenirs we had been given in the different handicapped homes, our medals from Italy and Germany and the three silver and one gold crucifixes and chains were missing.

Feeling totally sickened, I went to break the bad news to Max. We decided to keep it from the good nuns, for fear of upsetting them, but were thwarted in our plan when the man in whose drive the caravan was parked came to report to Sister Gabriella that it had been damaged. She came at once and asked me what had been taken. I told her it had little value. I did not add that it had, nevertheless, great sentimental value to us. She sent for someone to fit new locks and tighten all the bolts on the undercarriage. Somehow, news of the robbery spread and people called to offer condolences.

That evening, at 5 o'clock, a man arrived with a big, blue box containing spanners. He said he worked at the mountain ski lift and when he and his colleagues heard about the robbery they wanted to make amends by giving us the spanners.

The most moving incident happened when a young boy aged about twelve, who had been hovering round us most of the day, came up and handed me a box about four inches square and brightly painted. I opened it and saw something electronic lying inside. I thanked the lad, although I had no idea what it was I had been given. Max looked at it and said it was an electronic alarm for the caravan. It had been made in West Germany and must have been a most treasured possession. I felt the emotion welling up inside me and I went to the boy and kissed his cheek. He had given me his most valued possession to prevent us from being robbed again. The sight of Gabriella's kindly face peering out from under her headdress brought the tears flooding from my eyes.

Our next stop was Borovits, to a hotel in the mountain ski resort. It lay somewhat off our route, but Vili felt we should try it, and we had an enjoyable day going by ski lift to the mountain top while Action rested in the hotel grounds below. Vili turned up in the evening to tell us there was no reply yet from Moscow and there was no ferry from Varna to Odessa, although he offered instead to try and get us passage on a cargo boat. He spent the evening with us, full of energy, planning our trip and drinking. He wanted to retain our passports, which he said he would need in order to get us our visas. Max was unhappy about this, but did not make an issue of it.

When Vili left next morning, we set off for the Hotel Elbas at Pazardik. When I had spoken to Vili earlier about our intention to enter Romania, I had also said that if anyone gave us things to take for the people there, we should be happy to deliver them. He had warned me off the idea of visiting that country, so it came as a great surprise to find a crowd of children, dressed in their best clothes, waiting for us at Pazardik, to give us toys to take to their brothers and sisters in Romania. Adults pressed on us cakes, biscuits and jars of honey and soon the horsebox was so full we could accept no more.

Another visit planned by Vili was to Stameoliyski, to look round one of Eastern Europe's largest canning factories. To get there we had to drive through many miles of cultivated land where vegetables and fruit were grown to supply the factory. The economy of the whole town revolves around it. On the edge of town, two workers were waiting for us, to take us to the factory, I supposed, but they led us several miles along cobbled roads before turning down a track leading through a small village. The caravan's wheels had taken punishment from the cobbles as usual.

The track went some way into a wood and came, after half a mile, to a clearing containing a tin house outside which stood a sunburnt old man clad only in trousers. In his hands he held a shotgun aimed at me. The two workers spoke hastily to him, he lowered the gun and came over to shake my hand. He began to undo Action's harness, and I tried to prevent him, not knowing what was in his mind. He shoved me away, wanting to do everything himself. He intended for us to spend two days with him.

I learnt that he had been a major in the Bulgarian Army, serving under General Stoichev. He was to tend Action as though he were his own horse. The workers then led us through the woods until we came to three man-made lakes, each covering a good two acres. By the side of one stood a tin shed in front of which was a good sized wooden table surrounded by chairs. A group of men were standing there and we were introduced to them all. One was to be our interpreter.

"You are to stay here and rest. Everything you need will be provided. More people will arrive this evening and we shall have a feast of roast pig and fish and cheese followed by melons, wine, brandy and beer," they told us.

Two of the men began lighting a fire under a small pig suspended on a spit, and others were busily catching plump carp from the lake.

I was happy when they offered me the chance to try some fishing for myself, using pieces of tomato for bait and a lead sinker, but no float. The lake was teeming with fish and I had a catch immediately, followed by fish after fish which were saved for the feast to come. It was a very hot day and Max was still complaining that he felt unwell and giddy. Most of the time he lay in the sun, taking occasional short walks among the surrounding fields where tall, green plants with thick stems grew. My interpreter told me the land we were on belonged to the canning factory and the old major with the shotgun had instructions to shoot trespassers. He also said the top manager was coming out to meet me. I could keep an eye on Action, who was with the old Major. The horse was tethered to a tree and the old man fetched him water from a stream flowing a short distance away.

The feast was almost ready; and melons, beer, wine and brandy were being kept cool in the waters of a stream feeding the lake, when a large, Russian-made car came lurching along the track. When it stopped, a smartly dressed man got out and came up to us. The interpreter told me he was Mr. Stollan, Manager of the canning factory. We shook hands and Mr. Stollan made a speech of welcome, which our interpreter repeated in English. He was followed shortly by the Mayor and Mayoress and several other people. Most of the men wore their work uniform of blue smock tops and matching trousers. I was surprised when the director stripped off his best suit and also donned the factory uniform, probably to make himself seem like one of the boys.

The roast pig, served with tomatoes, spring onions and cucumber, was delicious. Carp cooked on the open fire came next, but Max ate very little and went off from time to time to be sick. He had been ill for three weeks now and I was getting increasingly concerned about him, as he could not keep his food down. I had also had a few bilious turns lately, and only the previous night had woken up in the early hours to vomit.

Our companions began to drift away slowly, many of them quite well oiled, and Max, the Major and I were finally alone by eight o'clock. When we got back to Action, we saw that he had trampled down several of the cultivated plants.

"Dad," Max whispered, "Do you know what these plants are?"

"No," I said. "I haven't a clue."

"They're cannabis. This whole area is filled with it. No wonder they want to keep people away. It's a good thing Action has only been eating grass growing between the rows."

The next appointment made for us was on Monday, at the Hotel Asenovgrad, in the town after which it was named. The receptionist asked for our passports, which we did not have. This fact puzzled and upset her and she conferred with her colleague at the switchboard while Max fumbled for the note Vili had given us. He gave it to her, she read it and then said,

"Police come. Wait."

"Now we're in trouble, Dad," Max said. "No passports, no vehicle documents, no stamp on our cards to show where we stayed each night and no receipts for the currency we changed."

"We can always ask to speak to Vili in Sofija, if we do have trouble," I replied.

The police came and started to talk to the receptionist. A Bulgarian man stood listening to all this and then asked me what our problem was. We explained that Vili was holding our passports in order to get visas for us to visit Russia. He believed us and tried to persuade the police that we were genuine. We let them look through the folder, expecting to be asked for the rest of our papers, but they merely asked where we intended spending the night. Another man arrived and spoke to the receptionist before telling the police that he knew all about us and asking if we could park in front of the hotel, which was in the main square. They raised no objection.

There was no grass to be seen, only gardens surrounding the square, so I tethered Action to the caravan and declined the offer of a room in the hotel, explaining that I would sleep in the caravan for security reasons. Max, however, decided to make use of the room.

We soon gathered a crowd, as usual. For a while, we had kept a visitors' book just inside the caravan door, into which people could write messages and leave their names and addresses. It had already acquired many hundreds of entries. Sometimes we would put it out on a card table along with publicity about the handicapped. It had some lovely messages from people of twenty different nationalities and had become my most treasured possession. A large man, who had been reading the material displayed on the caravan, wrote a long message in Bulgarian, and when he finished he patted me on the shoulder and said,

"Tonight, you drink with my friends in the bar just around the corner. Come at seven o'clock."

A young couple came up next, and spoke in good English. They put their address in my book and told me they came from Romania. They implored us to visit them there. We felt elated at having got our first invitation to visit people in their own homes. How mistaken we were to feel thus.

Max was still feeling ill when we entered the bar full of men seated at tables and drinking some sort of clear liquid out of tiny glasses. Our friend was sitting with a dozen others. When he saw us, he beckoned us to join them and ordered drinks for us. His companions looked as if they had been there some time already. I noticed that they took their drink in one gulp. I was given a glassful and took a good pull. It almost blew my head off. Max and I downed several more and spoke English to those of our companions who could understand it. The room was growing steadily more noisy, until the door opened and the whole place fell silent.

Two high ranking military officers strode towards the bar, and our friend spoke to the most senior of them while the rest of the men sat as if frozen. The officers shook me by the hand, said something in Bulgarian and moved to the bar. They each tipped back a single drink and then left. As the door closed, my big friend blew a raspberry and his companions jeered. Clearly, the military is unpopular through being used, in the Communist fashion, to keep control of civilians.

As the drink took hold of me, I started to talk politics in a loud voice and silenced the whole room by saying, in one breath, "Mrs. Thatcher, Ronald Reagan." All eyes swivelled in my direction, as though I had dropped a bomb. We left, feeling tiddly, but not drunk.

Our next stop was at Khaskovo Monastery, where we hoped to see the Bishop, certain that Vili would have arranged this with him. We were told, however, that the Bishop was at a meeting with a man from the Ministry of Internal Affairs, so we settled down to a wait of three hours outside the monastery. Then some men came out, got into a limousine and drove away. Minutes later, a priest emerged and told us to leave immediately. We left, to avoid trouble, and returned to our hotel. The receptionist explained that the police had requested us to stay there until our passports were returned. She said Vili was coming next evening at six o'clock.

Max was still suffering from sickness and diarrhoea, and the hotel staff sent for a doctor to come and look at him. I was very worried when the doctor called an ambulance and had him taken to hospital, but he was back two hours later. He said he had been told to return the following evening for more injections, but he had no intention of doing so. When I asked why, he said the ambulance had been more like a large delivery van, totally devoid of equipment, and the hospital room where he had been taken was like a dormitory and held eight other people suffering from the same sort of thing as he was. He said the beds were old and had no partitions, but most alarming was his conviction that the syringes and needles were not clean and sterile. He had been given a drip containing glucose, the same as everyone else. It had been suspended on an insecurely fixed hook in the wall. There were cigarette butts and discarded swabs on the floor and an unpleasant and unclean sort of smell pervaded the room.

He went on to tell me about the almost indescribable squalor of the toilet facilities, which he had had to use when he wanted to be sick. Having made one visit to this disgusting place, he left the hospital, determined never to set foot there again. His story convinced me that we have very little to complain about in Britain by comparison with Bulgarian health care and its amenities.

In Max's absence a Turkish Gipsy came to re-shoe Action and Vili came to give us back our passport and two forms in Bulgarian, which he had already completed and we just had to sign and take to an office in Plovdiv to get our extended visas. The one thing he did not have for us was permission to enter Russia. In the evening, he took us to Pamparovo ski resort to meet an old friend, Ivan.

We had noticed that the Bulgarian bars were rather short of beer, but good old Vili was able to find a few bottles for us from somewhere. We grew to have a healthy appreciation of the Balkantourist organisation and their people after this. It was usually at one of their places where we made camp and where we were entertained.

We were glad to get to Plovdiv and the camp site, where the receptionist telephoned Mr. Ivantov, our contact in Plovdiv. We took Action with us to the office where we were to get our visas extended, a job that took a trifling ten minutes. We had previously been given a yellow card to get stamped at all the places we stopped at, and although we had collected a number of stamps, we could not account for every single night we had spent in Bulgaria. The woman in the office proposed letting us have a new visa valid for thirty days, but it would cost us £3 at the official exchange rate, or £1 – 50 unofficially. We were warned to make certain we had a stamp for every night we spent in the country from now on, as any gaps in the dates could lead to problems when we tried to leave Bulgaria.

The camp site at Plovdiv was very much like the others we had stayed at, with a mixture of Libyan Arabs, always hospitable; East Germans, ever ready to chat; and Russians, who stayed together. There was also a small sprinkling of Western tourists present.

Chapter Twenty

Vili Leaves Us To Our Own Devices

Our guide, Violet, took us to see Vili again at the Balkantourist Office, and we learnt that arrangements had been made for us to tour the town with horse and caravan, after which we could stay outside the Novo Hotel, as the camp site was a little way out of Plovdiv. Max was concerned about the police being after us for not staying on an appointed site, but Vili produced a permit issued by the K.A.T., Bulgarian Traffic Police, which seemed to satisfy him. Then Vili said he would not be seeing us for a couple of weeks, as he was off on a visit to Czechoslovakia, South Korea, Hong Kong and Moscow. His aim was to promote Sofija as a venue for the 1994 Winter Olympic Games. We offered to carry posters to this end and distribute leaflets for him. We already carried publicity for Balkantourist holidays, and many very interesting places of interest to visitors had been included on our itinerary. There has been a great Turkish influence on Bulgaria in the past. The Turks ruled the land for 500 years, until their expulsion, with help from the Russians, in the late 1800s.

Violet took us to do a radio interview and we visited an institute for the deaf: an impressive place complete with workshops and factories. We needed to change some drachmas into local currency and Violet conducted us to a Balkantourist hotel that has this facility, but we discovered that only low denomination notes, up to 500 drachma face value, can legally be exchanged. This restriction is supposed to prevent black market currency dealing. We had 80,000 drachma in large denomination notes that were now, according to the rules, valueless. We told Violet that the Bulgarian Embassy in Thessaloniki told us to carry high value notes, and this had been confirmed by the manager of the National Bank of Greece. Violet shrugged and said,

"Well, that's politics for you."

We went to the Greek Bank in Plovdiv and asked for the notes to be replaced by those of smaller denomination, and were told it would take several days to do. Next, we telephoned the British Consulate in Sofija to see what they could do. They said they had someone returning to England and he would give us Sterling in exchange for our drachmas, and change them back when he got home, if we could bring our money to Sofija. We said we would ponder it and let them know later.

In our tour of Plovdiv we saw a Roman amphitheatre, discovered by accident in 1968. It stands on a hill above the entrance to a road tunnel not far from the town centre. The old part of Plovdiv covers about 47 hectares and has a population of 3,000 as well as many beautiful buildings. Everywhere we saw excavations in progress, the ancient town emerging and contrasting starkly with modern buildings, underpasses and walkways. Great care had been taken to provide access for handicapped and elderly people in all parts of Plovdiv, which is a lovely town with many trees and open spaces.

We were scheduled to spend the night outside the Hotel Moritza, where we met a waiter and a waitress, with whom we made friends and who cared for us well. Max fell into conversation with a young man who had been working on the Black Sea coast. He warned us to be very careful not to exchange currency at black market rates as the police sometimes act as decoys to trap illicit dealers. He then went on to explain exactly how the black market works and to stress its importance to the man in the street in Communist countries. His name was Valentine, and he invited Max to go with him to his apartment, meet some of his friends and see exactly how the black market functions.

Some of Valentine's friends were going, next day, to visit Sofija and meet shopkeepers who would buy goods, for lev (Bulgarian currency), which had been purchased in the Free Shop, selling Western goods for Western money (dollars), in Plovdiv. The dollars had been obtained by black market currency deals with tourists in Plovdiv or on the Black Sea coast. A network of contacts bought western goods for lev and sold them to friends at an under the counter profit. The profit would be exchanged for western money again and divided between the group. Some of them were saving the currency in order to try and escape from Bulgaria when they had enough put by. It is a cycle that has been going on for years. The goods that change hands are usually denim jeans, American cigarettes, batteries, soap and deodorants, small things that can be split down.

When we were leaving the Hotel Moritza in the morning, our waiter and waitress friends brought us tomatoes, cheese, butter and bread to take on the journey. Other Bulgarians had made us gifts of money, one lev or more at a time. I was told that the average monthly income is between 200 and 250 lev.

We stop in Karlovo to visit the Vassil Levski Museum. Levski was a revolutionary of the mid 19th century and both he and his wife were executed for their beliefs.

Near Kazanlâk, I imagined myself back in time 200 years. There were peasants harvesting maize by hand and loading it onto horse-drawn carts. I pulled up to watch them for a brief moment. Max had gone ahead to park the horsebox, and I saw him walking back towards me. He thought there must be a problem when he saw me stationery.

"I just pulled up to record these people on video tape," I explained.

Suddenly, as if from nowhere, a man carrying a stick with a round STOP sign on the end appeared out of the hedge and blew a whistle. An armed soldier, brandishing a machine gun, also burst on the scene and the first man unleashed a torrent of Bulgarian at him, of which I only caught the words "video camera". Looking about me, I saw to my horror that there was a military installation a few hundred yards beyond where the peasants were working. It must certainly have figured in the background of our pictures. Max hurriedly produced the folder, which now contained articles in Bulgarian, and letters from the Institute for the Blind and from General Stoichev. The soldier read it from end to end and then told us to go. In English, he warned us to pay more attention in future to what we were filming and reminded us that it was forbidden to film anything pertaining to the military. We left quickly.

Two policemen met us in Kazanlâk and suggested we park everything outside the police station and Action could go in their yard. We were allowed to tour freely in Kazanlâk and talk to many people; the police were always in attendance to keep drunkards away from us. The usual Bulgarian tipple was a powerful, home-brewed plum brandy, and many people were almost always in a state of inebriation. Beer was in short supply everywhere we went.

Our guide took us to see an ancient Thracian tomb dating back to the third or fourth century B.C. and supposed to be the finest example of its kind anywhere in the world. It is one of only four monuments in Bulgaria covered by U.N.E.S.C.O.

Our next visit was to a convent, used as a hospital for Russian troops in the war against Turkey in 1878. Outside the convent, a man and a little girl came to speak to Action. The man was smartly dressed and he asked if we remembered him.

"I was the man in military uniform who stopped you the other day, when you were filming. It was a very serious matter to film a military installation, especially as you are from the West," he said.

Max assured him I had only intended filming the workers in the fields and had been unaware of what lay beyond.

"Have the police here been looking after you?" he asked next.

At this the penny dropped. They had been detailed to keep an eye on us.

"I wish you good luck," he added and left.

We began to climb up towards Shipka, and visited a beautiful Turkish mosque, the gleaming, golden domes of which could be seen from miles away. We were aiming for the Balkantourist Shipka Hotel, high up on the pass. Action had grown used to selecting his own time and place to stop for a breather, never anywhere dangerous, and we made a few stops on the long climb uphill. He would stand at the verge of the road and let the caravan go back in a right hand lock for about three feet until its rear wheels rested in the drainage gully at the road side and the weight was no longer on him.

On top of the hills overlooking the valley stands a huge, square monument approached by 890 steps cut into the hillside. It commemorates the Russian soldiers who died fighting the Turkish army. This battle is said to have claimed the lives of 7,900 soldiers and Bulgarian volunteers. When ammunition was running low, the bodies of the dead were thrown down the hill at the advancing Turks. Across from here, on the top of another hill, it is possible to see another monument. This marks the site of the first meeting of the Communist Party, in 1897.

From Shipka, which stands 1,330 metres above sea level, one can see, on a clear day, across northern Bulgaria as far as the Danube, some 140 kilometres distant. The sunlight reflecting off the river, made it look like a silver thread.

A guide had been appointed to accompany us for the next two days, to take care of our arrangements and to translate for us. We continued north, travelling downhill again, towards Gabrovo. On this stretch, the brake on the rear caravan wheels failed and the sudden shove from the weight of the vehicle almost knocked Action's legs out from under him, but he managed to hold it safely.

When we got to the camp site, it was decided that Max must go back to Sofija and exchange our remaining Greek money for Western currency. It was risky for him to travel alone, but one of us had to stay and take care of Action and our belongings. Our guide tried to divert my thoughts from Max by taking me to visit a museum, but the ploy failed to work.

While I was still in bed, at 4.15 on a chilly morning, Max took 49,000 drachma and boarded the taxi waiting to drive him to the station, where he would catch a train for Sofija, where Mr. Cobden, at the British Embassy, had promised to exchange the Greek money for British pounds and re-exchange it when he got home to England.

The train left at 5 o'clock. Its somewhat less than first class accommodation was fairly crowded with workers going to outlying factories and co-operative farms. Many carried large bags, the contents of which Max was curious to discover. Finding an empty compartment, Max sat down, but he was soon joined by a middle aged couple with piles of baggage, and two young girls. The couple made themselves comfortable and fell asleep, while the young girls talked endlessly, so that Max could not also take a nap. After half an hour's journey through the mountains, dawn broke and revealed absolutely magnificent countryside. Having absorbed enough of the view, Max began to read a book.

"Hey, Max," said one of the girls. "How is Action? Where is Bill? Do you like Bulgaria? I have read about you in the newspapers."

This was the beginning of a conversation that lasted until the train arrived in Sofija and which was to satisfy Max's curiosity concerning the bags people carried. They contained home-made articles or things bought from tourists in Gabrovo which would be sold in Sofija, and the money raised would go towards the cost of buying things they could not get at home. The bags contained all manner of things, from soap, chewing gum and chocolate through to articles of clothing. There were gangs of young men, who would split up in Sofija, some to exchange lev for dollars, others to buy electrical goods and scarce commodities in the Free Shop, which they would take back and sell at a profit for Bulgarian lev. The lev would serve to exchange for more dollars when the next batch of tourists came through Gabrovo. Others were just doing personal shopping for things they could not buy in Gabrovo. Max's two young girl friends had a bag full of rabbit skins which they wanted valued and they also wanted to know how much it would cost to have a coat made out of them. Their brothers caught and skinned the rabbits, and when they had enough to get a coat made, it could be sold for dollars to a tourist and yield a good return, in Bulgarian terms.

Max was approached on several occasions by people suspecting that he had foreign currency, who asked if he wanted to do a deal with them. The two girls came to his rescue and explained who he was and what he was doing in Bulgaria. They also helped him book a seat on the return train, leaving later in the day, and offered to take him to the British Embassy. He wisely refrained from explaining his business there, having felt uneasy about carting such a large sum around with him. Anyone who recognised him for a foreigner automatically assumed he would be carrying a bulging wallet stuffed with dollars and pockets full of cigarettes, even though he had neither. What he did have represented eight months' wages for an average Bulgarian, even if it was in drachma and not something more universally acceptable.

He had seen police and military officers patrolling the train and asking for identification cards, and he hoped they would not question him too closely about his journey and its purpose. His two friends, Svetlana and Svetesmira, assured him, correctly as it transpired, that he only had to show his British passport and he would not be troubled further.

They gave him directions for the British Embassy, but he had two, hours to kill before it opened for business, so he strolled around trying to look inconspicuous until, with a glad heart, he could go inside and have a good cup of coffee with Mr. Cobden, who said he could give Max £115 for 30,000 drachmas, as that was all the English money he had. It was a fair rate of exchange, but left him with 19,000 drachma in large denomination notes. Mr. Cobden suggested asking at the Greek Embassy if the money could be changed for smaller value notes. He confirmed that there was still no response from Russia about our visas.

The Greeks said they would give him lev in exchange for drachma, but the man refused to co-operate when Max said he was happy with drachma, but wanted smaller value notes. Max assumed he was on the fiddle. He could use the drachmas himself, send them home for later, and he could offload some lev he had acquired elsewhere. Max tried to explain that he was not a tourist, that he was on his way to China and would be on the road for another eighteen months at least, so the Bulgarian money would not be of any use. He produced newspaper cuttings to prove his story. The Greek questioned him closely, and it came out that he was once a scout himself, in Greece. A useful compromise was reached at last. The drachma could be exchanged for dollars at the official exchange rate. Max said he had 19,000 drachma and the man did a few sums and offered $120 dollars. Then, Max told him how the bank in Thessaloniki had advised him to take high value notes to Bulgaria, and he confessed that many tourists arrived at his office with the same problem.

"Our banks ought not to do it, and our government does not care because we get rid of the large denomination notes in exchange for the tourists' dollars, Deutschmarks and Sterling, and the drachmas always come back to Greece in the end. It's unfortunate for some, though. We always try to make them take lev in exchange. Communism only works here because almost everyone in Bulgaria is onto some sort of fiddle or other."

Max felt quite elated at having acquired £115 and $120 for a morning's work, although he had mild misgivings about the legality of it all. With his business transacted, there were some hours to spend before the train back was due to leave, so he had a meal and looked round Sofija until 3.30, when he returned to the station. On the way, he picked up the two girls at a previously arranged spot and they had to run for the train. The ticket inspector found them seats together.

I was waiting at Gabrovo to meet Max, who brought Svetlana and Svetesmira over to meet me. We chatted for about half an hour, then Max said,

"Dad, all I want now is a quiet drink and somewhere to relax.

Chapter Twenty – one

Low on Luck, Water, Diesel and Everything Else

Max had not telephoned his mother and sister since Christmas, mainly because it is not very easy to make international calls from Bulgaria, but also because he knew they were about to move house at this time, and he had no new address.

We were on the road to Veliko Tarnovo when we noticed the wheel spokes getting loose again, and the wheel we had had rebuilt in Sofija was beginning to show signs of serious trouble, for the metal part of the hub was parting from the wooden part. Max noticed it and made me stop and take Action from the shafts while we took a closer look. The wheel had almost come right off, so we lashed it back with ropes, making it secure but no longer able to rotate. This soon led to another problem: the metal rim dragging on the road caused friction, heating the metal. Then smoke began to come from the wooden blocks beneath the rim and Max again yelled for me to stop.

We tried to get water to extinguish the fire, but all the water had been turned off in this area, so we resorted to the dire extreme of using our last bottle of beer for the job. People stared in amazement and I poured in disgust, but it had to be done. What a sacrifice!

We went directly on to a large school and factory serving 300 young men and girls aged between fourteen and twenty and with varying degrees of speech and hearing impediment, which makes it difficult for them to learn in a normal school environment. The girls make all manner of clothing and the young men learn woodworking and machining. Their day consists of four hours work and two hours study, and many are resident at the institute. There had recently been a devastating earthquake in the district, so we found several old people, who had lost their homes, living there also. Our translator explained their plight in a most moving way, and said that none of them knew what plans were being made to rehouse them.

When the director heard of our wheel trouble, he quickly set some of his maintenance staff to the task. We, meanwhile, went to the front of the building and listened to the assembled staff and students sing the "Bulgarian Peoples' Song" for us, after which girls in traditional costume served us cakes and wine. Any conversation between Max, the director and myself was conveyed to the students by sign language. It was amazing to see the totally hushed crowd all showing such interest in us.

They had done their best with the wheels, but they were in a bad way and we decided to keep going as best we could. The metal hub on one wheel had split and needed welding, the diameter of the metal rims had to be reduced by 12mm and the gap welded, to compress the rim blocks together and thus make a better bed for the spokes, but we had no idea how long the wheels would last now. Every night we had to cover them with wet sacks to keep the wood moist. When the work was finished, two of the men concerned mentioned dollars, but the director jumped up to say we must pay nothing. He would sort it out later.

Sliven lay 100 kilometres away, and when we came to the village of Elena, which lay on our route, we called at the police station and did our best to explain that we urgently needed someone to attend to our wheels. They wrote down an address of someone they thought might have been able to help, but when we got there, the man did not want to know anything about it. Two young men, seeing our predicament, offered to take us to a barrel maker, but this man also wanted nothing to do with us.

We parked on the railway station car park for that night, and the owner of the station restaurant fed us and then introduced us to a man employed at the Balkantourist Coach Depot. He told us to have our wheels ready for him at nine o'clock in the morning. We offered him $20 to shrink the metal rims on each wheel by cutting a small piece out and running a saw into the wooden rim block joints.

We got up early and took the wheels off and checked the bolts on the undercarriage of the caravan. The bolts were satisfactory, but we noticed that the metal brackets between the frames and the end of the springs were beginning to bend forwards as a result of all the weight of children we had been carrying and all the bumpy roads we had been on. The bracket on the very bad wheel was in the worst state, having taken the most punishment. When our man had not arrived to collect the wheels by eleven o'clock, we decided to press on towards Sliven.

On the way, we spotted a Gipsy encampment in a remote piece of countryside. The Gipsies had tents made of bent sticks covered with canvas and blankets, and their horses were all tethered to carts or caravans, and they had all manner of other animals wandering around loose. All the women were busy cooking or washing while the men stood in small groups, talking and drinking. No sooner had we stopped than we were surrounded by people of all ages asking us for things. We gave the men two bottles of wine we had brought from Italy. One woman was particularly interested in our red metal mugs. I gave her one and she grabbed it and ran to the middle of the road, trying to hide it in her bag quickly, but four other women saw her and began to fight her for it, but she clung on tenaciously. One old woman gave us four lev for having given the men something to drink.

We moved on again and saw people gathering vegetables from their gardens, ready for winter, and men cutting firewood. There were many outdoor, wood burning stoves on which plums were being boiled to produce the local brandy, which tasted horrible and was very, very strong. All the plum trees had been stripped of fruit.

When we got to Sliven, we parked outside the Balkantourist Hotel and Max went inside to speak to the Director, only to discover that he was away for two days and nobody else knew anything about us. We got permission to park outside and wait for Vili to get back from his trip abroad. Until something was done about the caravan wheels, we could travel no further.

Action went missing during the night, and we thought he might have been stolen, but before we panicked, a man arrived, leading him. Action had managed to snap his rope and find himself some grass in a nearby park. Then women from the hotel brought out a bag containing salami, bread and cheese for us. Max was feeling ill, but thought he had caught cold, so he went to sit in the warm inside the hotel. He was wearing his Tee – shirt with the slogan "1994 Sofija Winter Olympics", and someone came up to say that a town in Norway had been chosen to host the event. We imagined that Vili would not be happy at this news.

After two days waiting, we got a message that Vili would be arriving at eight o'clock on the following morning to sort out our problem with the wheels. Someone offered to try and contact him by telephone, but could not make the connection to Sofija, although we made international calls home without any difficulty at all.

Finally, arrangements were made for someone to look at the wheels, so I went to the police station with the hotel's interpreter, to get a permit to tour the city with Action and the caravan. They had never had this kind of request before, and said they had to prepare a special document for us. Then a man came to remove the two rear wheels. When he brought them back, he had replaced several spokes and made many new rim blocks. The old ones had been drilled and fitted with sleeves to make them hold the spokes tight. It was a very strong and neat job indeed, yet he refused to accept any payment for it.

Action enjoyed his stay outside the hotel, and all the attention and food from passers by. Just when we were trying to refit the wheels, however, he got an itch and began to rub himself against the caravan, causing it to topple off the blocks when he started pushing too hard. The caravan came down with a crash, but the only damage was to Max's foot, which was underneath the axle. I have never heard such bad language as he uttered while doing a dance and moaning.

When I went to collect the special permit, I found that the police had given up on it. They told me not to bother, but to go ahead and tour the town without it, so we spent four hours going round Sliven, stopping for a while in different parts of the town. There seemed to be a good number of people of Gipsy origins in the place, and many of the men pulled at Action's mouth to see how old he was. In the end I had to put a stop to this, when the horse began to nip people. I can hardly say I blamed him, either. When the men were expert horsemen, Action was all right, but some of the others just did it because they wanted to, until some of the older men told them to leave him alone.

In the evening, a young and very beautiful waitress came up and began to grow friendly, but when she started talking about dollars and jewellery, we made a hasty departure, not least on account of the four men who were watching her closely and were probably with her.

Sliven, Vili's home town, has a monument to his Father, a hero of the second world war. When we left there, we headed for Burgas, on the coast, where Vili had promised we could have the wheels overhauled free of charge by the Balkantourist coach depot engineers.

The journey went smoothly, except that we had to be careful with the front pair of caravan wheels, which were now loose all over. We spent one night at a restaurant on the way there. They were expecting us and we were able to change some more dollars into lev. The rate of exchange was $20 to 90 lev. Stefan, the restaurant manager, contacted Vili in Sofija for us, only to be told that Vili was ill and in hospital with a heart complaint. Our only chance now was to try and get help in Burgas with obtaining visas for Romania, since Vili could no longer be of assistance. He sent a message wishing us well and confirming that arrangements had been made for us at the Sunny Beach Hotel in Burgas, so we went straight there.

Christou, our Co-ordinator, and Maria, who was to translate for us, were waiting for our arrival, and they took us directly to the place where we were to have the wheels inspected. We plastered the caravan with publicity material and made a tour of the Sunny Beach Holiday Complex before parking up outside the Hotel Burgas. A young couple on holiday from England with a young man friend, showed great interest in us and told us that there were several English tourists in the resort with whom we could spend some time.

Maria, our translator, took us to a lovely coastal town called Nesabâr, which is classed as a museum town on account of all its restored historical buildings and churches. She said her parents had forbidden her to enter any of the religious buildings, because they are strict Communists. She admitted that she knew very little about any religions. This admission made little sense to us, in view of her job as a tourist guide.

The caravan and Action attracted a lot of public interest, as always, and we spoke to people from England, Germany and Italy, who had seen us before, or had heard of us at some time in our travels. One man said, in a broad Lancashire accent,

"Get the kettle on then, for a brew."

We did just that, in the middle of the street.

The weather was still good, and we saw that there were still plenty of tourists at the resort, walking along the beach in the mornings. The beach and the whole town was noticeably tidy everywhere, and from morning until night, Gipsies, mostly women, went round picking up every scrap of litter, including cigarette ends, then the beach was raked over by a tractor pulling a metal grid, so that one could not see so much as a footprint.

We met a group of Russians in a nightclub, when we went there with our English friends and an Irishman. From this moment, we spent a great deal of time together in the holiday complex during the next few days. One evening, when I had drunk just one too many, I left Max in the hotel foyer with about a dozen friends, English and Russian, and went off to bed. One of the Russians said that the hotel was really intended for Westerners and wealthy Communists, and he ought not to be inside and fraternising. Nobody else was bothered, however.

Two of the English people woke me up at three o'clock in the morning and said I should go and see to Max, who was in a bit of a state. His troubles had started when he began drinking good champagne, that cost about £1 – 50 a bottle, paid for with money exchanged on the black market. All tourists do their bit of trading in currency, encouraged by the hotel staff, who regard this as a good reason for working in the hotel, since they can get foreign currency in exchange for lev. Max had begun to talk about Valentina, and grown a trifle sad at being parted from her. I sat down and tried to sympathise, saying I understood how he felt, because I had similar feelings concerning Beth. We both ended up in tears and being comforted by our friends, who brought yet more champagne.

Some time after this, we all decided to go down to the beach for a swim in the sea; all except some of the Russians. One Russian girl said with a laugh,

"Communism does not allow us this much freedom."

Next morning, Max looked somewhat the worse for wear, but we had to get the wheels down to the coach depot, where five men set about them immediately. In the next six hours they literally stripped them apart and rebuilt them for us. The chief mechanic asked us to bring the horsebox along, too, for a thorough overhaul, which was good because it had been misfiring and was low on oil.

We took Action for a swim in the sea in the evening, and Christou arrived and said he would try to telex Moscow, in the morning, and ask if our visas were ready.

In the night, Action had trodden on a nail and it went about 30mm deep into the frog of his hoof until he was unable to stand on that foot. We decided to try and remove it, but when we pulled the nail out his hoof began to bleed and we had to call a vet. He arrived an hour later, cut into the hole to let the blood flow and then put a dressing on the hoof. He promised to come back later with something to put into water, in which Action must hold his hoof for half an hour, three times a day. He warned us not to let him stand on the hoof or get sand in it. Max and I both knew that a nail in the hoof can be enough to stop a horse working ever again, depending on the internal damage it causes and whether the wound gets infected and leads to blood poisoning.

There was great activity in the hotel during the afternoon. Cleaners scurried about and flowers appeared everywhere. Then some areas were closed off to the public, and at about three o'clock, a number of police officers and armed soldiers arrived, shortly followed by some black limousines. These parked next to the caravan, to which Action was tied. Later, we found out that the Vice President of Bulgaria had arrived for some sort of meeting.

Meanwhile, the vet had come back. He took Max out of sight round a corner of the hotel and gave him a small packet containing some white powder to use on Action's hoof. They were together for about fifteen minutes, and when I next saw Max he was rather shaky.

"What's up?" I asked.

"The vet gave me the powder and said he ought not to have given it to me really. I don't quite know why not, but he didn't ask for any payment. I had just peeped into the packet and slipped it into my pocket when two soldiers with machine guns stepped out of nowhere, maybe off the beach. One of them put the barrel of his gun against my pocket, then the vet said something in Bulgarian, presumably explaining what was happening. The police and soldiers were certainly hot on security."

"You and your Father had better go into the hotel reception area and wait there until the officials have left. The security guards will double check everything, just to be sure you are not terrorists," said the vet, before he left us.

Christou had no luck in getting information about our visas for Russia when he tried on the following morning to get news for us. It was a case of typical Russian bureaucracy, we were informed. They had not done anything about them yet. This left us needing an extension to our Bulgarian visa, which was something Christou could and did sort out.

When we bathed Action's foot, people gathered round to watch, which did not upset him, since he was continuously fed with tasty titbits by them. He certainly looked funny, standing with one foot in a bucket of water. Some of the waiters came out every morning to bring him sugar on slices of bread served off a tray.

Something upset Action one morning and made him jump backwards, pulling the caravan, to which he was tied, towards himself. Each time he moved back, he took the caravan a little further, until it came into contact with a huge plate glass window at the side of the hotel. The window must have been 3 x 2 metres, and the sound of it smashing was terrifying. The hotel manager came out and said,

"Forget it. It's perfectly O.K. In fact, I've never seen so much activity here as we've seen in the few days you've been here. You can stay here as long as you like. It's quite exciting. Something different happens every day."

We spent another night drinking champagne with our friends and getting to bed in the early hours of the morning. With Action unable to walk, we spent three days joining in the fun and bathing his hoof regularly. The treatment worked well, and soon he was able to stand on the foot without limping.

One of the Russian women had given Max a gold necklace as a present, but later she asked for it back. Apparently, when she left Russia to take a holiday in Bulgaria, she had had to sign a form declaring any valuable jewellery she took with her. She had to take the necklace back, as the idea behind the form was to stop people selling valuables to Westerners for Western currency. This restriction applied to all Russians leaving Russia. Max quite understood why she wanted it back after all.

The Irishman told us that two of the Englishmen we had been

spending time with had had a fight in the hotel reception. One had been arrested by the police and locked up, but the hotel manager had spoken for him, mainly because he had been a lavish spender of Western money in the hotel. We went up to the man's room to see him when he was released, and found that he had been given a good beating by the police for causing trouble. He also said they had taken $100 from his wallet and told him he could go if he forgot about the money, in which case, they would forget about the disturbance. There was a courier in charge of the group he was travelling with, and the courier said he had been lucky to get off so lightly, as the police do not like Western tourists causing trouble in public. They could have detained him for months.

One other Englishman was in trouble. He had been caught by the police when exchanging money illegally. It was going to take several months and some high level diplomatic intervention to sort him out.

Our next stop, after those eventful few days, was to be at the Golden Sands holiday complex, near Varna, where we decided we would try not to get involved with so many people or in so much activity.

One of the caravan's back wheels was still giving trouble as we trundled along the coast road. The wooden hub had begun to part from the metal sleeve again; this was nothing to do with the previous repairs being substandard, but rather the punishing roughness of the road surfaces. We had to stop in a village and have some large, metal washers fitted behind the retaining bolt holding hub to axle. This ensured that the wheel could not come off, but it was still very loose. To be on the safe side, we also fitted washers to the other three wheels at the same time.

Golden Sands Holiday Complex was similar to Sunny Beach except that it stood on a hill overlooking the beaches. When we stopped on the road to check the wheels again, a police car came up and the driver, on hearing our story, went to find someone to help us. By coincidence, this man had already met us in Sunny Beach and had written in our visitors' book, which by this time contained messages from people of many countries. We were eagerly looking forward to getting it translated once we were back in Britain.

The kindly policeman also arranged for us to stay overnight at the house of his friend, who lived about 5 kilometres away. We spent a convivial evening with the friend and his family, and did not get to bed until the early hours. We had no common language, but we all had a good time together.

Before we reached Golden Sands, we pulled in at a café, and while we were inside a car must have reversed over the caravan's shafts and snapped them. Once again, Balkantourist came to the rescue. One of their coach drivers, who had already seen us several miles further back down the road, picked up the shafts and took them in his coach to the hotel to which we had been told to go.

When we got there, the staff knew nothing about our arrival, but had seen us on television in a broadcast we had made in Sofija, so we were soon accommodated. Meanwhile, our shafts were taken to the coach depot for attention, and a promise was given that an attempt would be made to make our caravan wheels more secure in the morning.

Early next day an English speaking official from Balkantourist came to see us. A strange incident occurred then, too, when an English tourist told us she was the daughter of the Chairman of Balkantourist. We were unable to fathom the depths of this yarn, true or not. However, our wheels were fixed for us.

We wanted to telephone Vili and see if he was getting better, and during our discussion we must have mentioned Romania in the hearing of some tourists. They were aghast when we confirmed that it was our intention to go there and they implored us to think again. One woman told us her reasons.

"We have just been on a four day tour," she said. "There seems to be very little food and very much begging, especially people wanting to change their currency into Western currencies. One one occasion, when our coach broke down, we had a crowd clamouring round us within minutes wanting things. People of all ages were banging on the windows and some of the younger men entered the coach. It was very frightening. As for getting fuel for your horsebox, that looks like being difficult. The only garages are outside towns. There are none in the villages. Those garages we saw had queues kilometres long waiting to be served."

This woman went on to warn us to watch Action closely all the time we were there, as there was a risk of having him stolen. She explained that this was because he was such a beatiful, big, strong horse, unlike the puny animals of Romania, a country that relied heavily on horse power to pull its carts. She also added that punctures are common, since so many horses lose shoe nails on the roads. She told us what to expect if we had to stop and repair a punctured tyre. Vili had already given us a similar grim warning of what to expect, and we wished he had been able to arrange a ferry direct from Bulgaria to Russia, but the die was cast and we would go via Romania. Max was afraid it would be a dangerous exploit and I nursed pangs of guilt about pressing ahead.

In the night we had heavy rain and in the morning Action was filthy, but looked happy enough. The horsebox was not performing well, however, until the hotel staff arranged for it to be overhauled by the men who maintained their amusement equipment. They also repaired the exhaust, which had been blowing. While they were at it, these men straightened the caravan's springs, tightened the bolts and attended to one or two other minor defects for us, including the locks and bolts on all our doors.

One of the maintenance men told us that food was scarce in Bulgaria and what they got was of inferior quality, for all the best was reserved for Western tourists. He said things were worse in Romania.

That night Max was violently sick in spite of having almost nothing to eat during the day. He had been ill for three months by now, and I was worried that something serious must be wrong with him.

Knowing that fuel was short in Romania, but that we had a Balkantourist coach station to hand, I thought it might be wise to make a few advance preparations. Even in Bulgaria, fuel was short and had to be queued for, and without the good offices of Vili, we had to rely on kind people obtaining supplies for us, as we had no coupons, which Western tourists need to buy petrol or diesel. Where we had not been able to manage in any other way, we had stopped passing cars and bribed the drivers with foreign currency or goods to part with some of their fuel. It had always been successful. I mentioned my worries to the men mending the caravan, and they promptly filled my tank and gave us an extra 20 gallons in cans and they would not let us pay a penny towards it.

Morfi Scarlotov had arranged for us to visit the Union of the Blind in Russe, and when we got to the gates the director was waiting to welcome us. He was totally blind himself, but he had mastered English by means of Braille. The place was not a home this time, but a factory employing 650 blind and physically handicapped people in the manufacture of electrical items such as plugs and leads. We were given a guided tour of the factory and then taken into the yard where all the employees came out and listened while we told them our story.

After this, we were presented with a baby rabbit to take away with us. My first thought was that this was another animal to get through customs, but I accepted it with due thanks and said nothing about the touble it might give us. I mentioned to the director that we were still waiting for news of visas to enter the U.S.S.R. He telephoned the Russian Embassy in Sofija, and was told that we would just have to carry on waiting. When he pressed them to say how long we must wait, they said it could be a week or two, a month or two or a year or two. They could not be more specific.

I suspected the reason for this delaying tactic lay in the fact that when we had been asked to specify our route through Russia, we had mentioned Georgia and Azerbaijan, and passing close to Armenia. This part of the Soviet Union had recently been the scene of uprisings which Gorbachov had tried to quell with soldiers and tanks. There was no way we could be permitted to go through that area.

Turning my mind to the present, I knew that the caravan wheels were still not up to scratch, in spite of having had some fifteen lots of repairs. I discussed this with the director and told him the wheels either needed rebuilding or replacing, and whichever it was it must be under our supervision. He quickly organised a team of men who set about rebuilding the wheels completely, and for once I had confidence that it was good job well done.

Our director took us to see the River Danube, which forms the boundary between Bulgaria and Romania. The spot he chose for us to view this river was some way from Russe, out in the country. As we stood gazing across the steely gray waters towards Romania on the far bank, he told us about the hundreds of people who had swum across it to find a better life in Bulgaria or even in the West. Most of them had been shot by Romanian guards while they were still swimming. Many who made it to the Bulgarian side were returned to Romania, if caught by the authorities, and these people probably faced death. Having seen something of the hardships to be endured in Bulgaria, I wondered how truly awful Romania was that people should take such risks to escape from the one to the other.

Our guide took us with some of his blind friends to a restaurant where they sang traditional Bulgarian songs accompanied by a blind man playing the guitar. On another occasion, here in Russe, we went to the director's home with some other friends and had a meal. We had met some of the kindest people ever while in Russe.

On Sunday afternoon, with our director friend, we came to the bridge that crosses the Danube. One one side was the Bulgarian customs post and on the other lay Romania. Our friend guided us through the Bulgarian customs inside five minutes, having explained the lack of stamps on our card recording stopping places. As I left him standing at the barrier I was saddened by the thought that I might never see him again.

I urged Action forward and we rumbled on over the stone bridge towards Giurgiu. At this point the Danube is several hundred yards wide and yet no other vehicle passed me in either direction. It was a dull, gloomy day and the river rolled sullenly below us. Two men in uniform watched me approach and stepped forward to stop me when I came close.

"Cigarette. Cigarette," they said.

I handed them a packet of Bulgarian cigarettes, little knowing how often I should hear this word "cigarette" again in the days ahead, then they signalled us to move forwards to the customs post.

Bulgaria, our first East European country, taught us something of what to expect in Romania and Russia. Georgi Dimitrov, who was elected Premier in 1946, when the monarchy was abolished, had been in power ever since, and the time for a change was approaching. We found the people sombre and serious in their everyday lives, but in spite of their low living standards, they showed great kindness to us. Once, when we had been doing a live television interview, the interviewer asked what the Bulgarian people could do to help us reach our goal. I told him we still had a long way to go through Bulgaria and across Romania, and we needed all the support we could get. I said how the people of Romania were hungry, in need of clothing and fuel, and I offered to take to these Romanians anything that anyone wanted to donate.

As a result of this appeal, I was overwhelmed by people pressing on me gifts of food for which they must have queued for hours, and hay and fodder for Action. People with very little themselves gave us toys and clothing for Romanian children. The response was very touching indeed.

The fact that we were robbed and had to endure a considerable amount of pestering for Western goods, was understandable under the circumstances. We found the going cheap, and fuel, if not plentiful, was always available, even if a lot of it came through the black market. The country was strikingly clean and there was a total absence of litter and graffiti. It is an agricultural society, with manpower making up for lack of farm machinery and providing employment for all, including school children and soldiers, who are brought in to help.

The scenery in Bulgaria is beautiful. It has plains, and mountains, and the water in its rivers and streams is said to be the purest in all Europe. Most housing is found in small rural communities and consists of cottages straggling along the main roads between towns, with blocks of flats and high rise blocks on the outskirts of urban areas. The cottage gardens are cultivated and produce vegetable crops for use by the owners' families.

Nowhere would we see better facilities for the handicapped than in Bulgarian towns. The handicapped homes and hospitals might not have the best equipment and many were old and damp, but they did their best with what they had.

I was struck by the lack of colour in the streets, caused by the fact that there are no advertisements on buildings or vehicles, and all motor vehicles and horse – drawn carts are painted the same colour, creating a drab overall effect. It might explain our popularity to say that the people loved our colourful caravan plastered with bright publicity material. We were often asked how we could get away with such a display. This sort of thing was simply not done in a Communist state.

Given freedom from Communism, I feel sure Bulgaria would fit well into Western style politics.

Chapter Twenty – two

Into No Man's Land – Romania

A few cars and lorries were waiting at the border customs post in Russe, and I had my faith pinned on our trusty folder, which now contained our most up to date credentials, when I took Action to join the queue that ended no more than fifty yards from the office block ahead. I knew it would not be long before we were approached by someone, as it was obvious they had been notified about us by the sentries on the bridge. A solitary customs official came up and walked round the caravan and horsebox. Rather than wait, I decided to jump down and approach him with our passorts and folder in my hand. He looked at me, shrugged his shoulders and said,

"Moment."

In my experience, customs men can always determine one's nationality by looking at vehicle number plates. This customs officer brought another man back with him, a tall, handsome man with more signs of rank than himself.

"English, yes?" he asked.

Max came forward, fiddling with an unopened pack of Benson & Hedges cigarettes. Both men looked, but said nothing. These cigarettes would buy plenty of things in Romania, so we had brought 200 in from Greece.

"Passports, please," said the senior man.

We handed them over.

"Move over there," he said, indicating a wide piece of road.

He needed to let other vehicles get past us if they were to avoid having a long wait. However, by this time many of the other drivers had got out of their vehicles and gathered round the caravan, reading the publicity posters liberally displayed on every surface. The two officers went away again, and Max was showing visible signs of deep anxiety. Romania was an unknown land, reputed to have one of the most severe Communist regimes of any country in the world. The warnings we had been given by everyone who knew it was our intention to go there kept whirling round in my head. The poverty there made the people dangerous to travellers. We had heard a barrage of gloomy tales about people running out of petrol, stranded without food and getting no help from the authorities. The Romanians were under orders not to fraternise with Westerners, and we had been advised to expect to lose everything we possessed when we passed through their land. In the event of trouble, people said, we would be totally alone.

The previous evening, when Max telephoned his Valentina, in Venice, she had implored him not to enter Romania, as dire tales had recently been broadcast on the Italian news media about people suffering hunger, thirst and deprivation after running out of petrol there. I could understand his trepidation, but we should soon be finding out for ourselves. A coach from Greece was leaving Romania, and when it waited to cross the border, its passengers got out to stretch their legs. I could see them, bedraggled, unshaven, untidy and depressed, handing over their passports for checking. They soon piled back aboard and the coach trundled over the border and pulled up beside us. The faces were transformed. Smiles and tears of relief and joy, arms waving, hands being shaken, all because they were out of Romania.

Some of the delighted Greeks got out of their coach again and came to see us, to read our posters, those that were in Greek, and tell us about their ordeal on a coach trip, via Bucharest, to Constanta. They had run out of diesel and could only obtain a gallon here and a gallon there. They had been condemned to push the coach between times, or wait for days without food and water, continually subjected to harassment by young men and children, who pestered them for currency, for things to barter, who threatened them if nothing good was forthcoming, and who stole what they could snatch and get away with. One young woman summed it up for us.

"It has been torment for us and we are forty people. You are two. Please turn round and go back to Bulgaria."

Max was aghast. I was uneasy. We had come so far already.

"Let's go back, Dad," Max pleaded.

"We can't go back, Max. I can't give in now. You go back if you must, but I'm not," I shouted angrily, sick to the stomach with this tricky situation.

Max turned and made his way to the horsebox, climbed in and slammed the door shut. His nerves were shattered, as I could see, and he sat with his head resting wearily on the steering wheel. We had had an audience for this angry exchange and most of the watchers understood what it was all about. The young woman who had uttered the dire warning, tried to attract Max's attention by tapping on the horsebox window, but for a while he seemed oblivious to her. Then, he wound down the window and they began a conversation. I walked away out of earshot.

Presently, five men: three customs officers and two young soldiers, came over and walked round the caravan, chattering together. Then the officer we had met earlier came back to say he was fetching a vet to look at the horse and we must wait. This was the first good news we had had for a while. At least, something was about to happen. I went across to tell Max, fully expecting him to say he was not coming any further with me, but his reply was quite the contrary.

"That's good. Let's hope he is not too long coming. We must get Action out of the shafts soon," he said, almost as though nothing untoward had happened. He had changed his mind after all. I could wait to find out why when he felt like telling me.

The officer asked me to open the tail–gate of the horsebox, which was a worrying development, for we had the vehicles crammed full of clothing, toys, blankets and stuff given to us in Greece and Bulgaria for distribution to the Romanian people. It also contained boxes of our own equipment and about 200 souvenirs we had been given by the public or people from the various homes we had visited. They had been removed from the caravan and put in the horsebox for safety, to avoid getting them stolen. We also had our rabbit in a wooden box: one more animal and a lot more regulations to contend with, I supposed.

The two soldiers, one of the customs officers and Max went inside. The men began to rummage through all the boxes, except the one dirty old box that held the rabbit. One of the customs men kept saying "narctotics, drugs, firearms" to Max, and he repeatedly said we carried nothing like that. They moved to the cab next and asked Max to open that. They seemed very concerned about the door with a broken lock being wired shut. The lock had been broken when we were burgled in Bulgaria. They made us open the door by undoing the wires. Then they wanted the door panel taken off, although I insisted we had no drugs hidden behind it. In the end we levered the panel off with a screwdriver, they peered round the door with a torch and then seemed to be satisfied at last.

I had been scared stiff. In one corner, wrapped in black plastic, was a small parcel containing my money, much of which was Deutschmarks or dollars. Other hiding places for money were in a hollow strap on the horse harness and in my shoe. It was not that importing currency was illegal, but I was afraid of being robbed and losing all we had. Western currency confers almost godlike status on its possessor in this country. We had learnt our lesson in this subject during our time in Bulgaria. I also had a lack of trust in the customs officers.

The caravan was also subjected to examination. Our video camera in its case I had left in clear view hanging by the door. A soldier touched it, but left it hanging. A great deal of conversation was taking place all around us and the English speaker said they wanted to remove the canvas cover, which made me groan inwardly at the thought of what that entailed. They wanted to be sure we had nothing hidden between the canvas outer cover and the lining. I put my head in my hands, to convey my plea to be excused this one request.

I was saved by the timely arrival of a woman in a white coat, who asked me for the horse's documents. She was the veterinarian come to see Action. I was hardly expecting to find my papers adequate for Romania. She gave the horse a brief look over and then went into the office block.

Back at the caravan, I found one customs man on the outside of the canvas, tapping all over it with his knuckles and shouting to a man inside who was doing the same. Having completed the canvas, they began on the floor, still tapping happily inside and underneath, knuckle to knuckle, and still muttering "drugs, firearms" in our direction.

The veterinarian came back and told us a doctor was being sent for to come and examine us. We looked incredulous and I asked why.

"In case you have brought any horse diseases from another country," she said.

We had already been hanging about for five hours, it was now dark and cold and the poor horse still had not been taken from the shafts, but we resigned ourselves to the inevitable. An icy wind blew off the nearby Danube.

"Max, I think we should put Action inside the horsebox with his food. There's nowhere here we can tie him up," I said.

Max pulled down the tailgate, but an obstruction lay in Action's path: the box containing our rabbit. Max was unthinkingly lifting it out at the very moment the veterinarian returned. The box had a wire mesh across the front and the grey rabbit was clearly visible inside. She must have seen it. I was just about to confess all, when she held out a document and said she had no other objection to us proceeding.

"What about this?" I asked.

She lifted her eyebrows and sighed deeply, then said, "Remove it." After which, she walked away.

"What about the human doctor?" I asked the English speaking officer.

"Injections," he replied.

"No way!" exclaimed a horrified Max, who made for the horsebox with the intention of leaving immediately.

I followed him.

"There's no way I'm going to be injected again, Dad," he said. "Not by this lot. I had enough of that in Bulgaria. Never again!"

The officer told me to go to the office and collect a visa, and when I went inside, an English speaking woman advised me the visa would cost 146 Deutschmarks. She added that we must each change 30 DM into Romanian lev every day we spent in the country, keeping all the receipts to show when we left again. Then she asked for a further 10DM, and when I asked what that was for she slid it into a drawer and said, in perfect English,

"Five for me and five for the man."

We were allowed to pay Romanian lev for the green card needed for the vehicle. The English speaking man came in and said we could now go, but we must park overnight by the petrol station, which he pointed towards, and in the morning we must purchase our petrol coupons there. He showed us a stamp that had been added to our passports, then handed them back to us. The barrier was lifted and we drove through into the darkness beyond. There was a restaurant there, but it was closed. The time was nine o'clock at night.

In my relief, I threw my arms round Max.

"Thank God for that, Max. Are you all right?"

We woke up to a cold morning. Action was still tied to a post and the horsebox and caravan were still side by side.

"Hey! Look at that," I cried, suddenly spotting a huge pile of corn on the cob stalks and leaves half dry, and sugar beet and maize leaves beside the caravan. At this point a policeman came over and made it clear he was responsible. I had no idea how he managed it.

Later, we met a German who had travelled 6,000 kilometres across

Eastern Europe, and he warned us to be vigilant over our belongings, especially when young children and youths were about.

We set course for Bucharest in the hope of finding someone at the Embassy to whom we could explain our situation, which was admittedly somewhat vague, even to us. The lady veterinarian, for instance, had given us no written confirmation that she had made a satisfactory inspection of the horse. Neither had there been any further mention of a doctor to inspect us.

The roads were a bit rough in places, lined on either side by fruit and nut trees, and we saw no trace of litter anywhere. We came through two attractive villages, but it was like being way back in time. There were very few cars, many horse – drawn carts, muddy lanes, wells and old houses. Even the people we saw in the streets were old. There was plenty of work being done on the land, everywhere we looked, but not a sign of decent agricultural equipment. In the evening, we saw young children leaving school and coming straight to work in the fields, in groups, under supervision, and we saw convicts in uniform, guarded by armed soldiers, also working on the land. Even parties of young soldiers were doing their share.

What cars we did see were mainly of the Renault 12 type, and the lorries and vans were of Russian or Romanian manufacture, most in bad working order and old. The buses and coaches were certainly death traps. There were few road signs and the road surface was deteriorating rapidly. There were shops, but from outside, it was hard to know what they sold, and they appeared to be poorly stocked. The bars, on the other hand, were mostly full of drunks. Beer was still in short supply and the customers consumed wine and brandy. We stopped to investigate and to try and buy a coffee.

Before we got as far as the bar we found ourselves mobbed by people. It was rather terrifying, with everyone, from the age of three to ninety, wanting chewing gum, balloons, books, clothes, toys, cigarettes, disposable razors, contraceptives, soap, deodorant, ball point pens and, of course, dollars. On top of this, there was no coffee to be had in Romania, so they said.

After much anguish, we made our escape, but only by behaving aggressively towards them. We only had a few sticks left on the caravan and horsebox, and even these had been torn off by the time we left. To this day, I do not know how we got out of that situation.

We were on flat roads with huge expanses of cultivated land on either side and horses pulling carts passing every few minutes, often singly and some with man and wife, or father and son aboard. There were a few convoys also, always the same V – shaped carts with either wooden or pneumatic tyred wheels. A few had makeshift roofs of sacking or canvas supported on sticks or pieces of scrap metal, and these, I knew, were Gipsy carts taking itinerant labourers from field to field. The people waved to us in passing, never asking us for anything. They were poor people and their horses were small compared with Action, most were chestnuts and a good few were lame. There were a few carts pulled by a pair of horses side by side. The harness was always tatty and held together by string and rope.

Autumn had come and it was still warm by day, but the nights had grown very cold. These workers, who lived in their caravan – carts, wore thick, vast, old overcoats, woollen hats and the women had many layers of clothing to keep off the chill. Those without coats wore layers of rags about their shoulders. I, also, had resorted to wearing an extra layer of warm things when driving along.

When we made our first night stop, we pulled onto a piece of hard ground just off the main road, and within minutes we were surrounded by people trying to beg things from us. Even some of the professional spiv types in cars pulled up to see what was to be had. They stood out from the average Romanian by their blue demin, gold chains and air of affluence. Most of them were young and they spent their time cruising the road like sharks waiting for Western tourists to come along. One would engage the unwary traveller in conversation while another reconnoitred to see what valuables he carried. They were the scourge of our journey through Romania. They rob, they con, they swindle and we found their like also in Russia. I regard them as the dregs of both places. Even their own people are not safe from their depredations.

We hastily decided to move on, which was made more difficult by the fact that one of the youths had removed Action's bridle. When this had happened before, it was usually some concerned farmer who had seen the horse trying to eat and had done it out of kindness. This time things were different. It had been done to stop us moving. Something had to be done, however, as we had also attracted swarms of children and other adults, who had moved away when told we had nothing for them, and we were left alone with the scum. I was already at a loss what to do next, and this was only our first night out on the road.

I saw, approaching from behind, caravan canvases in the distance. There seemed to be four caravans, and I guessed they belonged to Gipsies. So far they had not bothered us, but I felt I must try and get them to stop. I quickly conveyed my intention to Max, speaking fast to confuse our unwelcome guests, many of whom knew some English. Two of the men had been pulling at my jumper sleeves and asking me to give them something.

"Stop the Gipsies, Max, and ask for horse fodder," I said.

One caravan carried a large bundle of sweet corn stems, which they use to feed horses when travelling the roads. They use the same material for roofing and bedding when they make a stop at night.

Max raised his hand when the leading caravan was close and explained that he wanted food for Action. Romanian, when spoken, sounds much like Italian, which Max now understood very well, so he was able to talk reasonably easily. The elderly man sat in the driving seat climbed down and went to the rear of his convoy. He gave us a bunch of the stems. The crowd of scum still hung round watching. I got out of their sight and took the old Gipsy by his arm, ran my finger across my throat and said,

"Bandeedos, Probleme, Bandeedos." Then I pointed to the youths.

The man understood that we needed help and by this time several other Gipsies had dismounted and stood admiring Action. Max replaced the bridle while the youths were standing back from us. No sooner was it in place than I jumped onto the caravan and we took off, the Gipsy convoy following behind us.

After two miles, the lead caravan went ahead and the driver signalled to me to follow him down a turn-off ahead of us. We went a short way until we came to a field and I followed him in. A second caravan came after me while the remainder continued along the road.

Max said they wanted us to stay there with them, and although I was a bit nervous about this idea, it seemed the lesser of two evils and I was not to regret making the choice to stick with them.

The man in the lead caravan had his wife with him, a plump, round lady in a flowered frock and a grubby apron. Her dusty feet peeped out from dirty sandals, evidence that they had been working all day in the fields. There were also two young teenage boys under the canvas. The second caravan held two men and a dog. Soon they had lit a fire, using the centre of the corn stalks for kindling. I started to light our own fire and get a brew made. We had little left to eat, however, except stale bread, small cucumbers, four soggy tomatoes and some feta cheese made from ewes' milk.

One of the young boys signed to us to come and eat with them, which we were happy to do. While the men tended the horses, I watched the women cut up carrots, onions, peppers and potatoes and put them in water with a handful of herbs to boil for about half an hour. The boys prepared a bed for themselves on a layer of corn stalks covered with a crocheted quilt. They used a piece of canvas and sacks held up on sticks to make a shelter over it.

The stew was served out in crock bowls and eaten with fresh bread. I found it lacking in flavour, but filling. Afterwards came bread and feta cheese, which I declined, but Max ate. The last course consisted of small fresh plums. We still had some bottles of wine we had been given in Italy, Greece and Bulgaria, most of it home-made and in unlabelled bottles, so we had no idea what was what. I sent Max to fetch some and we shared it with our companions, drinking from cups or mugs.

Not much talk took place, as everyone was tired, and we turned in at 10 o'clock, leaving a pile of glowing embers in the still, cold night. Max used to enjoy a good read when he got into bed, but our torch batteries had run down and we had not been able to get replacements in Bulgaria. Until now, this had not mattered much, as it stayed light well into the evening.

In the morning, when I woke, there was the sound of people talking outside and the fire was already burning, although it was barely light yet.

"Max, let's give them a tin of coffee as another small present," I suggested, knowing we had several tins that had been given to us at different times.

I gave the tin to the lady and she smiled her thanks. Next came our sugar and our tinned milk. I think they could hardly believe their eyes at this bounty. The two boys regarded us as if we were a pair of magicians when we produced all these smart tins and packets. Our final gift to these kind friends, I gave them as we were about to take to the road; it was some of the Spillers High Protein Feed for their horses.

Max drove ahead, only a mile at a time, as we followed the E20 road towards Bucharest. We stopped at midday for food, again given by the Gipsies, a pale, insipid salami type sausage which is not one of my favourite things, but which went down with bread and tomato to help it.

We moved off again and Max went ahead. When I caught up with him he had a crowd of children jumping up at the horsebox while a crowd of adults stood back and watched. He was being pressurised by beggars, and the minute I drew up they turned their attention to me, pestering me for all the usual things. Even women came and begged for deodorants and Bic razors. Max was glad to see me.

"All I did, Dad, was throw out that old chocolate cake," he said. "When I wound down the window, they nearly tore my arm off. I let go and it broke into tiny bits all over the ground. The children swooped down like vultures. I've never seen anything like it. They must be starving. I had to lock myself in the van and wait for you. No way was I going to leave it and live."

We stuck close to our Gipsy friends as we continued our way towards Bucharest. The filling stations we saw were either closed for lack of fuel or else had long queues, up to two miles in length, waiting for hours to get served. We had purchased our petrol coupons at the customs post and besides having a full tank, we also had two 5-gallon containers, enough to get us a few hundred miles. In the villages we saw pavements filled with old people waiting patiently for a battered van to come with bread, apples, preserved fruit in jars or other simple things. I was struck by the orderly manner in which they waited. There was no pushing and shoving even when the van arrived, as if the people had been trained to queue and wait. It was the pattern of everyday life for those too old to work, who had to queue patiently for food to give those members of the family labouring in the factories and fields all day.

On the outskirts of each village was the communal farm where most of the adults found employment. Many farms specialised in a particular type of crop, cereals, vegetables or stock rearing, and some were mixed farms with something of each. Huge haystacks stood in some of the fields, and enormous straw ricks, sometimes three or four at a time, stood side by side. Old men and women herded at the roadside, one cow or, perhaps, four or five goats each. Pigs roamed the verges, too. These verges provided a piece of common pasture for all manner of farm animals, and it was a rare sight to see beasts grazing in fields, although there were some herds on rough moorland, tended by herdsmen and women, who travelled with the animals and slept at night under tin sheets and hedges, on brushwood beds covered with sacking and old rags.

Another common sight was women washing clothes on the rocks in rivers and streams. Soap and detergents are unknown in this part of Romania. Most small towns had a market place with tiny stalls selling carrots, onions, potatoes, small cucumbers, spring onions, fresh herbs and a few tomatoes. There might be no more than one bucket of potatoes, or ten small bunches of spring onions on a stall. When a new batch of food was delivered to a stall-holder, the crowds would make a dive at it, the late comers not getting within touching distance, as it was sometimes sold off the cart, before it actually reached the stall. It was all done, however, in the same, zombie – like, patient manner, without any hustling or impatience. My heart went out to these old folk, queuing from six in the morning until something turned up many hours later, if it arrived at all, or if it had not all been sold before they reached the front of the queue.

When we visited shops, we found stale food and a sour smell. The small amount of food on sale was displayed on shelves, while glass fronted counters held large rolls and the local, fly covered, salami type sausage, consisting of more fat than meat, but there were no refrigerated units to be seen, and detergents and cleaning agents were equally impossible to find. The cut edges of the sausage were dried up and discoloured and the trays it stood in were chipped through years of wear. The other items on display were scarce, unappetising and, in my opinion, inedible. They usually amounted to no more than a few jars of preserves and a foul tasting fruit juice, plus some tomatoes, peppers and plums.

Bread was sold in bakery shops and mostly baked on the premises, but there was a continual shortage of flour and yeast. When supplies were adequate, which was seldom the case, the baking capacity was insufficient. Milk was also sold in specialist milk shops. We were just outside Bucharest when Max spotted a delivery of crates being made to a shop and he went to buy two bottles, for he loves milk. He handed me one of the bottles and the outside of the glass felt sticky and had smears of milk all over it. Max's bottle was just the same. The absence of detergents meant the bottles had only had a quick rinse in cold water. I opened the bottle and put it to my lips, but the top edge was also greasy and the milk had a taste that I cannot adequately describe, being a thin, foul mixture of cow, sheep and goat milk, almost transparent and enough to put us off Romanian milk for good.

The bread was good, however. It was heavy, had a light brown colour and was filling, but its one drawback was that after four hours it went hard as rock. I was interested to see under what conditions it was produced, and I found out in a suburb of Bucharest, when we were walking past a shop with a queue outside and a strong aroma of baking bread in the air. There was a fence running alongside the bakehouse and our investigations revealed a pile of dead, dying and decomposing rats beside it. Like other Romanians, we had no choice but to eat bread or starve.

The food shortage was less noticeable in the large towns, and it seemed to be Ceauçescu's policy to feed the towns and let the villages survive to the best of their abilities. But his days were numbered. The next time we came to Romania was after the revolution, when the people had a new degree of freedom and the villagers were able to keep more of the food they had grown for themselves.

We saw three types of housing in Romania. In the country there were cottages on the roadside or along mud tracks. They had no running water and several cottagers shared a communal well for personal and livestock needs. Many of the cottages had vegetable gardens which were worked with primitive hand tools and provided extra food for the families. There were other cottages inhabited by the old and the sick. These were almost derelict, with boarded up windows, tin roofs, their gardens overgrown from lack of care.

The second style in housing was found on the fringes of the towns and consisted of massive, poorly constructed blocks of flats, thrown up fast and cheaply to rehouse the agricutural community when Ceauçescu developed his ideas of population relocation that led to whole communities being uprooted and their villages abandoned. His reasoning for such massive translocation sounded sensible in theory. He said it was the best way to give the poor and underprivileged of the rural areas a chance to enjoy proper sanitation and amenities, and thus rid Romania of its Third World status. While people in the west criticised Ceauçescu for what he did, many of the peasants who now lived in the flats told me they much preferred their new homes, with running water, sewerage and warmth, to the old cottages that had none of these. Perhaps we have no room to complain about this aspect of Ceauçescu when we think what has been done in the 1950s, 1960s and 1970s to build unpopular, high rise blocks in our own inner cities, in place of much better, older housing.

The third style of housing was for the privileged, high ranking officials of the Communist Party, the Securitate, the Army or the Police, and ranged from luxury cottages to luxury apartments. The price the occupiers pay is twofold: loyalty to Ceauçescu and hatred from the populace.

That evening, we said goodbye to our Gipsy friends. Before we parted, the woman brought her husband to me and showed me the backs of his hands, which were covered in septic sores and open cracks exposing raw flesh. In a mixture of Romanian and Max's Italian, we understood that it was a common complaint in Romania and she was asking if we had any cream to soften the hard skin and give it a chance to heal. The two boys also had badly affected hands, but cream of any sort was unobtainable. The Wellcome Foundation had kindly given us some tubes of Drapolene, a cream for use on babies' bottoms, and I gave them three tubes of this and showed them how to apply it. I knew it offered no cure, but I hoped it would ease the soreness. Her gratitude was embarrassing. She fell on her knees and put her hands together in an attitude of prayer. I took her arm and pulled her to her feet. The two boys were already busy rubbing the cream into their hands. It was good to feel we had done something to help them in return for their kindness to us.

We pulled into a housing estate in the hope of finding a parking place and soon found ourselves besieged by begging children. Their clamour was deafening. Action took it in his stride, but Max was upset when they started trying to open the horsebox doors and began climbing all over it and up the back of the caravan. We could not control them and soon we should have nothing left.

"Let's get out of here, Dad," he said, brandishing a large steel bar, "Before I hit them with this."

Max always carried the iron bar and a sheath knife in the front of the horsebox, in case he needed them for self protection. It was this same knife that he would use to stab someone at a later stage of the journey.

By now, many adults had also moved in, and one hefty looking ruffian in baggy trousers and a white vest came forward menacingly. I thought our hour had come.

"Good evening," he said. "What are you doing with this?"

A hush fell over the children as Max handed over our folder, opening it to the English language articles and pictures of the handicapped. He quickly understood and began to tell the crowd, who started moving amongst the children, shouting and driving them away. Our defender had told the people to leave us alone as we had come on a humanitarian mission. Apart from a handful of hopeful youths still asking for dollars, the plea worked. Even the youths were now reluctant to touch our horsebox or caravan.

We spent the rest of that evening being treated like royalty. We ate chicken cooked by one of the families, had oranges for afters and drank red wine and beer. We should not have a feast like this again while we were in Romania, and our friend pointed out that it had all been obtained through the black market, run by so – called businessmen.

Typical of the way we were mobbed by Romanians every time we stopped in the street.

Family going to work by horse and cart

Wrapped up against the biting cold of winter

Typical Romanian peasant.

Watering cattle at a Romanian well.

Chapter Twenty – three

Romania Makes an Impression on Us. Action Leaves his Mark on Romania.

Our destination was the British Embassy in the heart of Bucharest, a city of old buildings, potholed roads and more traffic than we had seen for some time: old bangers belching smoke; lorries emitting bangs and pops; crammed commuter buses polluting the air; taxis racing hither and yon. The faces of the people were solemn, unenthusiastic about the working day ahead of them. Every road junction was manned by armed soldiers and police, and large lookout posts provided vantage points from which to observe the traffic and pedestrians below. I guessed they also served a more sinister purpose, and it was at one of these posts that we had our first real confrontation with the police.

I had seen men inside the lookout tower ahead of us, and as we came near it we noticed a police officer in the centre of the road crossing. He let the other traffic go on its way, but he signalled to me to stop. Max was following behind me and he also pulled up. Passers by stood transfixed when they saw the amount of publicity we carried, as such a display would never be permitted under normal circumstances.

I climbed down from the caravan and Max came up beside me. When the policeman spoke to us in Romanian, Max said "Anglisci", which the officer understood. He asked for our passports, read them and handed them back.

"British," he said, and then reverted to Romanian.

A crowd had gathered on the pavement, quietly observing the proceedings. Another officer came, from the lookout post, with a man aged about thirty clad in a coloured shirt and tie, denim jeans and a smart black leather bomber jacket. It was this man who spoke to us, in good English.

"Where are you going?"

"To the British Embassy," Max replied.

"What do you want in Bucharest?"

"Show him the book, Max," I said, feeling uneasy in this man's presence.

So far, we had come across all sorts of policemen, but there was something different about this man. Without uniform, he could have been anything: army, security guard, policeman or what? Max gave him the folder, which he looked at, speaking at the same time with the policeman at his side.

"I want to see in the caravan and the lorry," he said, as he handed back our folder.

He moved to the caravan, gazed inside and then climbed aboard. Another man, also in smart denims, had now joined the others. This one sported a gold chain round his neck and a gold watch on his wrist. He stood talking to the police. The man in the leather jacket emerged from the caravan with our video camera in his hand. I usually left it lying on the sofa bed when we were on the move, to save it from unnecessary vibration.

"Video camera?" he asked.

"Yes."

"You film Bucharest?"

"Yes."

He fiddled with the camera for a while, as if he had never seen one before and was rather intrigued with it. It was not an ideal spot for him to flash it about, with so many people watching. They would know we had it and that would make us a target. I had the impression that he would either confiscate it or damage it. He looked the type to do either. Instead, he handed it back to Max, exchanged a dozen words with the other man in denims, shook hands with the policeman and left. We lost sight of him when he entered another street.

When we were in Russe, the director of the Union of the Blind there, a Mr. Nedev, had promised to contact the director of the Bucharest Union of the Blind on our behalf, so we hoped to find a welcome when we arrived, but before then we had to get to the British Embassy. We asked our way several times and arrived at the Embassy at lunchtime. We found it at last in a narrow street. Beside its large gates was a sentry box manned by two policemen, who stared at the sight of us. One was a young man, the other, in his forties, stepped out and came over. I handed him our passports and said we wanted to visit the Embassy. He walked backwards in front of Action, beckoning me forward as far as a barrier and a No Parking sign. Our vehicles were still too long for the space, so he moved the barrier back to make more room. Once we were settled, he roamed round the caravan reading the publicity material.

As usual, we soon had a crowd of curious sightseers asking questions. Among the people returning from lunch were Romanian and British members of the Embassy staff. The policemen on the gate smiled and nodded as they went into the building. I gave Action his nosebag filled with horse nuts, but he needed water as well, so, armed with bucket and passports, I went up to the sentries. They understood what I wanted and directed me beyond the Embassy to an old house, with many subsequent additions, standing behind a tall iron fence. We went past the British Library, a prefabricated building on the right of the drive.

When we told our story at the Embassy, we were directed to take our troubles to the Consular Department next door, where we found a very attractive Romanian lady seated behind a glass screen. We told her about our wish to visit handicapped homes and asked her if she could confirm that we were expected by the Union of the Blind at the address we had been given. She said she could.

Next, we told her we had a thirty hour transit visa, and would like instead a thirty day visitor's visa. We had already been in Romania for four days, and we had not exchanged the obligatory sum of money every day and obtained receipts for it. She advised us to go to a hotel, exchange some dollars and get a receipt so that we were within the law. Meanwhile, she would ring the passport office about our visas.

"There is just one thing," I said. "I can't afford to change twenty dollars a day all the time I am in Romania. I do not class myself as a tourist. We came on a humanitarian mission. Can you do anything to help with this one? And, we need permission to travel freely in Romania with our caravan. There is yet another problem. Could I trouble you to contact the British Embassy in Sofija and ask if there has been any reply to our request to Russia for an entry visa? If there has not been any answer, would you ask them to chase it up. We really should like to get to our friends before the bad weather returns."

She showed great willingness to help with anything and everything, in so far as it lay in her power. I went back to the caravan and found a number of people busily reading the posters. A few men were after dollars and would give me a prod to attract my attention. They were reluctant to take no for an answer and continued to follow me about.

When we were called back to the Consular Office, the Romanian woman told us to take our passports to the passport office, where we would be issued with 30 day visas. She also gave us a letter requesting that we be exempted from making a daily currency exchange. She had already spoken to Mr. Craciun, Director for the Union of the Blind, and confirmed that he was expecting us. She had also obtained an assurance from the police that we could travel freely in Romania as long as we obeyed the law.

"I spoke to the British Embassy in Sofija about your entry visa for Russia. You will have to wait for a reply," she concluded.

She had been so helpful. I thanked her and said that I would telephone tomorrow and let her know the outcome of our visit to the passport office. At the same time, we hoped she would have firm news from Sofija.

We made our way through narrow streets until we came to the Union of the Blind, on a crossroads near a park. It was in a once grand old house with a steel fence and locked gates. To enter it one had to pass through a small building, so we parked Action by the gates and went up to this small building. Inside was an old woman watching us. We held out our folder and she opened the door. She seemed at something of a loss and indicated to us to wait. A man approached. He was deaf, but realising who we were, he escorted us to the director's office, where we met Mr. Craciun and some of his staff.

While they plied us with coffee and food, we spoke about our journey and said we should like to see round his institution and, perhaps, he might care to speak to other homes for handicapped people that we could visit.

"I cannot let you look round here until I have permission from the Ministry of Health. I will speak to them and ask about other hospitals in Bucharest you could visit, but until I have this permission, I cannot even allow you to bring your horse through the gates. I am sorry," he said.

He showed his good intentions by getting busy on the telephone right away.

We understood his predicament and appreciated what he was trying to do for us. An interpreter had been found and he told us where in the grounds to park. Apparently the police had been notified and were agreeable to the arrangements. We were shown to a small car park, large enough for about twenty cars and flanked on two sides by factories. We put the caravan and horsebox side by side in one corner and by the time we had done this it was already half past five. Apart from a few people who came up to read our publicity posters, it all seemed quiet enough. However, we had not yet got water for Action.

"I'll ask at the factory," Max offered.

When he returned he had water and a bag of bread. Now all we needed was some hay, or fresh grass. Taking an exploratory walk down the road, I came to a large park with good grass lawns, but Action would soon make a mess of them if we took him there. It would have to be hay after all, but where in the middle of Bucharest was it to be obtained? It would have to wait until the next day. For now, I tethered him on his chain between caravan and horsebox, gave him his water and some nuts and sweet corn stems, with which he was quite content.

Towards eight o'clock, things became busier in our vicinity. There was a bus stop on the corner and the passengers were watching us while waiting for one of the city's rickety old buses to stop. Passengers set down there came over and stared at us, but few spoke to us. I was puzzled by this, and wondered if they were shy or scared. The only limited conversation we had was with a party of twelve year old boys. They had picked up a smattering of English vocabulary, although they could not construct proper sentences. They knew the names of two British football teams: Liverpool and Manchester United.

Among the crowd was a number of youths, in their teens or early twenties and well dressed for Romanians. They began to indulge in rather rough behaviour too close to Action, and I ran up and shouted at them to stop. For a while they went away, then it all began again, while the people stood looking sympathetically at us.

"Dad, these men are dangerous. We had better call the police," Max said at last.

I did not think this was a good idea, and the harassment continued a while longer, until, luckily for us, a police car drew up, an officer got out and addressed the crowd. He said nothing at all to us. After a few seconds, he waved his arms indicating to the crowd to disperse. Everyone melted away and the policeman got back in his car, drove across the road, to where he could keep us in view, and parked. Two men started to talk to him through the window. They were smartly dressed and aged about thirty. The police car drove off and the two men went to stand by the bus stop. I thought they were waiting for a bus, but various buses came and went and still the men remained there, smoking cigarette after cigarette. It was now dark.

Night time in Bucharest means deep darkness. There are very few street lights and those there are are very dim. I wished there had been more light in our overnight location, as bright lights keep trouble away. For a while all was quiet. Poor Action wanted to spend a penny, but would not do it on hard ground. He also wanted a nibble at some grass.

"I'll just take him up the road to the park, Max," I said.

"Well, don't be away too long," he replied.

The park gates had been left open and we went inside. As Action ate his fill, I sat holding his rope, my back against a tree. Then he spread his legs and relieved his bladder. Finally, he began sniffing the ground and walking round in circles, a sure sign that he was preparing himself for a roll. This was when he was at his most destructive towards grass. It was not the actual rolling so much as his feet digging in when he stood up afterwards. Before I could do anything to stop him, he was on his back and snorting loudly. He got up and shook himself, leaving the lawn cratered with holes and spattered with divots. It was high time we left.

I got back and wanted to tell Max about what Action had been up to, but he was not concerned, being deep in conversation with a young man of about twenty–one or two. I wondered what was the matter this time.

"This is my father," Max began, introducing me to his new friend.

From now on, I shall omit some names and place names, in order not to make trouble for people whom we met and who were kind and friendly towards us. Even today, Romanians do not enjoy total freedom of speech and action. When Ceauçescu was still in power, as he was during our first visit, it was forbidden to fraternise with foreigners. I met some of these people again, when I revisited Romania after his downfall. One woman told me then that there was still a long way to go before they had democracy. This is what she said:

"We do not understand what democracy is here in Romania. What do we do to make it? We now have freedom of speech, but I still have to look over my shoulder, as the Government will not release the figures of how many soldiers, police and civilians were killed in the fighting, and, most worrying of all, we do not know how many of Ceauçescu's Securitate were killed or captured, or how many are still at large. I do know that many have been released and I will not feel free until these people are caught and brought to justice.

"You must remember that there were many Communists in good jobs, living off the fat of the land, under his regime. In many cases these people have been brought down or demoted. It must hurt them. We realise that these people will try to get back their old positions and living standards, as their tables were always full. They are a danger to our new democracy. They must never be allowed to get into positions of power again. But I fear they will.

"I do not condemn all Communists, as in most cases they had to join to get on in their work. Many would join the party who did not believe in its purpose. Even my Father joined the Party, but I knew he hated the system. Others will never give it up."

"I am pleased to meet you," said the young man, in excellent English. "How long do you stay in Bucharest?"

We stood by the caravan door for almost an hour, talking to together. At this late hour few people were about, but out of the gloom two men emerged and made for Action. I recognised them as the two who had been watching us from the bus stop earlier. They did not say anything to our friend, but he told us quietly that it was time for him to leave.

"Not good men. I see you tomorrow, three o'clock," he whispered, before melting away into the gloom of a Bucharest night.

I wondered what the two men were up to. When I got into bed, I lay thinking what a hole Bucharest was, with a palpable atmosphere of fear in the air everywhere. I had not eaten anything all day and the strain had left me overtired. I dozed off eventually, only to be woken by the sound of running feet, and distant laughter and shouts of "You English bastards". The sounds of running feet faded, but someone was walking about outside the caravan. I knelt on my bed and peered into the darkness beyond the window, but it was too black to see anything. The sounds of shuffling feet continued, and voices whispering. Then smoke began to fill the caravan and I saw the flickering light of flames through the window. Someone had set it on fire.

"Max!" I yelled as loudly as possible.

Until now, I had kept quiet, but when I shouted, there was the sound of running feet and voices calling. I got out into the street, my heart racing; smoke was in the air and lights were flickering under the caravan. A roll of paper had been set alight and placed by one of the wooden wheels. I quickly grabbed Action's water and threw it on the flames.

"Max," I cried. "The bastards tried to burn me alive."

Max had still not yet heard me. Because of his deafness, he sleeps with his head under the blankets, and I normally have to knock hard on the van door when I want to waken him. I banged hard, but got no reply. I banged again, but there was still no movement. I peered through the window, and could find no sign of him within. Where was he?

I untied Action and stood beside him for an hour. He was my first line of defence if anyone else wanted to have a go at me. I could easily make him angry or excited, if I wanted to. In my hand I held a big carving knife. There was a gap of eight feet between horsebox and caravan, and anyone approaching would have had to cross in front of or behind Action. Either way, I could make him move quickly by swinging him round in circles. I am sure he knew I was nervous.

Dawn was breaking when Max returned and found me sitting on Action's upturned bucket, tired out. I shouted at him, asking where he had been, ranting and raving in blind anger. I told him never to wander off like that again without telling me where he was going.

"I just had to get away, Dad. I couldn't sleep here," he said.

I could not understand him. I was too exhausted and angry, but he was hardly to blame for that. He moved away from my rage and locked himself in the horsebox.

My temper gradually subsided as I stroked Action, a sure cure for my woes when I was angry or scared about something. I began to feel sorry for abusing Max. I could see him sitting in the horsebox staring into space. He must have been feeling truly miserable.

I began a choking apology and Max came out, put his arm round me and said,

"There's only one way, Dad. Either one or other of us will have to stay awake all the time. We shall have to take it in turns to keep watch."

I grabbed a couple of hours sleep while Max stood guard. It would become part of the pattern of our existence while we were in Bucharest. It would also add exhaustion to the other pressures we would be under.

In the afternoon, the young man, who had arranged to return at three o'clock, came to say he could not stop now, but would come again at seven–thirty in the evening. He said he had a present for us.

Once again, crowds of people, many of them children, inundated us. Some of the hooligan element ripped off what was left of our stickers, but I had lost the will to stop them. By half past six, still without food and short of sleep, I locked myself in the caravan to have a lie down, but with so many people knocking on the door, voices calling for gum, chocolate or anything else they wanted, I saw no chance of getting any rest. Like a child expecting a good hiding, I buried myself under the bedclothes and hoped everyone would go away, but the tapping on my door persisted until I could stand it no longer.

I jumped from the bed and made a lunge towards the door, smashing it open and sending the nearest boy flying. I grabbed the carving knife, which was lying handy, and sprang from the caravan, brandishing it at the boys. One was slow making his getaway and I lunged at him. The knife just missed him. I stopped in my tracks, filled with shame. What was I doing?

I looked down at the ground for a moment and then turned to go back in the caravan. Two men stood a few yards off, waving their fingers as if to say, "That was uncalled for". I went back inside, wondering who else might have seen me besides those two men. I could find myself in deep trouble, I thought.

During this episode, Max had been away buying bread and anything else he could find. When he returned, he only had a stale loaf of yesterday's bread. We sprinkled it with sugar and sat down to make the best of it, but the nurse from the home suddenly appeared with two bags of something for us. Both were full of food. It was the usual monotonous stuff, but very welcome for all that. She said it had not come from the Union for the Blind, but she had brought it from her own home.

Our young friend reappeared at seven–thirty and we stood talking by the caravan door. All the while, his eyes roved restlessly over our surroundings and his nervousness showed visibly.

"This is for you," he said, handing me a book. It was a copy of David Copperfield, by Charles Dickens. "This is the only English book I have, and it is a prized possession, but I wish you to have it as a gift for your courage. Have you a pen? I should like to write a message in it for you."

I went inside the caravan to find a pen and invited him to come inside.

"No, no," he said. "It is a problem for me with those two men near me."

I looked across to the bus stop and our two minders were there again.

"They are from the special police, the Securitate," he said. "They watch us. Ah, well, they can only torture me," he added, bravely, as he came inside and began to write in the book.

He sat for a few moments on my bed, speaking rapidly.

"I don't care any more. Ceauçescu is evil and we must soon stand up to him. My country is ruined by his policies. Everyone that speaks out against his Communism is got rid of." He moved closer to the doorway. "When the special police have gone, I shall show you the new Bucharest."

It was dark by the time our friend told us it was safe to go and see the new city. He wanted us both to accompany him, but we explained that one of us had to remain on guard.

"You go, Max," I said. "But don't be too long."

"We'll be back by ten – thirty," promised our friend.

"See you later," I replied. "Off you go then."

I climbed onto my bed, trying hard to keep awake. Every little sound outside brought me back to wakefulness when I was nearly asleep. Then I came to again when I heard Action neighing loudly and felt the caravan shaking. I heard his shoes against the car park's surface and again the sound of running feet. Still half asleep, I rushed out to the horse and found a young boy standing close by making a stabbing movement with his hand. I touched Action's back and it felt wet. Again the boy made the stabbing movement and I realised the people I had heard had stabbed my horse. The wet on my hand was his blood. The young boy threw a punch in the air and touched Action's nose. When he removed his hand it, too, was covered in blood. Those men had not only stabbed him, they had punched his poor old nose. Anything I had done to upset Ceauçescu was hardly the fault of the animal. All he had ever done to anyone was good.

The stab wound was clean, about an inch deep, and the bleeding soon stopped, but his nose was very tender. I tried to look up his nostrils and he jerked away, in pain or fear.

Max came back alone and said he had parted from his friend just round the corner, but would be seeing him again at seven the following evening when he was coming to take me round Bucharest. I asked Max about his night out and what he had discovered. He said he had been given the history of Count Dracula, a bloodthirsty yarn that turned my stomach.

"I found it a fascinating story," said Max, "And my friend asked if I enjoyed fantasy and fiction. I said I did. He said he would show me the fantasy and fiction created by Ceauçescu, which took us on a walk, in darkness, through most of Bucharest. We found ourselves at a place I took to be a huge building site and a massive office block extending for about three quarters of a mile. We went through a passage and found ourselves in a wide boulevard with lawns and fountains, and walls lined with mosaic. The whole was lit with hundreds of lights, some on lofty columns, some in the fountains. What a contrast with the rest of the city!

"On either side of the boulevard were new blocks of flats with shops underneath. There must have been thousands of flats. I asked my friend what this place was. He told me it was Ceauçescu's eighth wonder of the world, his dream of the new Romania. Then he said how much it was costing the country, how all the income from Romania's exports went to pay for it. He reminded me of all the derelict villages there were and said the people who had once lived in them would never be rehoused here. These flats were built for the privileged few, the inner circle of Communists, Securitate, Police and Military, who kept his regime in power.

"At the far end of the boulevard was a brightly lit palace, which my friend said would be Ceauçescu's home and the seat of government. I had to admit that when the whole complex was finished it would put Romania on the world map. He told me there was much more yet to be built and he wanted to show me the sites where churches had been demolished to make way for the continued building programme. Then he said we ought not to be there, as no official pictures had yet been released to the West. The sight of a police patrol car made me suggest it was time to depart.

"On the walk back to you, Dad, he told me about the new underground railway and waterway that will run beneath the new city. What made the most impression on me, though, was the way it was all so brightly lit. I could see half a dozen people around and a few workmen, and all the time the rest of Bucharest is in total darkness after eight – thirty at night, because of lack of electricity."

When Max had finished regaling me with what he had been doing, it was my turn to tell him a horror story: what had been happening to Action and me while he was gone. It left us both feeling very uneasy and filled with forebodings, and I had to try and reassure him that the horse was not fatally wounded.

All seemed quiet by 1.30 a.m. and I told Max to take two hours sleep, promising to call him at half past three and get my own head down for a spell. He slept soundly while I paced around outside. Now and then, I walked along the road past some houses. If I had once sat down, I should have fallen asleep. I felt sorry at having to waken Max, but I also needed some rest. My mind had been filled with one question during the past few days: just how much more could Max and I take? I slept until he woke me at eight o'clock.

While I was feeding Action on some of his Spillers nuts, a crowd began to gather round. Three young boys also turned up, three of the well behaved boys, who chatted to me with their few words of English. The evening was quieter than usual and Max used the last handful of our sticks for a fire on which he brewed tea. People still stopped briefly to ask a question or two, but they all seemed reluctant to hang about near us for long.

We were expecting our young man back at half past seven, to take me on a tour of his city, but, at half past six, Max felt restless and asked if he could take a walk.

"As long as you get back here by seven," I said.

I fell into conversation with two young women, one of whom had some English and translated what I said for her companion. I spoke about the journey, watching Max wandering away, being pestered by the three young boys. He was back in less than ten minutes and seemed to be in a state of panic.

"Let's get out of here, Dad. They're f***ing mad," he gasped, trembling all over.

"Now what's happened?" I asked.

"I started to go for a walk, but changed my mind. I thought it might be too dangerous to leave you alone, so I sat down on a wall where I could keep an eye on you. Those three kids were trying to talk to me about football in their bits of English. A policeman with an Alsation dog walked by and overheard them. He came up to within a few feet of us and said something to the boys. I could tell he wasn't friendly. He suddenly let go of the dog and it sprang at the boys and pulled one to the ground. He pulled the dog off. It all happened so fast, just a few seconds. The boy got up, shaken, and the policeman took out his book and began to take their names and addresses.

"From what I could understand of Romanian, he told them not to speak to us as we are bad men. He reminded them that he had their names and addresses in his book now. He never said a word to me, and I sat there frozen. Let's get out of here, Dad," he pleaded.

At this point, his friend arrived and asked if I was ready to go with him. I asked Max what he felt, and he said I could go. He would be all right. I felt guilty about leaving him, but I had a burning desire to get acquainted with Romania, to find out why so many children, youths and young men were so hostile towards us. I promised not to be away for long.

The young man said he wanted to start by showing me the Bucharest night life. As we walked through the darkened streets, he told me of the oppression and misery of life in the last forty years under Ceauçescu; how he had gained absolute control of every citizen, all of whom once admired him for the good things he did. The change had been gradual; his brand of Communism turned away from Russia and towards the West; and his opponents were picked off secretly by his henchmen. The night life he showed me, at nine o'clock in the evening, was bar after bar tightly closed and empty.

"We can try a special bar where they sell beer, but it is very expensive," he suggested.

As we wandered, he continued his story of Romania.

"Ceauçescu did some good things at the beginning, before he became mad with power and greed. His wife, Elena, is even worse than he."

Whenever anyone came past, he would stop the flow of his narrative and wait until we were alone again. He walked me until I was dog–tired. My mind was not functioning clearly, from lack of sleep, and I cannot remember where this special bar was that he took me to. I can remember, however, that it had a magnificent interior and tall, gold decorated pillars. Although I cannot describe it in more detail, I remember being impressed by its beauty, and I recall that it was packed. My young guide found an empty table.

"We can get beer here, Bill. Max said you were a beer drinker."

There was no bar as such, but smart waiters in red jackets flitted round between the tables carrying trays of drink, much of which was served in large, blue and white china jugs. My friend ordered two jugs, gave me one and then said the place would be closing shortly. I took a pull and the beer tasted like piss.

That it was an expensive place could be deduced from the appearance of its clientele. I attempted to focus on the decor, but my eyes were blurred and my head was swimming. I finished the beer and told my friend I had to get out as I felt terrible. He understood and we got up and left.

"Now you feel like the rest us Romanians," he said simply.

On the way back, I noticed that the small groups of people we passed also stopped talking until we were out of earshot of them. Then it struck me how quiet my chum had been while we were in the bar, not talking much above a whisper so that I would not be recognised for a Westerner. By this time, I scarcely looked any different from anyone else in Bucharest. I could summarise his views on life under Communism by saying that in an ideal world it could be a Utopia, but in the real world those with special skills or that extra drive that leads to success in the West wanted some recognition for their labours over an above an equal share with the rest of mankind. In a time of national crisis, these people will do what they can to improve the lot of everyone, but afterwards they want their reward. One could love the theory if only it worked in practice.

Back at the spot where the caravan stood, he said good night to me. I invited him to step inside a while, but he declined. Lifting his eyebrows and inclining his head towards the bus stop, he drew my attention to the two men standing there again, in the gloom. I did not think they had seen us.

"Be careful, Bill. They know now that you've been talking with me."

I crossed the road, to put as much distance as possible between myself and the spies. I averted my eyes as I walked past them and headed for the caravan. I could see no sign of Max, but Action gave a small, welcoming neigh,

"Is that you, Dad?" came a subdued voice from the horsebox cab.

I peered into the cab, which was in darkness. Max was lying across the two front seats, an empty brandy bottle in one hand, an iron bar in the other and his sheath knife on his lap.

"Those bastards from across the road have been wandering around," he said. "They'll get this across their scalps if they come near me. Come on, Dad, let's go and sort them out."

He stumbled clumsily from the cab, the iron bar in his hand, and barged past me heading towards the two men.

"Come back here, Max," I shouted. "Come back and don't be silly."

He still continued to walk towards their position, so I ran and caught him.

"Come back, Max. I promise you we'll leave here tomorrow."

It was a hollow promise, but it had the desired effect. Max slowly calmed down and I prayed the Securitate guards had not witnessed his drunken outburst.

"I'll have the bastards," he yelled, before we reached the caravan.

He went to bed and I lay awake wondering what he was going to do next and if he intended having another go at the security men. I fell asleep and woke to the sound of Action's hoofs stamping on the Tarmac. It was daylight.

I lay on my bed willing myself to get up and have a wash, conscious that I was filthy and stinking, and that wafts of stale air were coming up from under my blankets. I got up and started the fire going under a pan of water. Max was still asleep. People occasionally walked past, and I squeezed between horsebox and caravan, stripped to the buff and had a wash in hot water with a squirt of washing up liquid. I had shaved and cleaned my teeth by the time Max appeared, bleary eyed and feeling rough.

After he, too, had washed himself, we felt more able to tackle the day ahead. Having waited so long, we were at last permitted to visit the Union of the Blind premises, but they would not let us take Action and the caravan inside, nor could we use the video camera. It was a woodworking workshop, where the blind made brushes and other items on machinery dating back to prewar times. We gained the impression that our visit had been carefully orchestrated. As we entered each room, the blind workers rose to their feet, and it had to have been in response to instructions given previous to our arrival.

That afternoon, we went to the British Embassy to ask if there had been any reply from the Russian authorities concerning our proposed visit, and again we were told that there had not. I grew angry at this and demanded an interview with the Ambassador himself. I cooled down when they said they would telephone and invited me to come back on the following day.

At 3 o'clock, our friend arrived, looking anxious, and said he could not stay long. He drew our attention to two people standing at the other end of the street and said they were his parents.

"They have asked me not to visit you again. They fear for my safety and I fear for their's," he said, hugging us both.

When he walked off it was the last we should see of this brave man until we came again to Romania and learnt of his involvement in the overthrow of the Ceauçescu regime.

The night was again quiet, apart from the menacing presence of our two Securitate friends, who stood dutifully observing us. Sometimes a police patrol car came slowly by or a policeman on foot, but I enjoyed a good sleep and woke again at 7.30 a.m.

A woman at the Union of the Blind had been letting me come inside the gates to fetch water for Action, but when I went this time she waved me away. Confused, I went to tell Max. He had no more success than I. The man who had acted as interpreter for us in the institute came up and said it was on instructions from the police that we were not to go inside the gates again.

"Take my advice and leave Romania," he added.

Just then, a police car drew up and the occupants sat watching us. The interpreter said how sorry he was, leaving Max and me in a state of confusion. Until now, everyone in the institute had been very kind to us; now they were turning their backs.

Two more policeman arrived, from a different direction, and the Securitate men joined them. The talked together for a while, then, for the first time, one of these men came over to me. His message was short and to the point.

"Leave Romania. You are not welcome," he said.

He turned and walked away. I asked myself, was I dreaming this or was it true? The interpreter had fled, as though he wanted nothing more to do with us either. Max and I were deeply shocked.

"I think they mean it, Max. We may have outstayed our welcome. Too many people have been talking to us and now they want rid of us," I said reluctantly.

Max was in a flaming temper as he banged and crashed about in the caravan.

"Let's leave, Max," I said.

"Where to, Dad?" he asked.

"Towards Russia," was my reply.

"Without visas? And we've been told to leave Romania," Max protested.

"I don't give a f***, Max. I'm going to Russia and these bastards won't beat me," I said defiantly.

Just before we departed, a young woman came up and gave her name. She wanted to invite us to have a meal at her home, but I thought this was hardly the done thing. She had the best command of English of anyone we had met on our travels.

"Please come tonight. I want to talk to you," she said.

"It is impossible. We have been told to leave Romania," I explained.

"Where do you go?" she asked.

"To the U.S.S.R."

"Which way?"

I was not sure of the answer, but I thought we could go to Buzau and from there to Galati.

"Then I shall come to you and bring my husband," she said, and showed us the main road leading to Buzau. "We shall find you later."

When she caught up with us, she was with her husband, like herself in his early twenties. He understood English, but spoke none. We pulled in to a rough, unmade car park and started talking, at first in the caravan, about our journey. We spoke, naturally, about life in Romania, and what follows is part of what she told me.

"Here in Romania, things are bad. We have no food, and what we have goes to feed fat Communist pigs. We have no freedom of speech. We are oppressed by the government. They send all our food to the U.S.S.R. and our people are starving. The worst affected are the weakest amongst us. Our handicapped have no rights. The government tells us they have none. They do not exist here. I know different. I can show you people who are dying from septicaemia after lying in bed at home, being cared for by relatives. The carers have nothing to clean them with, no soap, no dressings, nothing. They receive no state benefit and have to rely on their families to support them. Hundreds have died of septicaemia in Bucharest, and many more will do so. Our hospitals are bad. We have no medical supplies.

"Two years ago, I had an abortion. Abortion is illegal under Ceauçescu, and if you can find a doctor willing to risk performing the operation, you must pay dearly. I went into a clinic and had three lots of fluids poured into me. I know there was wine, vinegar and alcohol among them. This treatment was given three times and still the baby would not come away. I had to have it removed by an operation. As they wheeled me to the theatre, I could hear a woman groaning. She screamed, "Please let me live. Let me live, please."

"Then she fell silent. It was my turn next and I was terrified. Then, do you know what happened? They removed my baby without anaesthetic. It was awful. I will remember it for the rest of my life. I never want to have another baby, in case things go wrong and it has to be aborted."

Then she went on to tell us about conditions inside the hospitals.

"There were no bandages or dressings for me after the operation, just rags. The toilets were filthy and blocked with used bits of rag, and discarded dressings littered the floor. I know thousands have died from septicaemia due to lack of care and acute shortages of medication. The life of a woman in Romania is hard. How she manages to bring up a family I do not know. Milk is difficult to get if you have a baby. My reason for having an abortion, in spite of the risk of trouble from the authorities if I had been found out, was the fear that I could not support a child. I would have to have let it go, and having once given it life, I could not face losing it. We have no contraceptives here, and lovemaking is natural between men and women. Women are afraid of having more babies while they cannot support those they already have."

While Max spoke to the people who had crowded round us, she went on to tell me more.

"You know the new city Ceauçescu is having built. I have a friend who works on the construction of it. He told me that any workman who complains is beaten. Two of them he knows have been killed for speaking out. Nobody is allowed to utter a word of criticism here. A couple of years ago, in Brasov, there was a small demonstration against Ceauçescu and many of the demonstrators were arrested. For months nothing more was heard of them. When their families asked the police, they were warned not to ask again or they, too, would go missing. Those men have never been seen since."

Her words made me think it was high time we moved on, or they would go missing as well, if they were caught talking to us like this. We said farewell, with no idea that we should see them again and our other brave friend from Bucharest. These young people would also play a big part in the overthrow of the hated dictator, Ceauçescu.

From people like these I had learnt of the underlying current of dissatisfaction in Romania, and I knew they would not suffer these conditions indefinitely. My feeling was proved right when, two weeks after we left Galati, the uprising against Communism and Ceauçescu began.

At a handicapped home in Romania.

Author and Max with the Romanian police outside the British Embassy in Sofija

Farm between Bucharest and Galati with family that gave us shelter.

Inside the Romanian farmhouse.

Chapter Twenty – four

Towards Russia and the Cold

Bucharest seemed endless when we started off in a northeasterly direction towards Buzau. We had to get petrol, having used the last of our reserves, but we felt confident that our coupons and Western currency would save us having to queue. The first filling station we came to was on the outskirts of the city and had a kilometre long tailback of customers. Max drove slowly past this and cut in at the front of the line while I parked Action opposite. I watched an attendant direct the horsebox to a pump. People in the queue began shouting and jeering at him, and when I saw some male drivers getting out of their cars and approaching, I left the caravan and went across. Max had the window down to talk to the attendant, and several small objects lay on the windscreen ledge: a small, carved wooden house, half a packet of Bulgarian cigarettes, a pair of gloves, two maps and several of the small, soft toys we had been given by children in the West. Max had climbed out of the driving seat to complete the purchase, and when he got back, all these things had gone.

In my anxiety to cross to the filling station, I had left the caravan doors open. I glanced across the road and saw a car by the caravan, and two men were just getting inside it.

"Let's get out of here, Dad," Max said. "These people are upset at me jumping the queue.

I had every sympathy with them, for it often entailed a whole day waiting for the tanker to arrive with fuel. Max pulled out and I went to the caravan. One of my gloves was lying on the road. We had been robbed yet again, but now was no time to stop and inspect the damage. When we reached a village, later in the day, and I had time to look through our possessions, I found that my radio, a small Kodak camera, more medals and souvenirs and a large, waterproof coat were missing. If we went on at this rate, we should soon have nothing left.

The moment we stopped the crowd formed, everyone begging for anything we could give. The whole country seemed to consist of nothing but beggars and thieves, from small children to the very old, it made no difference. The people of this generation had, under Ceauçescu, been reduced to begging and stealing as a way of life.

When Max took the horsebox on ahead now, he hurried back and jollied me along, afraid the vehicle would be torn apart by the time he saw it again. We could see a crowd standing round it, some people looked rather menacing, and we began to quicken our pace. We could hear laughter and voices, but when we got near they all fell silent and began to stare in amazement at the caravan. Once again, we were asked what we could give them. Only the Gipsies took what we had to offer and left us in peace. The other people always wanted more and more, and pestered us until we relented and gave them something. After such an encounter, when we stopped, we would often discover that items had been stolen from us.

When we had nothing to give, there were always some who wanted to do some dealing, buy or sell something, and some of these people had large sums of money. The thing we had which was most coveted in Romania was our horse. Action was bigger and stronger than any of their beasts, and would have made a fine job of pulling their farm carts. Men would come up to him, inspect his teeth and feel his muscles. I tried to prevent them touching his mouth, which is a tender part of a horse's anatomy.

This time, when we came up to the horsebox, Max grew excited, trying to draw my attention to something happening up ahead. Two men were bending over a ditch in which lay something large, red and white.

"It's a horse, Dad. They've just skinned it," he said. "Look. There's another."

On the other side of the road lay the body of a horse, complete except for its skin. I felt a wave of nausea. We were still 30 yards away.

"What do you think they are doing it for, Dad?" Max asked. "And why on the side of the road?"

"Meat, I presume, and for the skin. What do you think?" I replied.

Before Max could answer, Action reared up, nostrils flaring. In my curiosity, I had forgotten how he reacted to the scent of blood. I tried to calm him, but he was shying away, head high, hoofs trampling the ground, but not moving forward. He was terrified. He would never bolt towards the dead horses, I knew, and his only course would be to go sideways into the ditch, taking me and the caravan with him. Suddenly, he began to back up, turning the caravan on its turntable. This is the most dangerous manoeuvre a horse in harness can make, and all a driver can do is shout and apply the whip. I have never carried a whip and had no control over him at all. Pulling him back by the reins made things worse.

By this time the caravan was sitting widthways across the road and making for the ditch. I yelled to Max to hold him, but every time Max made a grab for the bridle, Action reared up. I saw that I must control him myself. I waited for the right moment to jump down and run to the horse's head. He let me catch the bridle, but he was still stamping and snorting in terror. At last, he stopped backing towards the ditch and began to calm down, although he still held his head high and was breathing hard. I now became aware of a patient line of traffic that had built up behind us. It was fortunate that most of the drivers had had close association with horses and carts at some time in their lives, and understood my predicament.

We got him back on track and the caravan onto its own side of the road, but we still had to coax him past the dead horses.

"I'll turn him round, cover his head with a blindfold and take him past them backwards," I said, remembering something I had once been told.

The men who had been working on the dead animals, had seen all our antics and guessed the source of the problem. Max fetched a coat and, after I had turned the horse and caravan round, we covered Action's head with it and led him slowly backwards past the shambles. When we drew level, I saw one horse had had its belly slit open. Its guts were hanging out and there was a revolting smell in the air.

Somehow, slowly and with much gentle coaxing, we got Action past the horses and up wind of the smell, then I turned him round, removed the coat and walked him a short distance down the road. He was sweating heavily, so we stopped and I gave him some food. I sat down by the road and had a rest. Max returned to the men by the ditch to make a video recording of the horrible sight. Luckily, this gruesome record was among the items that were stolen later.

"I did that to show people in the West that there really is no meat to be had here," he said, when he came back to me.

Once again, out of nowhere, a crowd appeared round us. I urged Action forward and then I heard a scream from someone. He had trodden on the foot of a young girl. I expected to be lynched by the mob, but I jumped down to see to her. She was already surrounded by a small crowd of people examining at her toes. A rough looking individual wearing a balaclava said in English that we should spend the night there. I said we were on our way to Buzau, but he said we were not safe and must come to his farm with him. I asked about the girl and said I wanted to see her mother and apologise, but after he called out for her and there was no response, he said she would be O.K. anyway.

At this point I made a fatal mistake. In the horsebox I had a bundle of stickers with the British Union Flag on. I told Max to get some and distribute them among the children. Max had not stepped down when the children and adults attacked him, not maliciously, but with hands thrusting, pulling, grabbing, snatching until he was totally engulfed in humanity. Unable to handle this situation, he flung the whole lot in the air and set the crowd scrabbling about like wild dogs after a bone. It was an unbelievable sight, sad in its degradation. Soon, the crowd was standing still, everyone examining their small trophies.

"God, Dad, that was frightening," Max said, scrambling thankfully back to me.

Ivan, the man who had invited us to stay with him, told us to follow on behind while he led us down a track to a cluster of houses and other buildings. Dusk had fallen and I nursed an uneasy suspicion about being taken somewhere I did not know by someone I did not know, but consoled myself with the thought that it could hardly be worse than taking our chance on the side of the road. We came to a small yard surrounded by tumbledown sheds, and Action was taken by Ivan to a field. I could hear the frost crackle under his feet as he galloped across the grass.

A narrow dirt track separated the yard from a small house into which we were taken. Ivan introduced us to his wife. Beside her stood an old lady, probably looking much older than her years. She was short and plump, but a pinched looking face peered out from under a ragged headscarf tied under her chin. She wore a long, black dress that looked as if it had been worn for many years. Over this she wore a dirty apron. She offered me her hand, grimy and work roughened, cold as ice, and shook my own with warmth.

"You stay here tonight, and my Mother will give you her bed," said Ivan.

"Where will she sleep?" I asked.

"In our room," he said. "I should like to have asked you to spend some time here with us, but we Romanians are not allowed to have foreign visitors, so I must ask you to leave before daylight."

The family gave us hard boiled eggs, some of their awful salami and stale bread. Ivan apologised on behalf of his womenfolk for the poor fare, but explained that it was all they had. He said his mother would prepare warm food for us in the morning. We slept in the mother's bed between clean sheets, that had turned grey through lack of proper detergents and soap.

The sound of wheeled carts rumbling along the road woke me. I dressed quickly and went through the open door. White frost covered the ground and the cold hit me. I could see oxen pulling a cart loaded with sweet corn stalks approaching. A small, wizened man, with small hands and feet, walked beside the oxen, his clothes shabby, his features weathered and worn after years of toil in all weathers.

Ivan's old Mother was busy making a fire outside the house. It was surrounded by bricks and stones and covered with a sheet of steel mesh on which sat a pot of what looked like dirty water. The old man stopped and spoke to her. He looked down at the plates and cutlery sitting on the floor, gave me a friendly wave and moved on. This ox cart, with its wooden wheels, the wrinkled old man and the mother in her peasant clothes, the fire outside the cottage, the wooden shacks, the dirt track leading to other farms, all served to bring me in my mind to a time fifty years or more back in the past. This was the face of modern Romania and people doing their best to cope with squalor and poverty.

Ivan was in the farmyard tending his stock: four goats, two pigs, two heifers and a cow. He had hay in the loft of one building, and he fetched a bundle for Action. Max came out with Ivan's wife and a small baby, no more than three or four weeks old, wrapped in a crocheted blanket. She had come to tell us breakfast was ready. We sat round the fire while the old lady poured some clear liquid from the pot into bowls, and Ivan handed round the aluminium spoons. I looked into the liquid and thought I could see some small pieces of potato and onion. Max and I exchanged wordless glances and I began to eat gingerly. The only flavour I could detect was that of onion.

Ivan apologised once again for having nothing better to put before us, and explained that there was no meat to be had, for most of the livestock production that did not find its way onto the black market, went to feed Communists at home or was sold to Russia.

Sitting dipping stale bread into the thin soup, he began to speak out against the regime under which he lived.

"Things are getting worse. We cannot get milk for the baby. My wife tries her best, but she has little, not enough for her. My mother has not eaten meat for months. What little comes our way she makes me and my wife have, so we can work and feed the baby. I do not know how we shall survive the long, cold winter ahead. Soon it will snow and the wind will blow from Siberia. We have no heat, our well is dry and all our water comes from a stream. Come. I shall show you something."

He took me to back of his house where there was a ditch. Unlike the white and frozen surroundings, this carried a flow of sewage from the dwelling.

"We have no way to dispose of it. Most houses here are the same. Romania is finished," he said helplessly.

Ivan knew we intended going to Burzau and he offered to give us a letter of introduction to a farming friend, whom he would ask to help us.

"If you get stopped by the police, make sure they don't see it," he warned. "Tear it up, if they get close. I wish I were as brave as you and Max, then I might do something about our living conditions."

He filled Action's bag with hay and we were ready to depart.

"Dad," said Max, "Let's give them our tinned milk."

We had about half a tin of Cadbury's tinned milk left, and Max gave it to Ivan with our thanks for his help. Many of the neighbours came out of their cottages to wave us off. This was the first place we had been in Romania where we had been asked for nothing and been given all the people had.

In the afternoon light snow began to fall, and I was frozen as the wind blew icy cold over the flat road along which we travelled. We saw more Gipsy caravans than usual, laden with crops off the fields. We saw whole families huddling together under their canvas, often swathed in blankets. I could not make out what was different about them.

The farm belonging to Ivan's friend was behind some large gates. A man in blue overalls came out and I gave him the letter Ivan had written. He swung open the gates, looked up and down the road and hurried us inside to the safety of a yard surrounded by farm buildings. In the centre was a well and by this stood a trough with four horses tethered beside it. Action sniffed the air in anticipation of making new friends. Two of the horses still trailed harnesses, as if they had just finished working. On one side of the yard stood three carts, one with a roof made from sacking and other material. The horses had been working with them. Still silent, the man fetched hay for Action and led him into a shed. He threw the hay in after him, followed by a bucketful of small carrots like the ones we had seen on the market stalls.

In Romania, most of the horses lived on carrots for much of the winter, their diet supplemented with maize and oats when available. I had the feeling that our friend was worried about us staying. He made a great show of bolting the gates and indicated that we should not open them on any account. That night we sat without food, wearing all our clothes, topped off by scarves and hats, swaddled in blankets and smoking Romanian cigarettes in the darkness. At nine o'clock, still fully clothed against the cold, we went to bed.

For several days we had only been able to wash our hands and faces. I had some irritating spots on my wrists and arms, which I scratched.

At dawn next morning, I shouted to waken Max. I had told him my idea that our host was frightened about having us on his farm, and I wanted to leave early to avoid putting him at risk. When the man arrived, at eight o'clock, I signed to him to open the gates for us and we departed. There were people on the streets, some leading lone cows to graze on the roadside, children going to school, people queuing for bread and milk and other food. Dogs roamed the pavements, scrawny animals sniffing in doorways. The track leading to the main road was deeply rutted and dark traces of sewage in evil smelling hollows led to streams, some of which had a trickle of water, others were dry. Where the streams described a bend, the banks were black. Bobbing in the evil current were tins, scrap and rubbish thrown in over the years. Some places had methane gas pumps working in the fields, bringing gas supplies to industry.

The continuous flow of Gipsy folk was still puzzling me when we stopped north of Buzau on a freezing cold afternoon. We were on a straight piece of road. On the right were many caravans congregated in a field, clearly an encampment of some kind. As we came close, they spotted us and people came running to the roadside, men, women and children. There must have been about thirty of them altogether. We heard the familiar cries of "Cigarettes, chocolate?"

A man in his thirties came forward and caught hold of Action's bridle.

"Here we go again," I thought, as I tried to urge the horse forwards.

The man pulled the bridle in such a way that I had no control and led him through a gap and into the field towards their caravans. Max ran after the man and caught him by the arm, trying to get him to loosen his hold on the horse.

"No problem, no problem," said the Gipsy. "You our friends."

He took us to the back of the caravans, where we would be shielded from the road.

"*Probleme Polisi*," he explained.

The people made us very welcome and shared their salami, bread, cucumbers and tomatoes with us. The boy had a few words of English, and through him we conversed. He had a good understanding of the language, and I wanted to know what all these caravans had come here for.

"Most of us make for home in the early winter. We travel in the spring, summer and autumn, working in the fields. It is not possible in winter. We should freeze to death. It drops to 40°C below zero. No-one in a caravan can survive that. The horses cannot pull the caravans on the ice and snow."

This conversation was, for the most part, conducted with liberal use of hand signs and gestures. I wanted to show our appreciation of their generosity, but we only had one thing left to offer. Whispering to Max, I asked him to go quietly to the horsebox and fetch out some clothes, blankets or toys. To distract them from what he was doing, I handed out some stickers. They were eager to receive them, but not at all unruly.

Max came back carrying three plastic bags full of goodies. As he tipped one out onto the floor, the women made a dive. It contained small items of clothing, jumpers, vests and shirts. I tried to get them to take things easy, to explain that we had enough for all. The man who had invited us to the camp now intervened. He knew I wanted to give something to everyone. As he explained this, they fell silent. Next, he tipped the other sacks out onto the ground and the women came and picked up clothing while the children sorted out the toys. To me, it did not seem as if it had all been shared fairly, but no – one else was bothered by this. They were all so pleased to have something.

During the next five days we were to dispose of all the goods given us in Greece and Bulgaria. We would stop, often near old men and women, in a quiet spot, or by children tending animals at the roadside. We had occasional difficulties, when people wanted more than we could give. On the other hand, I had great satisfaction in handing out the things to those who needed them and not letting them fall into the hands of black marketeers.

We reached Galati uneventfully, except for the usual beggars. The spots on my wrists and arms had become septic, some swollen to the size of boils, and I had a sore throat most days. At night I could not get warm. Max, too, was not well. He complained of noises in his ears and some pain. We had both lost weight. I estimated that I had lost some three stones, partly from the heat, partly from lack of food and the rest through exhaustion. We were both in rather a bad state as we circled Galati, a mere six miles from the Russian border. I went to bed resolved to try and make a border crossing in the morning, permit or not.

When we stopped that night people again gathered round us. I asked how to get to the border post and kept hearing people mentioning Albita Husi, a place several hundred miles to the north. Max understood. They were telling him the only way into Russia from Galati was by ferry, and there was no way we would be allowed to get through with our caravan and everything. It was sickening news.

Late that night, when I had a chance to talk to Max, it was bitterly cold and we both felt sick with fatigue and physical illness. We realised that we could not possibly get to Odessa before the bad weather. It was already – 10°C and getting worse. I felt we must decide on the spot to give up the journey unless we were given permission to cross the border on the next day. I knew in advance that any permit we got would be for a crossing at Albita Husi. Money was running very low. We had not been able to telephone home except for the one occasion when I waited four hours to get a line. While I was talking, moaning about what an awful place Romania was, they cut me off. I should have remembered that international calls are tapped.

I could not have money transferred to me here, even if my bank manager had been willing to help. Things would be no better if and when we reached Odessa. I asked Max how much cash we would need to get back to Italy with Action in the horsebox, and he reckoned it would be about £100, assuming we could get fuel for the trip. All our coupons and reserves of fuel had been used up.

I had been advised that it was a requirement on entering Russia to declare how much currency one carried, to prove that one was self-supporting. There was certainly not enough to last us for the six months we had said we wanted to spend there. We had £240 between us, and even in Russia that was far from enough. Things were pretty well stacked against us and it only took two small nudges of fate to make up our minds for us. So far, all I had spoken about to Max was the idea of returning home. It was quiet when I turned in. We had little hay and no pony nuts left, and Action, tied to the caravan, shuffled his feet from time to time.

I sat up in bed and listened when I heard a car pull up and the sound of whispering, so familiar to me since we arrived in Romania. Then I felt someone trying the caravan doors. Outside was an inky, impenetrable blackness. Then there was a tremendous bang. They had tried to open the horsebox tailgate. Action bolted and when he got to the length of his tether chain, his brute force tilted the caravan until it almost fell on its side. It bounced back on the undercarriage and I heard men running, a car engine burst into life and Max's voice shouting oaths at the car, as he raced after it, brandishing the iron bar.

It was going to be necessary to start our system of watches all over again. I told Max to get to bed and I would stay on duty until four in the morning. Still fully clothed and wearing his shoes, Max went to sleep while I sat shivering in a pile of blankets. I thought we might freeze to death if I fell asleep. I woke Max at four, but all was still, so I told him to go back to sleep. At eight, I woke to find the bottom of my bed frozen solid. Even the spare clothing hanging on pegs was stiff right through to its linings. Outside, the wind cut my face like a knife. Action stood motionless, not making his usual morning neighing sounds. A line of frost stood on his back, icicles hung on his long body hairs; his chin hair, his whiskers and even the hairs in his nostrils were frosted and white.

"Max, get up. We're going home," I yelled.

He sat up in bed, his blankets wrapped tightly round him.

"My ear is driving me mad. I feel as if a war is being fought inside my head."

I looked long and hard at my son, his sockless feet thrust into his shoes, his trousers hanging like a sack round his body. They were not even his trousers. He was wearing a pair of mine. I felt sick to see what I had brought him to. He peeled off the blankets to reveal a dirty jumper, also one of mine. Most of his clothing had been stolen at one place or another. For a scarf, he had a filthy towel wrapped round his neck and tucked into the jumper. I was in no better condition. I was in a state of filth, everything on my back was smelly and we had run out of toiletries in a country where they were unobtainable.

"I've decided to go home, Max. We can't survive here in this cold and neither can Action. People have told me plenty of times that it can take up to two years to get an entry permit and the Romanians have told us to get out of their country, so who knows what might happen if we don't get out now."

For the next hour we packed up and prepared to leave, both of us in deep despair at having been beaten at last by the Communist system.

"Listen, Dad, I know you are disappointed, but no-one could have done more," Max said.

His words brought a lump to my throat and I turned away, to stop him seeing the expression in my eyes.

"You know, Max, I never told Action, when we left Scotland, that he was going on a long walk. Let's go and tell him this time he's going home," I said.

We rushed out and told the horse, both of us filled with an overwhelming rush of emotion. What we omitted to tell him was that, in a few months time, we would return, walk around Romania and, at last, enter Russia. We did not know about it ourselves at that moment.

Thanks, Max.

Thanks, Action.

Thanks to everybody who helped me achieve the first leg of my journey.

THE END

Caravan leaving – it will come back in Volume Two